THE
CASE
FOR
PEACE

Books by Alan Dershowitz

THE

CASE

FOR

PEACE

How the Arab-Israeli Conflict
Can Be Resolved

Alan Dershowitz

WILEY

John Wiley & Sons, Inc.

Published by John Wiley & Sons, Inc., Hoboken, New Jersey
Published simultaneously in Canada

Maps used by permission: pp. 22 and 23, Martin Gilbert, *Israel, A History* (New York: William Morrow and Co., 1998); pp. 37 and 38, Daniel Ross, *The Missing Peace: The Inside Story of the Fight for Middle East Peace* (Farrar, Straus and Giroux, 2004); pp. 42 and 43, Doug Suisman et al., *The Arc: A Formal Structure for a Palestinian State* (Santa Monica: RAND Corporation, 2005), accessible at www.rand.org/pubs/monographs/2005/RAND_MG327.pdf

Design and composition by Navta Associates, Inc.

For general information about our other products and services, please contact our Customer Care Department within the United States at (800) 762-2974, outside the United States at (317) 572-3993 or fax (317) 572-4002.

Wiley also publishes its books in a variety of electronic formats. Some content that appears in print may not be available in electronic books. For more information about Wiley products, visit our web site at www.wiley.com.

Library of Congress Cataloging-in-Publication Data:

Dershowitz, Alan M.
    The case for peace : how the Arab-Israeli conflict can be resolved / Alan Dershowitz.
        p. cm.
    Includes bibliographical references and index.
    ISBN-13 978-0-471-74317-0 (cloth : alk. paper)
    ISBN-10 0-471-74317-8 (cloth : alk. paper)
    1. Arab-Israeli conflict—1993—Peace.   I. Title.
    DS119.76.D47 2005
    956.9405'4—dc22

                                                                    2005013731

Printed in the United States of America

10 9 8 7 6 5 4 3 2 1

This book is dedicated to moderate Israelis and Palestinians who are on the side of peace and who reject those extremists who are more Israeli than the Israelis and more Palestinian than the Palestinians.

CONTENTS

viii CONTENTS

ACKNOWLEDGMENTS

Books about peace can be quite contentious. My excellent staff of research assistants fought with me about peace, some thinking I was too accommodating, others that I was not accommodating enough. My greatest appreciation goes to Alexander Blenkinsopp, Aaron Voloj Dessauer, Danielle Sassoon, and Mitch Webber, especially for their willingness to work long hours on a tight schedule without diminishing either their enthusiasm or their brilliance. I extend my usual appreciation to my family for reading drafts and setting me straight, and to my assistant, Jane Wagner, for tolerating my frenetic pace and keeping me on schedule. Finally, thanks to my editor, Hana Lane, for excellent editorial suggestions (even the ones I didn't accept) and for her belief in this project, and to my agent, Helen Rees, for making things happen.

Introduction
The Case for Peace

To everything there is a season,
and a time to every purpose under heaven: . . .
a time to kill, and a time to heal;
a time to break down, and a time to build up; . . .
a time to cast away stones, and a time to gather stones together;
a time to embrace, and a time to refrain from embracing; . . .
a time to love, and a time to hate;
a time of war, and a time of peace.

Ecclesiastes 3:1–8

The Israelis and the Palestinians have lived—and died—through too many seasons of warfare, hatred, destruction, and recriminations. They have thrown too many stones and bombs. They have killed too many dreams and dreamers. The time has come for compromise, reconciliation, healing, and a permanent end to the violence. The season of peace may be on the horizon. But unlike the seasons of nature, which come and go without human intervention, the season of peace will not arrive without the participation of many people, with different agendas, aspirations, memories, and worldviews. It will be hard in coming, and if and when it does come, it must last for many seasons of nature and become a permanent change in climate.

1

The good news is that the elements are all in place. The outline for the solution is obvious to all reasonable people:

1. Two states based on Israeli withdrawal from all of the Gaza Strip and nearly all of the West Bank, with territorial adjustments consistent with Security Council Resolution 242 (see chapter 1 for a full discussion of Resolution 242) and the existing realities on the ground.

2. Some symbolic recognition of the rights of Palestinian "refugees," including a compensation package and some family reunification, but no absolute "right of return" to Israel of the millions of descendants of those who claim refugee status—a questionable "right" whose exercise would produce the great wrong of quickly turning the Jewish state into yet another Muslim Arab state. All Palestinians should have the right to "return" to what will become the Palestinian state.

3. A division of greater Jerusalem, with the Arab part becoming the capital of the Palestinian state and the Jewish part the recognized capital of Israel.

4. A renunciation of all forms of violence, including terrorism, and an undertaking by the Palestinian state to dismantle terrorist groups and take all reasonable efforts to prevent acts of terrorism, just as Israel has undertaken to prevent and punish Jewish terrorism against Palestinians.

5. An end to the singling out of Israel for demonization and delegitimation—and to the hatred directed against the Jewish state and its citizens and supporters—by international organizations, many academics, religious leaders, and media pundits; and the normalization and acceptance of Israel as a full and equal member of the international community.

This solution, a variation of which was offered by Israel in 2000 and 2001 and then proposed by a group of Israelis and Palestinians at Geneva in 2003, is consistent with the "road map," and it holds the best prospect for real peace. It gives neither side everything it wishes. Nor will it immediately end all terrorism. Like Churchill's case for "democracy," this case for peace may be "the worst possible" solution, "except for all the others" that have been tried—and have failed—over the many years of bloodshed.

In *The Case for Israel* I responded to false charges directed against the Jewish state by the enemies of Israel. I told my audiences that I wished I could have written *The Case for Peace* instead, but the season was not right. Nor was it right when the paperback of *The Case for Israel* was released. As I wrote in the introduction to that book, "I plan to continue to speak and write in defense of Israel so long as unfair accusations persist against the Jewish state. My current plans include a new book, entitled *The Case against Israel's Enemies*, on which I am currently working." In that sequel I planned to show how so many of Israel's enemies care more about the destruction of the Jewish state than they do about the creation of a Palestinian state or about the welfare of the Palestinian people. My focus was going to be primarily on radical academics, both in Europe and the United States, who have made a career out of demonizing Israel and singling it out for unique condemnation.

The death of Yasser Arafat and the initiation of what appears to be a genuine peace process caused me to change the focus as well as the title of this sequel. But one reality has not changed: the enemies of Israel are also the enemies of peace. Those whose primary goal is the destruction of the Jewish democratic state of Israel are generally opposed to the two-state solution and the peace process that is leading in that direction. *The Case against Israel's Enemies* has now become *The Case against the Enemies of Peace* or, to put it more positively, *The Case for Peace*. *The Case for Israel* dealt primarily with the conflict between Israel and the Palestinians. Today the conflict is a different one. Mainstream Israelis and mainstream Palestinians, along with their respective governments, are now largely on the same side: they all want peace, compromise, and a two-state solution. There are, of course, real differences in the particulars of proposed compromises, but a process is underway for resolving these differences. The current conflict is between those who favor a compromise peace based on the two-state solution and those who oppose such a peace. With regard to this conflict most Israelis and many Palestinians are on the same side—the side of peace. The other side consists of Palestinian extremists who will never accept a Jewish state of Israel no matter how tiny, Israeli extremists who will never accept a Palestinian state no matter how tiny, and outsiders on both extremes—especially hard-left and hard-right academics, religious leaders, and politicians—who prefer the deadlock of ideological purity to the slow but steady progression toward an achievable compromise peace. The conflict therefore is no longer so much between the Israelis and the Palestinians as it is between those moderate pragmatists who favor peace and those extremist ideologues who favor a continuation of the conflict, with its resulting bloodshed. This book is primarily about this current conflict between the advocates of peace and the barriers to peace.

As I will show, those academics, students, political leaders, and pundits who rail against everything Israel does and is have encouraged people on both extremes who oppose compromise and insist on total victory. The enemies of Israel, such as Noam Chomsky, are also among the prime enemies of peace. It is not a coincidence that the German publishing house Europa simultaneously published German translations of my book *The Case for Israel* and Noam Chomsky's recent book on the Middle East. Chomsky's book is entitled *No Chance for Peace: Why It Is Impossible to Establish a Palestinian State with Israel and the U.S.* This contrasts dramatically with the title of my present book. Yet among many Europeans, Chomsky is seen as an advocate of peace and I am seen as, in the words of a leading German newspaper, a "militant"[1]—the same word often used for terrorists! This speaks volumes about the different standards applied to those who advocate peace (and especially the two-state solution) and those who favor the one-state nonsolution, which is a guarantee of continued bloodshed.

On the anti-Israel side, these naysayers to peace have sent a dangerous message to terrorists and others who believe that only the total destruction of the Jewish state will suffice: if they persist in the so-called "armed struggle" instead of trying to make peace through negotiation, they will continue to receive support from within the academy, the media, the international community, and other constituencies that matter to them. To the extent that this message encourages continuing terrorism, these ivory-tower spectators—who live, write, and lecture far from the killing fields—have blood on their hands. They bear some responsibility for the continuing terrorism that their support encourages. They have become barriers to peace and part of the problem, rather than part of a peaceful solution. Extremism is the enemy of peace, and those extremists have a stake in the continuation of armed strife, rather than in a compromise resolution. As I will show, they have become more Palestinian than the Palestinians. But in doing so, they fail to serve the interests of the Palestinian people.

These radical naysayers have also strengthened the hands of pro-Israel extremists who oppose compromise and define victory as Israel's retention of the entire West Bank and Gaza. Those pro-Israel extremists—who are more Israeli than the Israelis—point to the anti-Israel extremists who advocate continuation of the armed struggle as proof that peace is not possible and that the protection of Israelis from violence can only be assured by continuing the military occupation.

The enemies of Israel, who are also enemies of peace, exert a multi-faceted negative force on the prospects for a compromise resolution of the Israeli-Palestinian conflict. At the most enduring level, they are miseducating a generation of students to believe that if the anti-Israel rhetoric can be ratcheted up on university campuses throughout the world, they will control the future by having indoctrinated the leaders of the future. This will produce so great a lack of support for Israel over time that Israel's very existence will eventually be jeopardized. If peace can be postponed until that "messianic era" arrives, total victory can be achieved, Israel can be destroyed, and no compromise peace—which they deny is a real peace—will have to be accepted.

The unachievable one-state solution is the tactic offered up by these academics in lieu of the currently achievable two-state compromise they are trying to derail. They know that no responsible Israeli leader, and no reasonable Israelis, would ever accept the one-state ploy, because the one state would quickly become a Palestinian Muslim state. Israel would thus be destroyed politically, diplomatically, and demographi-cally, rather than by armed struggle—but it would be destroyed nonetheless. Everyone on the ground understands this, and under-stands that the one-state proposal is at best a tactical ploy, and at worst a deliberate attempt to sabotage any realistic prospect for peace. Even Noam Chomsky, one of the most extreme among the anti-Israel academics, and an ideological proponent of the one-state, binational solution, has recently acknowledged that it is unrealistic: "As to its desirability [the binational one-state solution], I have believed that from childhood, and still do. . . . By 1973 the opportunity was lost, and the only feasible short-term settlement was the two-state proposal. That remains true."[2] He still rejects the two-state solution in theory as a bad idea, but he grudgingly acknowledges that it may be "the best of the rotten ideas around."[3] Yet he dismisses current peace efforts as "impossible" and having "no chance."[4] The danger, of course, is that if people accept Chomsky's doom-and-gloom prophecy, it will become self-fulfilling and there will be no end to the bloodshed.

Despite his negativity, Chomsky has also acknowledged that those

Palestinian leaders (and presumably their academic supporters) who advocate the so-called "right of return" are pandering to their people and misleading them into believing that there is yet another "demographic" weapon that can destroy Israel: namely, the "return" of more than four million Palestinian "refugees" (this figure consists of the small number of actual refugees who are still alive, plus their millions of claimed descendants) to Israel, where they will quickly outnumber the Jewish residents of Israel and vote to turn Israel into another Palestinian state. This too would never be accepted by any responsible Israeli leader and is therefore not being demanded by any responsible Palestinian negotiator. Although Mahmoud Abbas insisted upon a full right of return during his election campaign,[5] he has, since becoming president, moderated his stance somewhat. The *New York Times* reports that Abbas is exploring ways "to limit any resulting immigration into Israel" following the establishment of a Palestinian state.[6]

As I will demonstrate in the chapters to come, the Palestinian people and their newly elected leaders hold the key to peace in their willingness to compromise and, along with the Israeli people and their elected leaders, to accept the half-a-loaf offered by the two-state solution. (In reality each side will get more than half a loaf from the two-state solution because the whole—peace, prosperity, and security—will be greater than the sum of its parts.) The major barriers to peace are the rejectionists among the Palestinians, the Arabs, and the Israelis, as well as the radical academics who insist on total victory (which is unachievable) and absolute solutions (which are not solutions at all). History is, I believe, on the side of the pragmatists and compromisers, since those with the most to gain from peace and the most to lose from a continuation of violence seem to favor the two-state solution.

On June 9, 2005, I spent an hour in private conversation with Israel's prime minister, Ariel Sharon, in his small office in Tel Aviv. Two things became clear: first, he was determined to reach a compromise peace based on a two-state solution and a division of land; and second, this compromise was deeply painful to him, because he realized that his "dream" of a larger Israel was inconsistent with an enduring peace. The only element he would never sacrifice was "Israel's security." Sharon realized that peace will be difficult to achieve, with so many naysayers on both sides, but he was confident that a real peace with security was in the best interests of both Israelis and Palestinians.

So I have written *The Case for Peace*. In it, I consider the prospects, problems, and plans that are most likely to bring about a workable resolution of this seemingly intractable dispute. The first part (chapters 1 through 13) deals with the geopolitical barriers to peace, while the second part (chapters 14 through 17) covers the various manifestations of hatred as barriers to peace. I propose ways of overcoming each of these barriers and reaching a compromise peace that is in the best interest of Israelis, Palestinians, and all people of goodwill who prefer achievable but imperfect solutions above waiting for unachievable perfect "justice" while the blood continues to flow. Extremists on both sides will reject my ideas, but moderates on both sides will, I hope, welcome them.

I wrote this book with equal degrees of optimism and pragmatism. During the latest campaign of suicide bombings, Israelis would define a pessimist as someone who says, "Things can't get any worse"—and an optimist as someone who says, "Yes, they can." I believe that unless things get better, they will get much worse. They will certainly not stay the same for very long. This is a season of hope. May it be turned into a long springtime of enduring peace.

PART I

Overcoming the Geopolitical Barriers to Peace

Until recently, the conflict between the Arabs and the Israelis was not over boundaries. It was over Israel's right to exist in peace as a Jewish democratic state. Muslim leaders refused to recognize any Israeli sovereignty over any land—even "the size of a postage stamp,"[1] as one Muslim leader put it—that they regarded as Muslim or Arab. In order to prevent the establishment of Israel, the Palestinians who testified before the Peel Commission in 1937 were even willing to deny themselves a state. When, a decade later, the United Nations partitioned the land into Jewish and Palestinian areas, the Arabs chose to fight rather than accept two states. In 1967, when the Security Council proposed an exchange of land for peace and recognition of Israel, the Arab states unanimously refused. Finally, when Israel offered the Palestinians a state on nearly all the land they claim, again Yasser Arafat responded with suicide bombings.

Now, following Arafat's death, the new Palestinian leadership seems interested in territorial compromise. The time is ripe therefore to focus hard on the specifics of such a compromise—the issues on the ground. In this section, we will explore the geopolitical barriers to peace and how they can be overcome. In the next section we will explore the even more difficult barriers of hatred.

1 The End Result
Two States with Secure and Recognized Borders

We all know what the final agreement will look like, but meanwhile young people are dying. That's what makes this so painful. It just breaks my heart.

—Former president Bill Clinton[1]

Like it or not, [Israelis and Palestinians] must recognize that their fate is intertwined. Their choice is either to live in perpetual struggle, with endless victims, pain, sorrow, and destruction, or to live in peaceful coexistence. From all the efforts I made over the years, I am certain that the mainstreams of both sides understand that reality. However, translating that understanding from an abstraction into a practical reality has proven far more difficult than I had hoped.

—Dennis Ross, Middle East adviser and chief negotiator
under Presidents George H. W. Bush and Bill Clinton[2]

[T]he question today is not what the final agreement will look like, but rather how much more time do we have before any agreement becomes impossible to implement.

—Marwan Jilani, executive director of the Geneva Initiative[3]

Sometimes it is better to start at the end. There seems to be more agreement among Palestinian and Israeli negotiators about what a final resolution will look like than about the steps that must be taken to get to that point. An absence of trust—the result of years of missteps, missed opportunities, and domestic posturing—has created a "chicken-egg" problem: each side wants the other side to show good faith before it is prepared to give up any important bargaining chips. Neither side can afford to give up too many chips without getting at least an equal number from the other side, lest it lose credibility among skeptical members of its own constituencies. Yet both sides understand that they will, eventually, have to exchange these chips if peace is to be accomplished. For example, all reasonable people acknowledge that the final borders will incorporate Israel's large permanent settlements (really towns—such as Maale Adumim) into Israel, and that these suburbs of Jerusalem will become contiguous with Jewish Jerusalem. That is the reality on the ground, as former president Bill Clinton, President George W. Bush, and Palestinian president Mahmoud Abbas recognize. But by announcing that Maale Adumim will be expanded in the direction of Jerusalem *before* a final agreement is reached, the Israeli government has usurped a bargaining chip from the Palestinians and engendered distrust among some Palestinian moderates.[4] At the same time, by announcing now these future plans for expansion of Israeli areas, the Israeli government has given an important chip to Israeli moderates on the right who are somewhat skeptical about the unilateral withdrawal from the Gaza Strip. Thus, even when it comes to gathering support among moderates, many steps have a zero-sum quality.

Also, opponents to peace on both sides understand how easy it is to exploit mutual distrust by provocative actions calculated to draw a response from the other side and create a cycle of recrimination. A disturbing instance of this exploitation was reported by the Associated Press on April 8, 2005:

> Tens of thousands of Hamas supporters paraded through downtown Gaza City on Friday, threatening to end a monthlong truce if Jewish extremists follow through on a pledge to hold a rally at a disputed holy site in Jerusalem next week. . . .
>
> Jewish extremists say that in July, when the Gaza evacuation is to begin, they will bring tens of thousands of people to the Temple

Mount, forcing police to divert their attention from the pullout to Jerusalem. . . .

Abbas said Friday that the Palestinians have been in contact with Israeli Defense Minister Shaul Mofaz of Israel about the rally.

"We have a pledge from the Israelis that they will prevent any aggression on Al Aqsa Mosque, and we hope so," Abbas said.[5]

So before we get to the difficult steps, and the order in which they should be taken, let us first address the end result.

The Arab-Israeli conflict should end with a two-state solution under which all the Arab and Muslim states—indeed the entire world—acknowledge Israel's right to continue to exist as an independent, democratic, Jewish state with secure and defensible boundaries and free of terrorism. In exchange, Israel should recognize the right of Palestinians to establish an independent, democratic, Palestinian state with politically and economically viable boundaries. For these mutually compatible goals to be achieved, extremists on both sides must give up what they each claim are their God-given or nationalistic rights. Israeli extremists must give up their claimed right to all of biblical Eretz Yisrael (the land of Israel) and their claimed right to maintain Jewish settlements on, or to continue the military occupation of, disputed areas that would be allocated to the Palestinian state. Palestinian extremists must give up their claimed right to all of "Palestine," including what is now Israel, as well as the alleged right of millions of descendants of those who left or were forced out of what is now Israel during the war of 1947–1949 to "return" to their "ancestral homes" in Israel. Unless these claimed rights are mutually surrendered in the interest of achieving a pragmatic, compromise resolution to the conflict, there can be no enduring peace. But if these claimed rights are surrendered, peace can be achieved. The remaining disputes—and there are many—will be much easier to resolve if agreement is reached on these fundamental issues.

It would follow from Israel's renouncing all claims to remain on Palestinian land that the military occupation would end and the Palestinian government would exercise political control over its land and the movement of its people. And it would follow from the Palestinian renunciation of claims to all of Israel and to any right of return that there could be no justification for terrorism, "resistance," or any other violence against Israelis, and that the Palestinian government would be responsible for preventing and punishing any such violence.

I do not mean to suggest that the occupation "justified" terrorism, only that even those who erroneously claimed justification could no longer credibly do so.[6]

The precise borders would, of course, have to be negotiated, but there is already in existence an agreed-upon international formula for resolving this divisive issue. Resolution 242, enacted by the UN Security Council in 1967, provides as follows:

> [The Security Council] (1) *Affirms* that the fulfillment of Charter principles requires the establishment of a just and lasting peace in the Middle East which should include the application of *both* of the following principles: (i) Withdrawal of Israel armed forces from *territories* occupied in the recent [1967] conflict: (ii) *Termination of all claims or states of belligerency* and respect for and *acknowledgement of the sovereignty*, territorial integrity and political independence of *every State* in the area and their right to live in peace within *secure and recognized boundaries* free from threats or acts of force.[7]

The "legislative history" of that important resolution provides guidance on how the borders should be determined. Soon after the end of the Six-Day War in 1967, the Soviet Union agreed to rearm Egypt. Egypt, in turn, embarked on an intermittent war of attrition against Israel. As Egyptian attacks escalated in frequency and severity, America's ambassador to the UN, former Supreme Court justice Arthur Goldberg (for whom I had, three years earlier, served as a law clerk and with whom I continued to consult on legal matters at the UN), drafted language that he hoped would frame subsequent peace negotiations. The United States found a willing cosponsor in Great Britain and negotiated language that eventually was adopted by unanimous vote of the Security Council.

Notably, the Security Council recognized that it could not reasonably ask Israel to return to the old armistice borders—agreed to as part of the end of the War of Independence in 1949—from which it had been threatened just months earlier. Resolution 242 demands Israeli withdrawal only from "territories," not "*the* territories" or "*all* the territories." This is no legal technicality; the definite article was omitted quite intentionally, and after extensive discussion, so that Israel would be free to negotiate reasonable and mutually secure borders with the defeated states that had threatened it.[8] The Soviet Union had insisted that the resolution demand the return of "all" or at least "the" captured territories, but that view was rejected.[9]

During the UN debate, Ambassador Goldberg argued, as described in Security Council records, that "[t]o seek withdrawal without secure and recognized boundaries . . . would be just as fruitless as to seek secure and recognized boundaries without withdrawal. Historically there have never been secure or recognized boundaries in the area. Neither the armistice lines of 1949 nor the cease-fire lines of 1967 have answered that description . . . such boundaries have yet to be agreed upon."[10] Goldberg explained further, "The notable omissions—which were not accidental—in regard to withdrawal are the words 'the' or 'all' and 'the June 5, 1967 lines'. . . . [T]he resolution speaks of withdrawal from occupied territories without defining the extent of withdrawal."[11]

Following the adoption of Resolution 242, in an address on September 10, 1968, President Lyndon B. Johnson stated, "It is clear, however, that a return to the situation of June 4, 1967, will not bring peace. There must be secure and there must be recognized borders." The *New York Times* even printed a correction of its coverage of the resolution: "An article yesterday about peace talks between Israel and the Palestinians referred incorrectly to United Nations resolutions on the conflict. While Security Council Resolution 242, passed after the 1967 Middle East war, calls for Israel to withdraw its armed forces 'from territories occupied in the recent conflict,' no resolution calls for Israel to withdraw 'to its pre-1967 borders.'"[12]

This legislative history clearly establishes that the pre-1967 "green lines"—the borders that contributed to the 1967 war—are not to be the "secure and recognized boundaries" contemplated by Resolution 242. Nor would *major* additions to the Israeli territory be consistent with the resolution. Relatively small adjustments, designed to assure mutual security would, however, be acceptable. This has been the operative assumption behind the two previous efforts to define new borders in the interests of peace: the Clinton-Barak and Geneva proposals. Both contemplated Israel's annexing the areas around Jerusalem on which thousands of Israelis now live in densely populated suburbs such as Maale Adumim, composed of large apartment complexes.

The Clinton-Barak proposals would have allocated to Israel small areas crucial to its security and made small adjustments to the Green Line amounting to less than 5 percent of the West Bank. In return, Israel offered to cede to Palestine certain areas inside Israel, adjacent to the West Bank. In the end, Israel agreed to an unspecified international presence and some early warning stations with virtually no permanent Israeli military presence.[13] The Geneva proposals, drafted by private Israelis and Palestinians in 2003, contemplated borders based on the 1967 lines "with reciprocal modifications on a 1:1 basis."[14] The difference between these proposals, though significant, amounted to a tiny portion of the total land at issue. It is, of course, uncertain what the final borders might look like now, since the Palestinians would no longer be negotiating with Barak or Clinton. That train left the station when Arafat rejected the Clinton-Barak offer, the second intifada was started, and both Clinton and Barak left office. The Palestinians will almost certainly get less now—after years of bloodshed and more than four thousand deaths—than they would have gotten had they accepted the Clinton-Barak offer or if they had offered a reasonable counterproposal. That is as it should be, if terrorism is not to be rewarded and negotiation discouraged. But if the Palestinians now enter into good-faith negotiations, and make best efforts to end terrorism, they will still get all of the Gaza Strip and nearly all of the West Bank.

A front-page story in the *New York Times*[15] analyzing Israel's building decisions concluded that the most Israel will claim is approximately 3 percent more than what was offered at Camp David. "Clinton was down to 5 percent of the West Bank, and here you are down to 8 percent before final-status negotiations," according to David Makovsky of the Washington Institute of Near East Policy. "It has to be modified and agreed upon by the parties, but before our eyes we see the rough shape of a two-state solution," he concluded. Under this plan, "99.5 percent of Palestinians would live" in the new Palestinian state, with "fewer than 10,000 of the two million [West Bank] Palestinians" living within Israel. Moreover, 177,000 of the 240,000 Israeli "settlers" who now live in the West Bank (not including East Jerusalem itself) would be within the new Israeli borders and the remaining 63,000 would be evacuated to Israel. The *Times* concluded that "the likely impact of the provisional new border on Palestinian life is, perhaps surprisingly, smaller than generally assumed."[16]

Once a permanent border is agreed on, the issue of a security fence diminishes in importance, because any such fence (like the existing Gaza fence) would be on the border, not inside Palestinian territory. To the extent that the Palestinian government could control violence from within its borders, the fence would become unnecessary, and eventually the borders could reopen without the need for security checkpoints. But until that time, the border fence would help make good neighbors by reducing both terrorism by extremists and retaliation by the Israeli military.

Until the death of Yasser Arafat, no Palestinian leader was willing to accept statehood for the Palestinians if it also meant acceptance of Israel. In 1937, the Peel Commission suggested, in essence, a two-state solution, with the proposed Jewish state (in which Jews would be a large majority) being tiny and noncontiguous, and the proposed Palestinian state being large and contiguous.[17] Although the Jewish Agency (the unofficial "government" of the pre-Israel Jewish Yishuv) was greatly disappointed by the proposal, and despite the strong opposition of many Jews, it ultimately agreed to the recommendation. The Palestinians, led by the grand mufti of Jerusalem, categorically rejected the two-state solution, arguing that establishing an independent Palestinian state would require acceptance of a Jewish state, tiny and noncontiguous as it would be. Such an acceptance of any Jewish sovereignty, regardless of the size of the land, would be inconsistent with Islamic law as the grand mufti interpreted it. Palestinian leaders "clung to the principle that Palestine was part of Syria" and that there should be neither a Palestinian state nor any Jewish self-rule, "political power," or "privilege." The grand mufti even refused to "provide guarantees for the safety of the Jewish population in the event of an Arab Palestinian state."[18]

It is not surprising in light of this attitude that the Peel Commission believed that it had no choice other than a division of the disputed area:

> On that point we would suggest that there is little moral value in maintaining the political unity of Palestine at the cost of perpetual hatred, strife, and bloodshed, and that there is little moral injury in drawing a political line through Palestine if peace and goodwill between the people on either side of it can thereby in the long run be attained. . . . Partition seems to offer at least a chance of ultimate peace. We can see none in any other plan.[19]

Once again, in 1947, the Palestinians were offered a state, this time somewhat smaller than the one offered a decade earlier, but still quite large. Again they rejected it, preferring instead to try, with the help of other Arab nations, to destroy the nascent Jewish state. Israel immediately accepted the United Nations partition, even though it was left with a small state in which large portions of its Jewish populations could easily be cut off from each other.

Twenty years later, after Israel won the Six-Day War, the Palestinians rejected Security Council Resolution 242, which could have provided the basis for a two-state solution. The Arabs rejected 242 because it required the recognition of Israel. They issued their three infamous "no's": "no recognition, no negotiation, no peace." Israel accepted 242. As Abba Eban characterized this unhappy result, "[The Six-Day War was] the first war in history which has ended with the victors suing for peace and the vanquished calling for unconditional surrender."[20]

It is interesting to speculate what the situation would be like today for the Palestinians if Israel had not captured the Gaza Strip and the West Bank in the 1967 war. There is no reason to believe that either Egypt or Jordan would have voluntarily ended their two-decade-long occupation over the Palestinians. Nor is there any reason to believe that the world would have cared, since the international community expressed virtually no concern over these occupations. It is even possible that the Palestinians would never have sought statehood from their Egyptian and Jordanian occupiers, since there was virtually no independence movement among the Palestinians during that twenty-year period. I am not meaning to suggest that Israel's capture and occupation of these territories has been good for the Palestinians. What I am suggesting is that it was no worse, and in many ways was probably better, than the preexisting occupation.

In 1979, during its negotiations with Egypt at Camp David, Israel offered to end the occupation of the Gaza Strip and return it to Egypt, which would then have been free to grant some degree of independence to the Palestinians living there. But Egypt refused to take back the Gaza Strip. Instead, it essentially gave up all claims to that volatile area[21] and agreed to the election of a Palestinian administrative authority and a process for negotiated autonomy. The Palestinians denounced this agreement and boycotted the subsequent autonomy talks, thereby assuring a continuation of the occupation.[22]

Then in 2000, Ehud Barak offered the Palestinians statehood on 100 percent of the Gaza Strip and more than 95 percent of the West Bank and the adjoining land. Arafat refused to accept the offer, because it would have required him to give up the so-called "right of return," which, if exercised by the four million Palestinians claiming to be descendants of those who once lived in Israel, would have quickly ended Israel's independent existence.

As the historian Benny Morris summarized the situation with regard to partition and the two-state solution:

> It is certainly true that neither side liked the idea [of partition], but in 1937, in 1947, and in 1993–2000 the Zionist leadership and then the Israeli leadership accepted—and in the latter years, even proposed—compromises based on the idea of partition, whereas the Palestinian leadership, under [Jerusalem grand mufti] Husseini and again under Arafat, rejected all proposals for partition.[23]

In *The Case for Israel*, I predicted that "[w]hen the Palestinians want their own state more than they want to destroy the Jewish state, most Israelis will welcome a peaceful Palestinian state as a good neighbor."[24] I also predicted that so long as Arafat remained in control of the Palestinian Authority, he would place his dream of ending Israel's existence above the pragmatic needs of his people for an end to the occupation and statehood.

Now, it seems, the pragmatic new leaders of the Palestinian movement finally do want a Palestinian state more than they want the end of Israel—or at least they are prepared to accept Israel, for now, as a means toward achieving Palestinian statehood. This is a step that no Palestinian leader was willing to take before the death of Arafat.

The precise borders of a Palestinian state should be decided by a combination of factors. First and foremost must be Israel's security needs. After all, it was Israel that was threatened with annihilation in 1948, 1967, and 1973. Israel poses no threat to its neighbors if it is not attacked. Resolution 242 expressly recognizes the need for "secure and recognized boundaries, free from threats or acts of force." That resolution also implicitly acknowledges that the pre-1967 borders—which were never "recognized" as final—were not secure. Border changes were expected, though not ones that were major in scope.

Fortunately, Israel's reasonable security needs can now be met without significant effect on Palestinian population centers. The Alon Plan, proposed by a former Israeli general and cabinet member following the 1967 war, contemplated security adjustments to the pre-1967 borders, including the retention by Israel of a "six–seven mile deep strip along the West Bank of the Jordan river" as a "security belt" against the

Jordanian army.[25] Not all of these security measures are still required, because Israel is no longer in a state of belligerency with Jordan, but some new ones may be necessary because of the increasing threat of terrorism. As we will see in chapter 3, the overall impact of any needed changes on Palestinian life will be relatively small and should not prevent the creation of a viable Palestinian state.

In addition to these minor security changes, there will have to be some border adjustments that recognize the new residential realities on the ground. Following the Six-Day War, Israel annexed several areas adjacent to Jerusalem and built large numbers of permanent apartment buildings on the land, which have now become suburban parts of greater Jerusalem. Forty thousand Israelis live in the southern Jerusalem suburb of Gilo;[26] thirty thousand Israelis currently live in Maale Adumim.[27] The reality—recognized by all reasonable negotiators—is that they are there to stay. As the *New York Times* reported on April 19, 2005, "[T]he Palestinians, in every negotiation so far, have seemed ready to cede Maale Adumim to the Israelis for other land."[28] This is probably also true of the other large settlement block outside of Jerusalem. The amount of land involved is relatively small, especially in comparison with the number of people who now live on it. In exchange for keeping this small amount of land, Israel should offer a comparable amount of Israeli land, consistent with security needs, to the new Palestinian state. More important, the vast majority of Palestinians—99.5 percent of them—now living on the West Bank would be living within the new Palestinian state and outside of the security fence. Their lives should not be affected in a significant way by the new borders.

It has been suggested that the exchange should also focus on Israeli land now populated by Israeli Arabs, who may want to become part of the new Palestinian state. That would seem a logical exchange—Israeli land populated by Palestinians becomes part of the Palestinian state, while Palestinian land (or, more accurately, disputed land) populated by Israelis remains part of Israel. Logic, however, is subordinate to democracy and Israel is a democracy in which Arab citizens have the same rights as Jewish and Christian citizens. Arab-Israeli citizens and their land could not lawfully be "traded" to the Palestinian state without the consent of these citizens, perhaps by a local referendum that supported such an exchange. At the moment, the vast majority of Israeli Arabs want to remain part of Israel.[29] The journalist Yossi Klein Halevi reported on this attitude on assignment to Um Al-Fahm, quoting a

Palestinian pastry shop owner as saying, "The Israeli mentality has become part of us. When I traveled in Egypt and Jordan, I realized I couldn't live in an Arab country. We've gotten used to speaking our minds." This attitude may change over time, were the Palestinian state to become economically viable, politically secure, religiously free, and protective of individual rights. If a majority of Israeli Arabs living in an area contiguous to the Palestinian state were to vote to become Palestinian citizens, and if annexing their land to the Palestinian state would not endanger Israeli security, then such a voluntary annexation—with appropriate compensation to those Arabs who chose to remain in Israel—might make sense. But this utopian solution is far in the future.

The other important considerations that must be factored into any final agreement regarding borders are ones of principle—and these are often the most difficult about which to reach agreement. It has long been a fundamental principle of Israeli, as well as American, policy that terrorism must never be rewarded. To the contrary, it must be disincentivized and deterred by punishment. The Palestinians should understand this well, since they have lost much by relying more on terrorism than negotiation. As Yossi Klein Halevi summarized the situation, "Under the Peel Commission, the Palestinians would have received 80% of the territory between the river and the sea; under the 1947 partition plan, 45%; under Camp David, around 20%."[30] They would have had a large state before the Second World War had they accepted the proposal of the Peel Commission. Instead, they responded with terrorism and with support for the Nazis. They were punished with an offer by the United Nations of a somewhat smaller—though still quite large—state in 1947. Again they responded with violence and terrorism. Again they were punished with a smaller landmass (which was quickly carved up between Jordan and Egypt). Then in 1967 the Arab states were offered Resolution 242, which could have resulted in an Arab state over nearly all of the West Bank and the Gaza Strip. Again they rejected the offer, and the result was a long-term occupation. Finally, in 2000 and 2001, the Palestinians were firmly offered a state on all of the Gaza Strip and nearly all of the West Bank. Again they replied with terrorism instead of negotiation.

Now many Palestinians would like the same offer they rejected in 2000 and 2001. But the principle of disincentivizing and deterring terrorism demands that they be offered less—and certainly not more—than they could have gotten had they opted for negotiation instead of

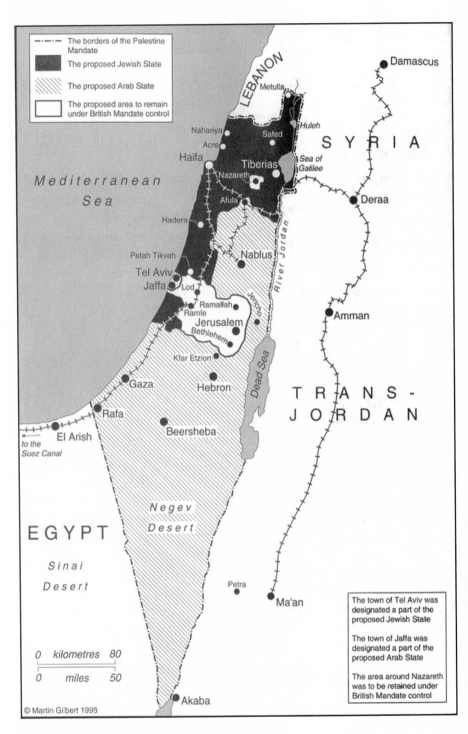

Peel Commission Proposal, 1937

22

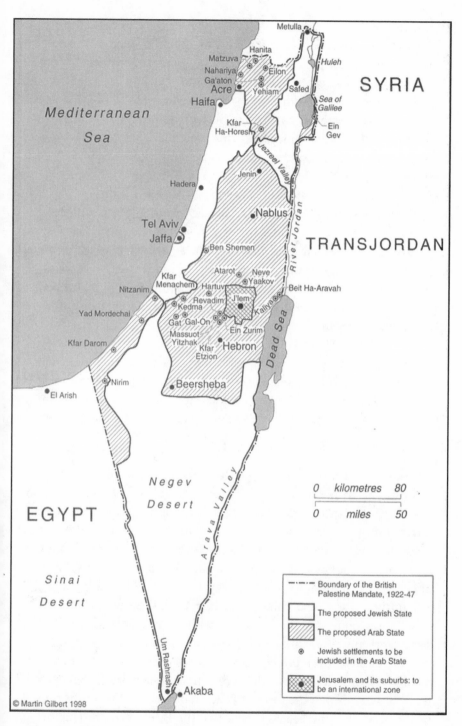

UN Partition Plan, 1947

suicide bombers in 2000 and 2001. If Israel were to offer the Palestinians *more*, after four years of terrorism, than they would have had by negotiating, a terrible message would be sent: namely, that terrorism produces better results than negotiation. Such a message would encourage resorting to terrorism by aggrieved groups all over the world and must be rejected as a matter of high principle.[31]

Many Palestinians understand this principle. The *New York Times* interviewed several residents of the West Bank and Gaza in February 2005, following the election of Mahmoud Abbas:

> [T]he Palestinians interviewed recognized with bitterness that their own political perspectives have narrowed, and that they had lost ground, despite so many deaths over the last four and [a] half years. They expressed nostalgia for the relative prosperity and freedom of travel they had before the outbreak of this last intifada, in September 2000—even though those conditions were onerous enough to fuel the intifada itself.
>
> "Before the intifada we used to go to Israel to work or to shop, and people had some money," said Nasir al-Bayouk, 41, sitting in a taxi in a long line at Abu Houleh, as cold rain and hail hammered down. He used to own a restaurant, but it failed. "We've lost a lot in this intifada," he said. "Before, we were negotiating for a state. Now we're negotiating over Abu Houleh, and that's it."[32]

Some Palestinians would prefer a different principle—one entirely inconsistent with the war against terrorism. They believe that they deserve to be *paid* a price, rather than having to *pay* a price, for the terrorism: "We hear Israel wants peace, and we want it, we want this cease-fire. But at the same time, all the sacrifices we made during this intifada can't be for free. People lost their loved ones, and we need a price for this."[33] In other words, they want a reward for having initiated a campaign of suicide bombings in which both Palestinians and Israelis died. This would be in direct conflict with the principle on which both Israeli and American antiterrorism policy is based.

This conflict over principles and perspectives will be difficult to resolve. Many Palestinians believe they have already paid a heavy price for their terrorism in the form of Israeli reprisals and the deaths caused by them, while many Israelis believe that the Palestinians, by employing terrorism, are responsible for all the deaths—those caused by the terrorists and those caused by Israel's legitimate efforts to prevent and deter terrorism against its citizens.

In the end, there seems to be widespread agreement that the only way to resolve these and other disagreements is by negotiation rather than by a renewal of the violence. The *New York Times* quoted a West Bank Palestinian as follows:

> "Everyone agrees that violence will not solve our problem, but worsen it," he said. "We'll never achieve stability unless we negotiate, and that's true with Israel and also with Hamas."
>
> People's desires are simple, Mr. Filfil said—live, work, travel freely and raise their children. "Most people don't want to die," he said. "But people don't want to be cheated or sold short. They don't want to forget the national issues—a Palestinian state with open borders, with its capital in Jerusalem."[34]

Even if the Palestinians and the Arabs recognize Israel's right to exist as an independent Jewish state with secure and defensible boundaries and free from terrorism, there will be no real and enduring peace until Israel's other enemies—academic, religious, political, and diplomatic— finally come to grips with the reality that Israel is here to stay and that its existence is a force for good in the world. Grudging acceptance of Israel, on tactical or pragmatic grounds, will not be enough, especially if such acceptance is seen as merely a "stage" in the ultimate object: namely, Israel's eventual replacement by a Muslim state. So long as Israel is treated or even regarded as somewhat less "legitimate," "normal," or "acceptable" than Australia, South Africa, the United States, Jordan, or Pakistan, there will be some who will remain dedicated to Israel's ultimate disappearance, and even some who will continue to take action calculated to achieve that destructive and bigoted goal. If such attitudes and actions persist, Israel will be required to remain on guard against its sworn enemies. This will, in turn, generate concerns among Israel's Palestinian and other Arab neighbors, thus continuing the cycle of suspicion—and belligerency.

This cycle must and can be ended, but it will take more than a cold peace between former enemies. It will require these former enemies to call off their extremist allies and to urge them to accept—really accept—Israel as a full and normal member of the international community. This will require an end to *all* efforts at divestment, boycott, exclusion, and every other form of singular condemnation of the Jewish state. (As I will show in part 2, these bigoted efforts to demonize and delegitimate Israel have persisted, sometimes even accelerated, as Israel has moved toward ending the occupation of Gaza and negotiating a full peace based on the two-state solution.) On the positive side, a real peace will require that Israel be invited—indeed welcomed—into all international organizations from which it is today, in fact, if not in law, banned. As Professor Anne Bayefsky, an expert in international organizations, summarized the situation in January 2005, "In March the UN will begin its annual session of the UN Human Rights Commission, at which Israel will be the only UN member state not allowed to participate in full because UN states continue to prevent it from gaining equal membership in a regional group."[35] Not surprisingly, the commission immediately condemned Israel but none of its Arab neighbors.[36] Other organizations from which Israel has been effectively excluded include the Security Council and the International Court of Justice.

No one can reasonably expect Israel and its former enemies to "beat their swords into plowshares," or to see the "wolf dwelling with the lamb,"[37] as the Bible prophesied. A real peace, based on universal acceptance of Israel, is feasible, but it will take more than Israelis and Palestinians alone to achieve it. It will take an end to the hatred directed against the Jewish state by so many academics, religious leaders, diplomats, and others determined to see it destroyed.

The writer and philosopher Amos Oz does not expect old enemies "to fall in love" with each other. "Let's not be sentimental." He sees the conflict as a "tragedy in the exact sense of the word"—a "collision between one very powerful claim and another no less powerful." Employing a literary analogy, he believes that tragedies "can be resolved in one of two ways: there is the Shakespearian resolution and there is the Chekhovian one. At the end of a Shakespearian tragedy, the stage is strewn with dead bodies and maybe there's some justice hovering high above. A Chekhov tragedy, on the other hand, ends with everybody disillusioned, embittered, heart-broken, disappointed, absolutely shattered, but still alive. And I want a Chekhovian resolution and not a Shakespearian one for the Israeli-Palestine tragedy."[38]

2   Is the One-State Solution a Barrier to Peace?

The very idea of a "Jewish State"—a state in which Jews and the Jewish religion have exclusive privileges from which non-Jewish citizens are forever excluded—is rooted in another time and place. Israel, in short, is an anachronism.

> —*Tony Judt, New York University history professor and director of the Remarque Institute*[1]

A bi-national state is not the alternative *for* Israel. It is an alternative *to* Israel.

> —*Leon Wieseltier, literary editor of the* New Republic[2]

[W]e must in the end come back to what has been socialist Zionism's standing offer to the Palestinian Arabs—reasonable partition of the country in accordance with demographic realities; recognition for recognition; security for security; self-determination for self-determination.

> —*Amos Oz, Israeli author and peace activist*[3]

Because the two-state solution requires the recognition of Israel's right to continue to exist as a Jewish democracy, those who oppose Israel's existence have been trying to sell the "one-state" or "binational" solution. I first challenged this ploy—and that's all it is—in a debate with Noam Chomsky back in 1973. Chomsky's proposal at that time was consistent with the PLO party line. He wanted to abolish the state of Israel and to substitute a "secular, binational state," based on the model of binational "brotherhood" that then prevailed in Lebanon. Chomsky repeatedly pointed to Lebanon, where Christians and Muslims "lived side by side," sharing power in peace and harmony. This was just two years before Lebanon imploded in fratricidal disaster. He also used to point to the former Yugoslavia as a model of a one-state solution.[4] This was before it too blew up into five separate nation-states.

This is what I said about this harebrained scheme in our 1973 debate:

> Putting aside the motivations behind such a proposal when it is made by the Palestinian organizations, why do not considerations of self-determination and community control favor two separate states: one Jewish and one Arab? Isn't it better for people of common background to control their own life, culture, and destiny (if they so choose), than to bring together in an artificial way people who have shown no ability to live united in peace? I confess to not understanding the logic of the proposal, even assuming its good will.

My counterproposal was that "Israel should declare, in principle, its willingness to give up the captured territories in return for a firm assurance of lasting peace. By doing so, it would make clear what I think the vast majority of Israelis believe: it has no interest in retaining the territories for any reason other than protection from attack."

Chomsky rejected my proposal out of hand. He characterized it as a mere return to the "colonialist status quo." Only the dismantling of the colonialist Jewish state would satisfy the PLO, and only the creation of a secular, binational Palestine in "all of Palestine" would satisfy Chomsky.

The violence in Lebanon and Yugoslavia relegated the Chomsky proposal to the dustbin of history until the PLO removed it from the trash and tried to dust it off and resell it in 2004. The lawyer for the PLO, Michael Tarazi, wrote an op-ed article for the *New York Times* in which he argued that Israel is both unwilling to disengage and incapable of disengaging from the West Bank, so that a de facto binational state already exists and only awaits international recognition.[5] Tony Judt, a New York University history professor, tried to give this nonstarter some academic credibility by publishing an article in the *New York Review of Books* that characterized Israel as "an anachronism" and called for "a single, integrated, binational state of Jews and Arabs, Israelis and Palestinians."[6]

It is rare for events to prove a historian completely wrong within a decade of his asserting historical truths. In Judt's case, it took less than a year. He published his anti-Israel screed in October 2003. In it he declared that "the Middle East peace process is finished"—not delayed or postponed, but forever *"finished."* He also believed that "the two state solution—the core of the Oslo process and the present 'road map'—is probably already *doomed."* Not endangered but "doomed"! And he criticized those who, in the spirit of "a ventriloquist's dummy, pitifully recite . . . the Israeli cabinet line: It's all Arafat's fault." These "dummies" included, of course, President Bill Clinton, U.S. chief negotiator Dennis Ross, and President George W. Bush, as well as Saudi Arabia's Prince Bandar, who represented Saudi Arabia at the negotiations.[7] Dennis Ross put it this way:

> Did we come close? Yes. Were the Palestinian negotiators ready to do the deal that was available? Yes. Did we ultimately fail because of the mistakes that Barak made and the mistakes that Clinton made? No, each, regardless of his tactical mistakes, was ready to confront history and mythology. Only one leader was unable or unwilling to confront history and mythology: Yasir Arafat.[8]

Well, it turned out the dummies were right and the professor was wrong. The peace process was not finished. All it needed to start up again was the death of Arafat, because its rejection was in fact "all Arafat's fault." Arafat's untimely death (untimely, because if it had come a few years earlier the Camp David negotiations would almost certainly have produced peace and a Palestinian state) immediately changed the dynamics and restarted the peace process. Rarely has history provided such a natural experiment: while Arafat was alive the peace process remained stymied; as soon as Arafat died the peace process continued. This alone should be more than enough to disqualify Judt from ever again being taken seriously about how to achieve peace in the Middle East.

But there is more, much more. The idea of a one-state solution comes as close to a crackpot idea as anything ever published in a serious intellectual journal, especially by a writer who claims to be interested in what's good "for the Jews." You see, Judt's basic point, as he wrote in a *New York Review of Books* article, is that "the depressing truth is that Israel is bad for the Jews." I've heard all that before. When Joseph Lieberman was nominated to be the Democratic vice presidential candidate in 2000, some frightened Jews worried that a Jewish vice president—or, God forbid, a Jewish president—would be "bad for the Jews," because *all* the Jews would be blamed for his mistakes. I recall once during a question-and-answer period following a speech in Los Angeles being asked by a woman whether having "so many Jewish professors and students at Harvard was bad for the Jews." (This was before Harvard had a Jewish president.) Jewish success, Jewish influence in the media, Jewish Nobel Prize winners—all bad for the Jews! Now comes Tony Judt:

> Today, non-Israeli Jews feel themselves once again exposed to criticism and vulnerable to attack for things they didn't do. But this time it is a Jewish state, not a Christian one, which is holding them hostage for its own actions. Diaspora Jews cannot influence Israeli policies, but they are implicitly identified with them, not least by Israel's own insistent claims upon their allegiance. The behavior of a self-described Jewish state affects the way everyone else looks at Jews. The increased incidence of attacks on Jews in Europe and elsewhere is primarily attributable to misdirected efforts, often by young Muslims, to get back at Israel. The depressing truth is that Israel's current behavior is not just bad for America, though it surely is. It is not even just bad for Israel itself, as many Israelis silently acknowledge. The depressing truth is that Israel today is bad for the Jews.[9]

In other words, the real cause of anti-Semitism is Israel, because non-Jews hold all Jews accountable for the actions of the Jewish state. This is no more than a modern-day variation on a very old theme: rich and powerful Jews, like the Rothschilds, caused anti-Semitism; communist Jews, like Marx and Trotsky, caused anti-Semitism; media-owning Jews, like Pulitzer and Sulzberger, caused anti-Semitism; poor Orthodox Jews caused anti-Semitism. It's all the fault of the Jews themselves, not the anti-Semites.

Leon Wieseltier answered Judt as follows:

I detect the scars of dinners and conferences. He does not wish to be held accountable for things that he has not himself done, or to be regarded as the representative of anyone but himself. It is disagreeable to be falsely represented by others. These are old anxieties. . . . Why doesn't he simply delete his Zionism or his support for Israel from his inventory of multiple elective identities? Why must Israel pay for his uneasiness with its life? . . .

For the notion that all Jews are responsible for whatever any Jews do, that every deed that a Jew does is a Jewish deed, is not a Zionist notion. It is an anti-Semitic notion. . . . But if you explain anti-Semitism as a response to Jews, and racism as a response to blacks, and misogyny as a response to women, then you have not understood it. You have reproduced it.

And bad for which Jews? Surely Israel is not bad for the Jews of Russia, who may need a haven; or for the Jews of Argentina, who may need a haven; or for the Jews of Iran, who may need a haven; or for any Jews who may need a haven.[10]

There is an even better answer: let "the Jews" decide what is good or bad for them. For too many years, others have determined the destiny of the Jewish people. It was an important part of the theory of Zionism to establish self-determination for the Jewish people, rather than elitist decision making by a handful of Jews who are embarrassed by Ariel Sharon or other elected leaders of the Jewish state.

It is not surprising that the overwhelming majority of Israeli Jews believe that Israel is not bad for the Jews.[11] The same, I suspect, is true of American Jews and even of European Jews who are the particular object of Judt's misguided and patronizing solicitude.

And they are right. Notwithstanding the anti-Semitic attacks on some Jews in some countries that may be attributable to hatred of Israel, the Jewish state has been good for the Jews. It has also been good for the world. And, difficult as Judt and his ilk may find it to accept, Israel will prove to be good for the Palestinians and the Arab world in general, because of the model of democracy and free-market economy it provides. King Hussein of Jordan told me as much during a conversation in 1996, and other moderate Arabs have also implicitly acknowledged beneficial effects stemming from the Israeli model. Many Palestinians also acknowledge this reality, as evidenced by polls showing that they favor the Israeli model of democracy, and especially its independent judiciary, over all other models, including the United States.[12] And the fact that most Israeli Arabs want to remain Israeli, rather than become Palestinian, citizens provides some confirmation as well.[13]

It would be a tragedy if the first modern democratic state to be abolished in the name of some abstract principle of "multiculturalism" were to be the world's only Jewish state, rather than one or more of the numerous Muslim, Protestant, Catholic, or Eastern Orthodox states. This is especially so because Israel, unlike many of these other ethnoreligious states, does not have a single "established" religion or any religious barriers to office holding, citizenship, or other rights. As Edward Rothstein put it in the *New York Times*:

> Perhaps then, despite Mr. Judt's embarrassment, the binational experiment might first be tried elsewhere? Say between Iran and Iraq? Or Pakistan and India? Or France and Germany? Until then attention might return to the real world and to the details that inspire such proposals of despair.[14]

In fact, Israel already *is* a secular binational nation, even while retaining its identity as a Jewish state, in much the same way as France retains its identity as French and Germany as German. "Jewish" is more than merely a religious identification. Judaism is a civilization and culture that began as a religion and has become, especially since the Enlightenment and the establishment of Israel by secular socialists, a largely secular civilization. Israel is more secular than any other Middle Eastern state or any Muslim state. It is far more secular, in practice, than the United States. Its 1.25 million Arabs are full citizens with representation in the Knesset and on the Supreme Court. Arabic is an official Israeli language and Israeli Arabs enjoy more rights in Israel than anywhere else in the Middle East. Israeli Arabs are better off—as measured by longevity, health care, legal rights, even religious liberty—than other Arabs in the Middle East.

Forcibly integrating Israel proper and the occupied territories into one political entity would be the surest way to destroy Israel's secular, democratic character. There would be an immediate struggle for demographic superiority. Every death would be seen as a victory by the other side and every birth as a defeat. Within decades, the different birth rates would ensure that Palestinians will outnumber Jews, and the binational state would become another Islamic state—Greater Palestine.

An Arab majority would bode ominously for a Jewish minority. Jewish life within Arab nations, as well as within the British Mandate of Palestine, has been marked by discriminatory laws against *dhimmi* (Jews and Christians), expulsions, and pogroms.[15] Considering the close proximity and history of hostilities between Israeli Jews and Palestinians, it is more than likely that Jews would fare even worse in a Greater Palestine than they have elsewhere in the Arab world. There would be, as Benny Morris puts it, "old scores" to settle.[16] And the wide economic gap between Jews and Palestinians would certainly not "make for peaceful co-existence."[17]

This binational state would be truly devastating to Israeli Jews, left defenseless once they had lost their sovereignty and military deterrent. It is for good reason that I have likened the proposed one-state solution in the Middle East to Hitler's one-state solution for Europe. Only this time, the Jews would be geographically concentrated and easier to identify. David Frum makes this point powerfully:

> If the day were ever to come when the Jews of Israel lost the power to defend themselves and had to submit to the rule of their neighbors, the outcome would not be "pluralism" but slaughter. . . . One must hate Israel very much indeed to prefer such an outcome to the reality of the liberal democracy that exists in Israel today.[18]

Five hundred thousand Hindus and Muslims died in the process of partitioning the Indian subcontinent. No one today recommends that those two ethnicities be reintegrated into a binational state in order to resolve the Kashmir dispute. Likewise, Israelis and Palestinians are already, for the most part, geographically distinct. It would be absurd to suggest that they both forgo their separate aspirations to self-determination as a testing ground for Tony Judt's failed multicultural fantasies.

What is certain, though, is that neither Israeli Jews nor Palestinians want to be subsumed in a Greater Palestine. A binational state would not only imperil its Jewish population, but would eradicate the one state in the Middle East that affords its Muslim citizens more expansive civil liberties and political prerogative than any other. As Michael Walzer observed:

> Every opinion poll shows that a majority of Israelis and Palestinians want the two-state solution. The US government is formally committed

to it; so are the Europeans. There is still time to enforce it. And afterward, when the French, Germans, Swedes, Bulgarians, and Japanese begin to worry about their anachronistic politics, Jews and Palestinians will be able to join them.[19]

The binational Greater Palestine solution is the far left's equivalent of the Israeli far right's Greater Israel. The late Rabbi Meir Kahane was rightfully denounced, his party even outlawed in Israel, for advocating the transfer of Palestinians out of the West Bank. Tony Judt's binational state would do the same to the Jews, only, we can reasonably assume, far more violently.

The one-state solution is an argument made in bad faith. It is an attempt to accomplish by law and demography what Hamas seeks to achieve by terrorism: the extinction of Israel. The practical consequences of such a state would be to leave millions of Jews geographically isolated, politically powerless, and physically defenseless. The one-state solution is rejectionism, pure and simple. But its proponents do not merely reject peace; they reject Israel's right to exist altogether.

In a world with numerous Muslim states, there is surely room for one Jewish state. The one-state solution will surely fail, but it is also important that it be taken off the table immediately, because its very advocacy poses a serious barrier to the only peace that has any realistic chance for success: peace based on the two-state solution.

3 Is a Noncontiguous Palestinian State a Barrier to Peace?

[I]n fact, Israel conceded only non-contiguous Palestinian areas which were all to have Israeli security posts and settlements surrounding them. In addition, there was to be no common border between Palestine and any Arab state.

> —*Edward Said, late Columbia University professor of English and comparative literature*[1]

Bill Clinton and Israeli prime minister Barak did propose an improvement: consolidation to three cantons, under Israeli control, virtually separated from one another and from the fourth enclave, a small area of East Jerusalem, the center of Palestinian communications. The fifth canton was Gaza. It is understandable that maps are not to be found in the US mainstream. Nor is the prototype, the Bantustan "homelands" of apartheid South Africa, ever mentioned.

> —*Noam Chomsky, MIT professor of linguistics*[2]

[The Camp David offer was] less than a Bantustan, for your information.

> —*Yasser Arafat, late chairman of the Palestinian Authority*[3]

To this day, Arafat has never honestly admitted what was offered to the Palestinians—a deal that would have resulted in a Palestinian state, with territory in over 97 percent of the West Bank, Gaza, and Jerusalem; with Arab East Jerusalem as the capital of that state (including the holy place of the Haram al-Sharif, the Noble Sanctuary); with an international presence in place of the Israeli Defense Force in the Jordan Valley; and with the unlimited right of return for Palestinian refugees to their state but not to Israel. Nonetheless, Arafat continues to hide behind the canard that he was offered Bantustans— a reference to the geographically isolated black homelands created by the apartheid-era South African government. Yet with 97 percent of the territory in Palestinian hands, there would have been no cantons. Palestinian areas would not have been isolated or surrounded. There would have been territorial integrity and contiguity in both the West Bank and Gaza, and there would have been independent borders with Egypt and Jordan.

—*Dennis Ross, Middle East adviser and chief negotiator under Presidents George H. W. Bush and Bill Clinton*[4]

So I want everybody to adjust to reality. So I say, no, here's the map you were offered. No cantons. Territory that was, in fact, contiguous with an independent border with Jordan, because we can't make peace until everybody admits what reality is. Maps are one way of demonstrating reality.

—*Dennis Ross*[5]

Some opponents of the two-state solution reject the idea that the proposed Palestinian state could be economically or politically viable, since its final borders are likely to leave portions of the new state unconnected geographically to all other portions of the state. The Gaza Strip, in particular, will be separated from the West Bank by approximately twenty-eight miles of Israeli territory. The Gaza Strip will, however, not be cut off from the Arab world. It will be contiguous with Egypt and, because it is a seaport, will have maritime access to all Mediterranean nations and the world. The West Bank will be contiguous with Jordan and, through Jordan, will have access to the Aqaba seaport and to the world. Even the problem of noncontiguity between the Gaza Strip and the West Bank is not insoluble. Creative solutions have been proposed,

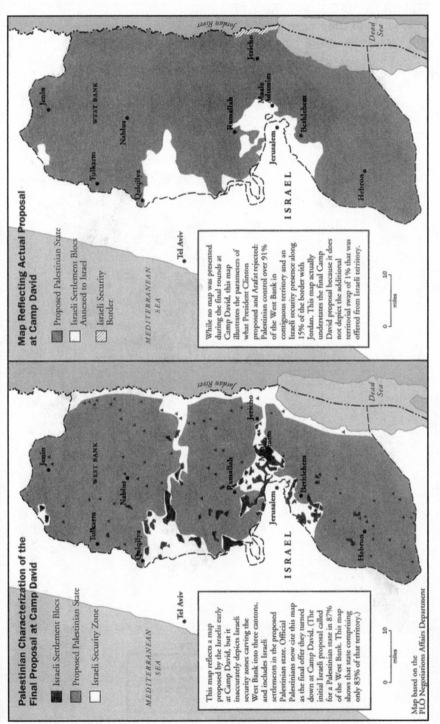

The Bantustan accusation versus Israel's actual Camp David offer

Map Reflecting Clinton Ideas

■ Proposed Palestinian State
□ Israeli Settlement Blocs Annexed to Israel

Haifa

Sea of Galilee

MEDITERRANEAN SEA

0 — 15
miles

N

Jenin

Jordan River

Tulkarm

Nablus

Qalqilya

Tel Aviv

WEST BANK

Ramallah

Jericho

Jerusalem — Maale Adumim

ISRAEL

Bethlehem

Gaza

Hebron

GAZA STRIP

Dead Sea

JORDAN

EGYPT

No formal map was presented to the Israelis and Palestinians in December 2000 by President Clinton, but this map illustrates the Clinton ideas—a Palestinian state in 95% of the West Bank and 100% of Gaza. This map actually understates the Clinton ideas by not showing an additional 1 to 3% of territorial swaps to the Palestinian state from areas within Israel.

The Clinton Parameters, December 23, 2000

including a secure elevated highway—connecting the two Palestinian areas, which would be deemed Palestinian territory, or an internationally recognized "easement" or "right-of-way" from one Palestinian area to the other. In 1999, Ehud Barak proposed the building of a highway "from Beit Hanoun [in Gaza] to Dura near Hebron . . . with four lanes, a railway line, a water pipe, a communications cable." Such a project would enable the Palestinians to travel between their territories without actually entering Israel. Barak estimated a cost of approximately $200 million.[6] And at the Taba talks of 2001, European Union envoy Miguel Moratinos reported that "[b]oth sides agreed that there is going to be a safe passage from the north of Gaza (Beit Hanun) to the Hebron district, and that the West Bank and the Gaza Strip must be territorially linked. The nature of the regime governing the territorial link and sovereignty over it was not agreed."[7]

Moreover, whatever noncontiguity remains between the West Bank and Gaza is *not* a result of Israel's occupation following the 1967 war. The West Bank and Gaza were essentially noncontiguous as a result of the United Nations partition of 1947. They became even more separated as a result of the Arab attack against Israel between 1947 and 1949. Nothing has changed with regard to this noncontiguity as a result of any unilateral Israeli actions. Indeed Israel has offered to ameliorate it—though it is not required to by international law—by compromising its own territorial sovereignty. Yet it is blamed for the problem of noncontiguity between the West Bank and Gaza.

Finally, both the West Bank and the Gaza Strip will be internally contiguous. Notwithstanding the overblown allegations of Bantustans (to use the politically loaded, but utterly inapt, terminology of current rejectionists who compare the lack of total contiguity of the proposed Palestinian state with the policy of the all-white racist South African regime that assigned its black population to ten separate "homelands" or Bantustans), the maps published by Dennis Ross and the more recent map by the *New York Times* show a completely contiguous West Bank. (There was never any claim that the Gaza Strip would be divided into Bantustans.) Every part of the Palestinian West Bank would be accessible to every other part. (Jerusalem raises some geographic and logistical issues of its own both for Israelis and Palestinians.) A Palestinian could travel from Bethlehem to Jericho to Ramallah to Nablus and to Jenin without ever encountering an Israeli, a checkpoint, or a security fence. The *New York Times* was correct when it reported that under the likely two-state solution, the potential "impact of the provisional new border on Palestinian life is, perhaps surprisingly, smaller than generally assumed."[8] Even the road connecting Ramallah to Bethlehem, and circumventing greater Jerusalem, would create little inconvenience. It would be similar to the circumferential highways that exist in many American cities (Route 128 in Boston is an example). Sometimes the quickest route between two points is not a straight line, especially through a major urban area.

Noncontiguity as a barrier to the two-state solution and thus to peace is largely a pretext. Many nations, including the United States, include noncontiguous areas.[9] Today's world, with high-tech Internet access and low-tech air connections, does not require contiguity for a state to be viable. As Bret Stephens has answered the argument: "[u]nless a Palestinian state has 'geographical integrity' and is 'sustainable,' it will inevitably lead to the 'one default option' which is a one-state, binational solution. But again, why?"[10]

Even in an era when contiguity was far more essential, the Jews of Palestine were willing to accept a two-state solution that left them with a noncontiguous state. The 1937 Peel Commission recommendation—accepted by the Jewish Agency but rejected by the Arab world—chopped up the Jewish state into several Bantustans. The Peel Commission proposed the following ameliorative to Jewish noncontiguity:

> [An open travel corridor] would also solve the problem, sometimes said to be insoluble, created by the contiguity of Jaffa with Tel Aviv to the north and the nascent Jewish town to the south. If necessary Mandatory police could be stationed on this belt. This arrangement may seem artificial, but it is clearly practicable.[11]

Even the two-state solution voted by the UN and accepted by Israel in 1948 created an essentially noncontiguous Jewish state, with Jewish Jerusalem and Safed effectively cut off from the rest of the state.

The Palestinians could have had an entirely contiguous and much larger state had they accepted the Peel Commission proposal in 1937. They could have had a more contiguous and larger state had they accepted the UN partition plan of 1948. Their leadership rejected both of these reasonable two-state proposals because they wanted the destruction of the Jewish state more than they wanted the establishment of their own state. They responded to these proposals with violence rather than with negotiation, and as a result will receive less than they would have achieved through negotiation. That is justice. It is also good policy.

If the Palestinians now really want their own state more than they want the destruction of the Jewish state, then geographic noncontiguity should not be a barrier to peace. Again, listen to Bret Stephens: "Palestinians could yet build a Monte Carlo in Jericho, a Vatican state in Bethlehem, a Luxembourg in Ramallah, a Cyprus in Gaza, a Singapore in Nablus, and so on."[12]

Stephens argues that the noncontiguity allegation, whether honest or not—and it is decidedly dishonest—is nothing but a pretext for Palestinians' unwillingness to say yes:

In fact, the entire issue of a Palestinian state's territorial viability is bogus—a substitute way of justifying why Palestinians won't settle for less than X-amount of territory. . . . But the significant point is that a country's viability, or "sustainability," is chiefly a function of the quality of governance, not the extent of terrain.[13]

In fact, the best predictor of a nation's viability is not its geographic size or contiguity. It is its democratic nature, its economic structure, its educational institutions, and its commitment to the rule of law.[14] These are all possible to achieve in the proposed Palestinian state, despite its lack of complete contiguity. Those who insist that noncontiguity is a barrier will never accept any two-state solution. The alternative they seek is the military conquest of Israel, its destruction as a Jewish state, and the establishment of an Islamic Palestinian state in what is now Israel. That is the "contiguous" Palestinian state they desire, and it will not happen. For peace to be achieved, the Palestinians will have to settle for a mostly contiguous state with functional connections, just as Israel was willing to settle for a noncontiguous state in 1937 and 1948.

In May 2005, the *New York Times* reported on a RAND Corporation study of how a Palestinian state could be functionally contiguous and viable as the result of a high-speed rail system connecting all of the major cities:

[The] high-speed railway would run for 70 miles along the West Bank ridges, linking Jenin in the North with Hebron in the south. The railway would then slip like a fishhook through the Negev desert to attach the West Bank to the Gaza Strip, running 130 miles in all

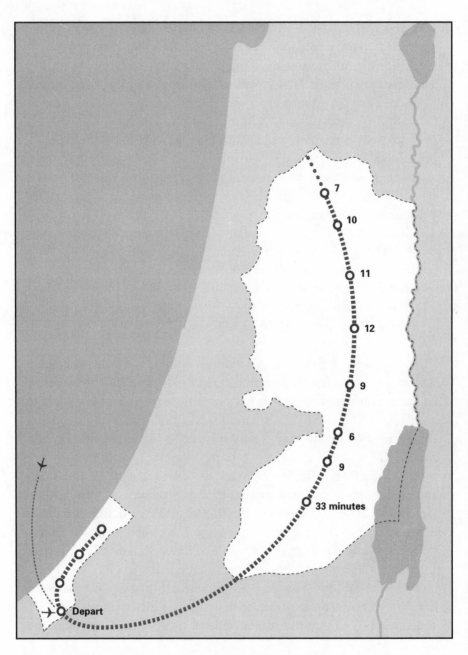

The proposed Interurban Rail Line. The critical infrastructure along the arc is a fast rail line linking almost all the primary cities of Gaza and the West Bank in just over ninety minutes. The rail line makes public transportation a national priority while establishing the "trunk" of the national infrastructure corridor.

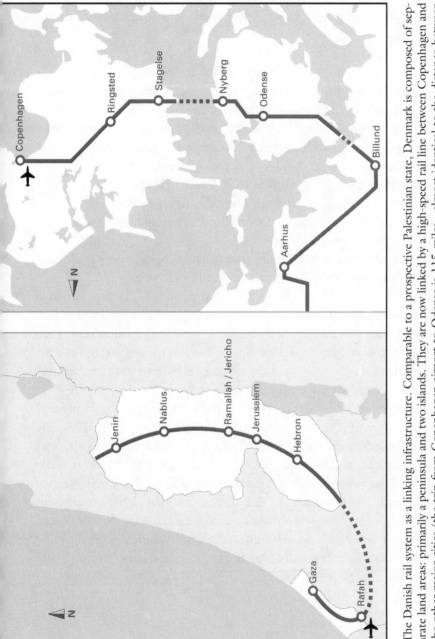

The Danish rail system as a linking infrastructure. Comparable to a prospective Palestinian state, Denmark is composed of separate land areas: primarily a peninsula and two islands. They are now linked by a high-speed rail line between Copenhagen and the other major cities (the trip from Copenhagen airport to Odense is 115 miles—almost identical to the distance between Rafah Airport and Nablus—and takes only 72 minutes). The final link across the Great Belt was accomplished by the engineering feat of building a rail tunnel and a vehicular bridge.

and establishing the connection between the two territories that development officials consider essential to a Palestinian economy. Alongside the railway, [the plan] proposes stretching a water conduit, a trench for fiber-optic cable, power lines, a toll road and a strip of parkland.

The RAND study has received qualified support from both Palestinian and Israeli officials. The deputy finance minister of the Palestinian Authority said, "I was very moved. . . . [I]t had that beauty of simplicity of design, and coherence, and comprehensiveness." The spokesman for the Israeli Embassy in Washington said, "The report has many elements that are positive, and we support the development of a Palestinian economy."[15] On June 7, 2005, *Haaretz* reported that "Israel has offered the Palestinian Authority to lay a rail line linking the Gaza Strip and West Bank that would enable passage between the two areas after the disengagement."

A map of the proposal demonstrates that complete geographic contiguity is not necessary for an economically successful state. There are other creative proposals as well, some that involve land swaps between Israel and Egypt that would result in a larger Gaza area and a link between Gaza and Jordan. Both moderate Israelis and Palestinians have a stake in the viability of a Palestinian state. Yet there are those anti-peace extremists who do not want to see a Palestinian state succeed and who will do and say anything to ensure its failure.

A leadership willing to use violence rather than settle for 95 percent of the loaf is not a leadership really interested in peace. This was demonstrated by Yasser Arafat at Camp David and Taba in 2000 and 2001. The only real hope for peace is that the current Palestinian leadership will be more like the pragmatic leadership of the Jewish Agency in 1937 and 1948 that put the real interest of its people before any ideological absolutes and was willing to accept far less than the whole loaf to which it believed it was morally, historically, and ideologically entitled. A Palestinian state will come about by compromise, or not at all.

4 Can Peace Be Achieved without Compromising Rights?

Hamas demands "the reinstitution of the Muslim state" on "every inch of Palestine," including all of what is now Israel. Any compromise, even if every Arab and Palestinian leader were to accept it, would be a violation of Islamic law. All peace initiatives or "so-called peaceful solutions . . . are . . . contrary to the beliefs of the Islamic Resistance Movement. For renouncing any part of Palestine means renouncing part of the religion. . . . There is no solution to the Palestinian problem except by Jihad."

—Hamas Charter[1]

There are no sweet compromises. Every compromise entails renouncing certain dreams and longings, limiting some appetites, giving up the fulfillment of certain aspirations, but only a fanatic finds compromise more bitter than death. This is why uncompromising fanaticism always and everywhere exudes the stench of death. Whereas compromise is in the essence of life itself.

The Torah says:

"Thou shalt opt for life."

Let *us* opt for life.

—Amos Oz, Israeli author and peace activist[2]

As long as any party to the Arab-Israeli conflict was obsessed with obtaining its historical, God-given rights, it was not going to be able to make decisions on the basis of its interests, which are ephemeral and derive not from the heavens but from the needs of daily life. It is impossible to exaggerate how important it is that Israelis and Palestinians have finally recognized each other's legitimate rights in historic Palestine, have set that issue aside, and can now focus on how to divide up the pie and their respective interests.

—*Thomas L. Friedman,* New York Times *columnist and author*[3]

The halakhah forbids transfer of land in Israel from Jews to gentiles. Whoever does so violates the Torah.

—*Rabbi Daniel Shilo of Kedumim*[4]

No government has the authority . . . to abandon parts of the Land of Israel to foreigners, and anything done to this end is null and void, in the name of the God of Israel. Israelis must do whatever they can "to prevent the implementation of the road map," though it is necessary "to avoid any violence, physical or verbal."

—*Statement by some five hundred members of the Union of Rabbis for the People of Israel and the Land of Israel, a group whose members include two former chief rabbis of Israel, Avraham Shapira and Mordechai Eliyahu, and other Torah authorities*[5]

"But we have the right . . ." This phrase, heard so often these days,[6] is intended as an argument-stopper. Rights are, in the words of the legal philosopher Ronald Dworkin, "trumps" over all other claims. They can also become barriers to compromise and to peace, since it is more difficult—for some impossible—to give up rights than to give up mere preferences or other claims. Amos Oz has offered the following distinction between a "right" and a "claim":

Perhaps rather than speak of a clash between "right and right", it is better to speak of "claim against claim". The term "right", at least in its secular sense, stands for something which is recognized by others, not for something that someone feels very strongly about. You may have the deepest conviction that a beloved person, place or object is exclusively your own, but as long as this is not the way others see it what you have is a claim, not a right.[7]

In the context of the Israeli-Palestinian conflict, "rights" are asserted—on both sides—that have made compromise difficult. Palestinians assert a "right of return" by all those (and all their descendants) who left—either by force or preference—what is now Israel during the 1947–1949 War of Independence that was started by the Arabs. The numbers that are now claimed—in the range of four million—would be enough to turn Israel into another Palestinian state. It is difficult to understand why Palestinians, given a choice between living in a Palestinian state or a Jewish state, would choose the latter, especially after so many years of insisting that Palestinian statehood is the only acceptable solution to the Palestinian diaspora. It would seem disloyal in the extreme for a Palestinian to prefer to move to a Jewish state and live as a minority than as a majority helping to build a new Palestinian state. Indeed, it has long been acknowledged—by Arab and Palestinian leaders—that the only justification for Palestinians opting to exercise their right of return would be a macropolitical, rather than a microhumanitarian, one. It would have to be part of a large-scale, carefully orchestrated plan to return millions of Palestinians to Israel in order to overwhelm the Jewish state with a Palestinian majority. On August 6, 1948, Emile Ghoury, the secretary of the Arab Higher Command, told the *Beirut Telegraph* that "it is inconceivable that the refugees should be sent back to their homes while they are occupied by the Jews. . . . It would serve as a first step toward Arab recognition of the state of Israel."[8] Shortly thereafter, the foreign minister of Egypt acknowledged that it is "known and appreciated that, in demanding the restoration of the refugees to Palestine, the Arabs intend that they shall return as the masters of the homeland, and not as slaves. More explicitly: they intend to annihilate the state of Israel."[9] In other words, the right of return was never seen as an individual right to be exercised by specific Palestinians, but rather as a group right (or power) to be exercised collectively or not at all.

A "collective" or "group" right is different from an individual right, in that it can be waived or compromised by the duly elected representatives of the collective or group when the general interest would thereby be served.

In order to achieve peace with Israel, the Palestinian leadership would have to waive or compromise the broad, collective political "right" to turn Israel into another Palestinian state by orchestrating a mass return of millions of Palestinians to Israel. They could still assert individual rights in particularly compelling cases of family reunification, for example, where nearly all of a particular family now live in Israel except for one or two members who wish to join them. Subject to legitimate security concerns, Israel should be willing—without necessarily recognizing the claim as a right or requiring the Palestinians to stop asserting it as a right—to negotiate a reasonable number of returns. This was approximately the formula proposed by Israeli and U.S. representatives during the Camp David–Taba negotiations in 2000 and 2001, and it is not unlike the proposals generated by the informal meetings in Geneva in 2003.

Virtually all reasonable Palestinians and their supporters understand that they cannot possibly negotiate a full macropolitical right of general return. Sabri Jiryis, a former Arab-Israeli lawyer who left Israel and became a member of the Palestinian National Council, has acknowledged that Arabs "must settle the Palestinians in their own midst and solve their problems,"[10] rather than deliberately exacerbate the problems by insisting on a right to return to Israel.

Virtually all reasonable Israelis and their supporters understand that no elected Palestinian leader can demand of his people that they give up *all* claimed rights of return, especially since this has been drummed into them for so many years. As Shimon Peres once told me, "You don't ask a people to give up their dream. You just don't let them turn it into our nightmare."

Sophisticated compromise is essential to an enduring resolution of this issue; the elements of such a compromise are already on the table and should be possible to achieve as part of an overall peace settlement.

There is a parallel right claimed by some Israelis, which may be called the "right to remain." This right is asserted by settlers who have long lived in government-sponsored settlements in the West Bank and in Gaza. Consider, for example, the claims made by residents of the Etzion bloc. These Jewish settlements had been established in the 1920s and 1930s. During the War of Independence, they were overrun by Palestinians and 240 Jewish residents were killed, many after surrendering. It was regarded as the Israeli Alamo: "Etzion is to Israel what the Alamo is to Americans."[11] When Israel recaptured Etzion in 1967, descendants of the murdered Jews, and some survivors, petitioned to "go home." The petition was granted and they have been living there for nearly forty years. Their familial roots in Etzion go back nearly eighty years. These, and other, claims are based, variously, on religious, political, ideological, and economic rights. They are also based on a transcendental right of the "Jewish people" to live in the biblical or historic homeland, as well as the right of Jews, as individuals, to live anywhere in the world, without any area being declared *judenrein*—closed to Jews, as many areas (including the entire nation of Jordan) have been, based on anti-Semitism.

These asserted rights to remain must also be deconstructed. Some are group or collective rights; others are individual rights. The collective rights claimed by Israelis as Israeli citizens may be compromised in the interests of peace by Israel's elected leaders. The collective rights of the Jewish people, whatever that may mean, may be more difficult to waive, but to the extent that Israel purports to represent the Jewish people, at least when it comes to geopolitical issues in the Middle East, these rights too may be negotiated in the interests of the even more fundamental right of the Jewish state and the Jewish people to live in peace. The individual rights of settlers, especially with regard to economic claims, must be dealt with legally and resolved by financial settlements of the kind that have already been offered and accepted by some. These settlers must be treated respectfully and generously, especially the ones who were encouraged by successive Israeli governments to move into the territories. But in the end, they must obey the law and submit to the overriding interests of the Israeli people to make peace. If they do not, they must be made to by lawful force.

There is yet a third claim of right made by many Sephardic Jews who were forced to leave the Arab and Muslim countries in which their ancestors had lived for centuries, sometimes millennia. These Jews were either expelled or frightened into leaving Iraq, Egypt, Yemen, Iran, Algeria, and other countries in the years following the establishment of Israel. Most were required to abandon their businesses, property, and other wealth without any compensation. Few, if any, want to return to inhospitable countries, but many seek financial compensation for their expropriated or forcibly abandoned property. Even Sabri Jiryis, of the Palestinian National Council, recognizes that the eviction of Jews from many Muslim countries is a serious issue: "the Jews of the Arab states were driven out of their ancient homes [and] shamefully deported after their property had been commandeered." Jiryis regards the expulsion of Jews from Arab countries and the expulsion of Arabs from some areas of Israel as a "population and property exchange." He believes that the best resolution is that "each party must bear the consequences."[12]

A global resolution of all of these claims of right will require pragmatic compromise, symbolic recognition, and good-faith willing-ness to focus more on the future than on the past. Much of the world today understands the Palestinian claim of right to return. It must also understand the settlers' claim of right to remain and the Sephardic claim of right to compensation in lieu of return. It must recognize that the Israelis as well as the Palestinians are compromising what they regard as important rights in the interest of peace. This is imperative because any compromise must not only *be* fair, it must also *be perceived* as being fair by the world and by those whose rights have been com-promised. Otherwise, grievances will remain, and festering grievances can become the seeds of violence. There must be a statute of limitations for the status of "refugee." Fifty years certainly seems long enough.

There is a wonderful Arabic word, difficult to translate into English, that captures the nature of the compromises that must be reached. The word is *taarradhin*, which, according to the wordsmith William Safire, "suggests the resolution of a conflict that involves no humiliation: our closest definition is 'a win-win outcome.'"[13] All sides of the Israeli-Arab-Palestinian conflict should strive for *taarradhin*.

There is also a wonderful Jewish story that recognizes that the perfect is the enemy of the practical. The Midrash has Abraham telling God that if you want the world to exist, "you cannot have complete justice; if it is complete justice you want, the world cannot endure." Or as Cicero put it: "Extreme justice is injustice." The peacemakers will never achieve perfect justice, but they can bring about a pragmatic peace.

5 Is the Division of Jerusalem a Barrier to Peace?

Jerusalem is Israel's eternal and undivided capital.

—Natan Sharansky, former Soviet dissident and
Israeli Knesset member[1]

You ought to let the Jews have Jerusalem; it was they who made it famous.

—Winston Churchill, late British prime minister[2]

First, we discuss Jerusalem—East and West. We are not ready to give up [any] of our rights in West [Jewish] Jerusalem, let alone East [Arab] Jerusalem. We have property there, as well as holy places and history.

—Palestinian Authority minister for Jerusalem affairs and
permanent status negotiation team member Faisal al-Husseini[3]

[N]o stone of the *Al-Buraq* [Western] Wall has any relation to Judaism. The Jews began praying at this wall only in the nineteenth century, when they began to develop [national] aspirations.

—Mufti of Jerusalem Sheikh 'Ikrima Sabri[4]

We rejected [Israeli praying privileges at Al-Haram] as well, but we agreed that they could pray next to the [Wailing] Wall, without acknowledging any Israeli sovereignty over it. [T]he Wall belongs to the Muslim *Waqf*, while the Jews are allowed to pray by it as long as they do not use a *Shofar*.

—*Mahmoud Abbas, president of the Palestinian Authority*[5]

Symbols have great power. Religious symbols have even greater power. It is particularly difficult to compromise religious symbols. And there is no religious symbol more powerful than Jerusalem—the "eternal capital of Judaism," Islam's "third holiest city," and the location of Christianity's "central event," the crucifixion and resurrection of Jesus Christ.

Yet Jerusalem must be divided if peace is to be achieved. Jerusalem must be divided politically because it is already divided geographically and demographically. Anyone who has visited the Holy Land understands that there is a Jewish Jerusalem, with a population of nearly half a million Israeli Jews. There is also a Palestinian Jerusalem, with a population of more than two hundred thousand Arabs.[6] Israel should control Jewish Jerusalem and Palestine should control Arab Jerusalem. That is easy to articulate in principle, but difficult to implement in practice.

The division of Jerusalem is difficult to implement because the demographic map is not easily turned into a political map. It is also difficult because some of the most powerful religious symbols are literally on top of each other—the Al-Aqsa mosque sits atop the traditional location of Solomon's Temple—and because other important religious sites are in close proximity to one another.

But pragmatic division is possible if there is a real desire for peace on all sides. Peace will require that with regard to Jerusalem, as with other divisive issues that have symbolic significance, the spirit of compromise must trump ideological absolutism. Compromise should include sensitive recognition by all sides of the symbolic importance of certain areas, structures, and histories. Yasser Arafat's constant refusal to acknowledge *any* Jewish religious or historic claim to Jerusalem in general, or the Temple area in particular, proved to be a major barrier to peace during the Camp David process. President Bill Clinton told me that after listening repeatedly to Arafat's "archaeological evidence" that Solomon's Temple was not even in Jerusalem and that Jerusalem was never a holy city to the Jews, he finally told him that he didn't want to hear any more about that nonstarter.[7] Jews believe that Jerusalem and the Temple with its Western Wall are at the center of Jewish history. (Archaeological excavations confirm this, despite Arafat's revisionism.) Any attempt to base negotiations on a rejection of this belief is not only doomed to failure but, as President Clinton realized, it is also calculated to produce stalemate—which is what Arafat wanted.

There are some Jews and Christians who similarly seek to denigrate Islamic claims to Jerusalem, arguing that it has become Islam's "third holiest city" only recently, as part of the political campaign on behalf of Palestinians. The conservative columnist Jeff Jacoby points out that

> [F]rom 1948 to 1967, when East Jerusalem and the Temple Mount were under Muslim rule, they were ignored by the Arab world: No foreign Arab leader ever paid a visit, not even to pray at the al-Aqsa mosque. Palestinians placed so low a priority on Jerusalem that the PLO's founding charter, the Palestinian National Covenant of 1964, makes no reference to it. Only when the Jews returned after the Six Day War did the Arabs grow passionate about Jerusalem.
>
> Nowhere in the Koran is there anything like the 137th Psalm with its aching love of Jerusalem. Indeed, nowhere in the Koran is Jerusalem even mentioned. For it is Mecca, not Jerusalem, that Islam venerates above all other places; Mecca, not Jerusalem, to which Muslims turn in prayer. Not for all the world would Muslims agree to divide Mecca—least of all with their enemies. To demand that the Jews sacrifice part of their eternal city is no less outrageous, and should be just as unthinkable.[8]

A local columnist at the *Albany Times Union* even disputes the Islamic claim that Mohammed ascended to heaven from Jerusalem:

> Mohammed died in 632 A.D. At that time, Jerusalem was a Christian city. . . . Jerusalem was captured by Khalif Omar in 638, some six years after Mohammed's death. At this time, there were no mosques in Jerusalem, only churches. . . . In or around 711, about 80 years after Mohammed died, Abd El-Wahl reconstructed the Christian-Byzantine Church of St. Mary of Justinian and converted it into a mosque. All he added was an onion dome on the top of the building to make it look like a mosque, which he then named El-Aksa so it would sound like the one mentioned in the Koran. . . .

Therefore, it is crystal clear that Mohammed could never have had this mosque in mind when he compiled the Koran. . . . So much for the Muslim claim based on the Aksa Mosque that Jerusalem is their third holiest city.[9]

These historical arguments too are nonstarters. Muslims hold these beliefs and they should be respected.

Despite all these, and other, difficulties, the negotiators at Camp David came very close to a compromise resolution that can still serve as a guide to future negotiations over Jerusalem.

At the start of these permanent status talks, held at Camp David in July 2000, President Clinton set out his framework for dealing with Jerusalem in a memo to both parties:

> On Jerusalem, we took a more conceptual tack. Jerusalem would be described as being three cities in one. It was a practical city that had to be governed and managed on a day-to-day basis; it was a holy city, holy to the world, holy to the three monotheistic religions, home to more than fifty-seven holy sites in the Old City alone; and it was a political city.[10]

Both sides were initially resistant on Jerusalem. Barak preferred to "expand" the municipal borders of the city to include the Arab town of Abu Dis, which could become the Palestinian capital Al-Quds. Arafat, for his part, "would accept nothing but sovereignty for all of East Jerusalem."[11]

Barak eventually agreed to Palestinian control over most of East Jerusalem and surrounding Arab neighborhoods—to become the Palestinian capital, Al-Quds—as well as joint authority over parts of the Old City, and official custodianship over Muslim holy sites on the Temple Mount/Haram. The proposed division included four main points:

1. Jewish areas outside Jerusalem's municipal boundaries would be annexed to the city, including such population centers as Givat Ze'ev, Ma'aleh Adumim and Gush Etzion. . . .

2. Arab areas outside Jerusalem's municipal boundaries would become the heart of the new Arab city of Al-Quds, including regions such as Abu Dis, el-Azaria, Beit Jala, Anata and A-Ram.

3. Arab neighborhoods inside Jerusalem's present boundaries would either be annexed to Al-Quds or would be granted extensive self-rule. Though some of these areas would remain formally under Israeli sovereignty, in practice Israel would have little authority over them.

4. Jerusalem's ancient, walled Old City would be divided, with the Muslim and Christian quarters offered autonomy under formal Israeli sovereignty, while the Jewish and Armenian quarters remained fully under Israeli rule. The Palestinian state would gain religious autonomy over the Temple Mount, though Israel proposed that an area be set aside for Jewish prayer on the site.[12]

The Temple Mount was a principal point of contention with Arafat. His insistence throughout the negotiations that "Solomon's Temple was not in Jerusalem, but in Nablus" was, as Dennis Ross described these remarks, "challenging the core of Jewish faith, and seeking to deny Israel any claim in the Old City."[13]

The December 23 Clinton Parameters, which Israel accepted and the Palestinians rejected, suggested that "the most promising approach is to follow the general principle that what is Arab in the City should be Palestinian and what is Jewish should be Israeli; this would apply to the Old City as well."[14] "On Jerusalem," according to Ross, "I said I thought the Israelis would have to accept Palestinian sovereignty in the Arab neighborhoods outside the Old City, meaning the inner municipal neighborhoods. This went beyond Camp David."[15]

President Clinton ended up recommending two approaches to dealing with the Temple Mount, both involving international monitoring systems. The first granted Palestine sovereignty over the Mount's surface, with Israeli sovereignty over the Western Wall and surrounding holy Jewish sites, along with a commitment by both parties not to excavate beneath or behind their own areas. The second suggested that the two sides agree to the same division of sovereignty with a "shared functional sovereignty over the issue of excavation under the Haram or behind the Western Wall." Under this joint regime, "mutual consent" would be necessary for any excavations.[16]

No official summary exists documenting the final negotiations at Taba. The results of the talks were largely kept secret and then invalidated when the understandings were never signed. Miguel Moratinos, the European Union's special envoy to the talks, however, released his summary of the opening stages of the talks, which both sides acknowledge presents an accurate picture of the ideas discussed at Taba. According to these notes, the creation of an "Open City," capital to both states, was discussed. The two sides reportedly agreed on Clinton's concept of Palestinian sovereignty over Palestinian neighborhoods and Israeli sovereignty over Israeli neighborhoods, but the Palestinians disputed certain Israeli neighborhoods in East Jerusalem and settlements created after 1967. The Old City would be divided between Palestinian and Israeli sovereignty.

The two sides discussed methods of "coordination" and "cooperation" within the Holy Basin and Old City and considered the idea of a special police force, and Israel proposed internationalizing the area (whereas Palestinians wanted to retain the area under Palestinian sovereignty). The parties agreed to cede control over holy sites along the Western Wall, though the exact length of the Western Wall remained contested. Palestinians were adamant about differentiating between the Western and Wailing walls. They also discussed the Clinton proposal that granted Palestinian sovereignty over Haram al-Sharif, and considered an interim period of international sovereignty over the area before transferring control to the Palestinians.

In the end, despite some passionate discussions, it was not disagreement over Jerusalem that doomed the Camp David–Taba negotiations. Even the Saudis, who regard themselves as the guardians of Islam, were prepared to sign off on the division of Jerusalem proposal by President Clinton.[17] It was Arafat's refusal to recognize Israel's right to continue to exist as a democratic Jewish state with a Jewish majority that led him to reject the Clinton-Barak proposals. He would not give up the "right" of Palestinians to destroy Israel demographically by "returning" millions of Arab "refugees" to their "homes" in Haifa, Jaffa, and Lydda.

Now that the new Palestine leadership seems willing to compromise over the right of return, as well as over other divisive issues, it should be possible to resolve the Jerusalem issue along the lines discussed at Camp David and Taba. Any such resolution should place primary emphasis on democratic principles—Israel should govern Jewish areas, while Palestine should govern Muslim and Arab areas. It should acknowledge the symbolic religious claims of all sides. The Western Wall (broadly defined) must remain under Israeli control so as to permit full, safe, and uncontested access to that place of prayer.[18] The Al-Haram area—which includes the Al-Aqsa and the Dome of the Rock mosques but also overlooks the Western Wall and includes the Temple Mount, which is holy to Jews—will require a more sophisticated and layered approach.

The mosques themselves should be under Islamic control and Palestinian sovereignty, but the Mount should be divided or shared. The surface of the Mount, on which the mosques stand, should be largely under the sovereignty and control of the Palestinians and Muslims, but with an area set aside for Jews who want to pray on the Temple Mount, and another security area from which to protect Jews praying below at the Western Wall. The "inside" of the Temple Mount, which is the traditional location of Solomon's Temple, should be under Israeli sovereignty, but this would be largely symbolic, since no one can get "inside" the Mount without excavating. All excavation should be subject to approval by some international excavation commission composed of recognized experts with no political agendas.

The rest of the "Old City" of Jerusalem is relatively easy to divide, since it is already divided into the Jewish, Armenian, Muslim, and Christian quarters. Israel should retain nominal sovereignty over all but the Muslim Quarter, but it should cede control over the Christian Quarter to Christian religious authorities and over the Armenian Quarter to Armenian authorities. The Muslim Quarter should be under Palestinian or Islamic authority.

Many technical issues remain, but creative legal, political, and religious formulae are available to help resolve them, if there is a good-faith effort to achieve a just result. Jerusalem, instead of being a barrier to peace, can become a city of peace, in which Jews, Muslims, and Christians live in harmony.

6 Are the Informal Geneva Accords a Basis for or a Barrier to Peace?

This document is virtual, but all of us are real, and our heartbeats are real.

—Former justice minister and Knesset member Yossi Beilin, Israeli "negotiator" at Geneva[1]

Today, we are extending our hands in peace. . . . The Palestinian people want peace, the Israeli people want peace. The world wants peace. Will we allow a few enemies of peace to destroy our dreams?

—Yasser Abed Rabbo, former Palestinian cabinet minister and coauthor of the accords[2]

[It's] a clenched-teeth compromise with painful concessions on both sides.

—Amos Oz, Israeli author and peace activist[3]

It's unlikely we shall ever see a more promising foundation for peace.

—Former president Jimmy Carter[4]

Israelis and Palestinians reached agreement in a meeting in Geneva this week on a settlement of all issues that have divided them for so many years. No one was acting in an official capacity, so the plan has no force of law. But the fact it happened at all is an encouraging sign for a region so bloodied by conflict.

—Former president Bill Clinton[5]

The good news, as I discovered in recent interviews with various Hamas activists, is that the movement seems ready to cut a deal along the general parameters of the Geneva Accords.

—Mark LeVine, assistant professor of history,
University of California at Irvine[6]

Our plan is the only hope of achieving a real and genuine break-through to peace between the Palestinians and ourselves. It is a plan which has been accepted by the majority of the world. Any deviation from it will release the Palestinians from the commitments they took upon themselves, and from the international demands made on them to uproot terror. Any such deviation will only encourage terrorist organizations.

It is no wonder that they are trying to renounce these commitments—and it is a pity that there are those in the world, and in Israel, who assist them by creating a false impression of alternative plans, without the Palestinians' making any effort to stop the terror directed at us.

—Israeli prime minister Ariel Sharon[7]

In 2003, a group of Israeli and Palestinian individuals—not representing their respective governments—met informally in Geneva to propose a possible resolution to the Israeli-Palestinian conflict. The resulting proposals, though immediately denounced both by Israeli and Palestinian officials, received widespread approval from many in the international community. But amid all the praise for the work of the individuals who hammered out these proposals two important points were largely missed. The first is that the Geneva Accords are strikingly similar in outline to what the Palestinians could have obtained at Camp David and Taba in 2000 and 2001. Had Yasser Arafat not simply walked away from the offers made by Ehud Barak and Bill Clinton, he probably could have negotiated a deal somewhat similar to, if not quite as beneficial to the Palestinians in its details, the one hammered out by Yossi Beilin and Yasser Abed Rabbo in Geneva. More than three thousand Palestinian and one thousand Israeli deaths could have been avoided, and the Palestinians could be celebrating their fifth anniversary of statehood, instead of continuing to bury their dead and blaming their deteriorating situation on Israel.

The extent to which the Geneva accords may be slightly better for the Palestinians than what they were offered at Camp David and Taba—and they are in some important respects[8]—raises the second problem. Resort to terrorism should never be rewarded by a better deal. If the Palestinians believe that Arafat's tactic of terrorism rather than negotiation is what got them their better deal, then the hands of radical Islamic rejectionists would be strengthened by the Geneva plan. This probably explains why Ehud Barak, Israel's dovish former prime minister who offered Arafat a similar deal, is so strongly against this one: "It is rewarding terror. . . . It will not save lives. It will lead to more deaths."[9] Every time the Palestinians want more—and they surely will—terrorist leaders will remind them of how they got more only after walking away from negotiation and restarting the terrorism. This will not only be bad for Israel, it will damage America's war against terrorism. America cannot fight global terrorism with one hand while encouraging the rewarding of Palestinian terrorism with the other.[10] As Thomas Friedman of the *New York Times* once remarked, if terrorism is rewarded in the Mideast, it will soon be coming "to a theater near you." Palestinian leaders have, as Friedman insists,

> adopted suicide bombings as a strategic choice, not out of desperation. This threatens all civilization because if suicide bombing is allowed to work in Israel, then, like hijacking and airplane bombing, it will be copied and will eventually lead to a bomber strapped with a nuclear device threatening entire nations. That is why the whole world must see this Palestinian suicide strategy defeated.[11]

Posthumously rewarding Arafat's tactical choice by improving the deal offered to the Palestinians in response to the threat of continuing terrorism will send exactly the wrong message to potential terrorists—namely, that terrorism works.

But what if the virtual agreement reached in Geneva is really the best possible solution for both sides, while at the same time giving the Palestinians more than they would have gotten without terrorism? Therein lies the conflict between achieving a just peace and avoiding the rewarding of terrorism. This conflict can be avoided only if the proposed agreement were to be ratified as a reward for serious Palestinian efforts to end terrorism and dismantle terrorist organizations. Thus, whatever deal is ultimately offered the Palestinians must be preconditioned on specific steps taken by its leadership to do what David Ben-Gurion courageously did in 1948 when he used force to prevent arms from reaching Israeli paramilitary groups such as Etzel (Menachem Begin's group) and Lechi (Yitzhak Shamir's group). This contrasts sharply with Arafat's decision to pay for a shipload of illegal weapons that were intercepted by Israel before they could reach Palestinian terrorists who were targeting Israeli civilians. It also contrasts with Abbas's refusal to take tough steps against Palestinian terrorist groups, even while calling for them to put down their arms.

The world will become a more dangerous place if the Palestinians get a better deal as a result of promoting terrorism, rather than as a result of ending terrorism. But it will become a less dangerous and more peaceful place if the Palestinians begin to dismantle terrorist organizations and then achieve statehood.

In the meantime, neither the Israeli government nor the Palestinian Authority has accepted the Geneva agreement. Neither have they categorically rejected its substance. Informal agreements among private citizens, even when encouraged by world leaders, do not by themselves end conflicts. But they can go a long way toward moving the official leaders back to the negotiating tables and making them more flexible in their demands, so long as they do not raise unrealistic expectations among the Palestinians. It is far easier for an individual who is not speaking for his government to make concessions than it is for an official negotiator who must obtain the approval of any concession by democratic consensus.[12]

As it turns out, the deal that will likely be offered to the Palestinians fits perfectly into the policy against rewarding terrorism. It is not better than they would have gotten by accepting the Camp David–Taba offers, but it is not significantly worse—certainly not in its pragmatic effects on Palestinian life. Those who opposed the Camp David–Taba offer characterized it as "less than a Bantustan" and a series of disconnected "cantons, under Israeli control."[13] Whether or not those were honest characterizations—and they were not—it certainly cannot be said that the likely current proposal, as reported by the *New York Times*, even resembles "Bantustans" or "cantons," since both the Gaza Strip and the West Bank will be internally contiguous and will likely be connected to the West Bank by some highway, rail line, or right-of-way under Palestinian sovereignty. Israel will get 2 or 3 percent more land, but that is as it should be since it was the Palestinian side that rejected a negotiated settlement in 2000 and 2001 and opted for terrorism instead. The end result of the proposed two-state solution would be far better than what was contemplated by the Geneva Accords. The Palestinians would not be rewarded for terrorism, but the slightly smaller amount of land they would receive would not adversely affect their lives.

The most serious substantive objection to the Geneva Accords is that they do not purport to resolve the Palestinian claim that four million alleged refugees have a "right to return" to Israel proper. Were this claim ever to be implemented, Israel would soon disappear and become another Muslim Arab state. It is easy for Palestinians to sign on to any accord that preserves this option, even in theory, because it leaves open the possibility that Israel can be destroyed demographically, if not militarily. Any real peace must necessarily include—indeed feature—an end of all claims that threaten the existence of Israel as a Jewish democratic nation. The Geneva Accords fail this test.

7 Can Israel Make Peace and Prevent Terrorism at the Same Time?

We shall fight terrorism as if there is no peace process, and pursue the peace process as if there is no terrorism.

—Yitzhak Rabin[1]

The restraint Israel showed in the Gulf War only emboldened the Arab world into thinking that the Jewish state was not as strong or robust as it once was, and whatever international goodwill that Israel had won quickly dissipated once the war was over.

—Michael Freund, columnist for the Jerusalem Post[2]

If American forces are used in Israel, they would never take on the suicide bombers, nor should they. Their sole function would be to prevent Israeli reprisals to terrorist attacks by Hamas and others.

—Former New York City mayor Ed Koch[3]

Previous steps toward peace between Israel and the Palestinians had been halted by terrorism. It is easy for terrorists to thwart a democracy's efforts to make peace. All they have to do is kill enough civilians so that the citizens of the democracy demand a military response. By their nature, military responses tend to be perceived as "overreactions" by those against whom the responses are directed. Inevitably, some civilians will be killed or injured in any response to terrorism, especially when the terrorists deliberately provoke those casualties by hiding among civilians.

The military response to the terrorism thus provokes (or is used to justify) additional terrorism and additional military reaction. The result is a so-called "cycle of violence." That term does not aptly describe the dynamics because the unlawful violence was deliberately started by terrorists who target civilians, and the response of the democracy is lawful, so long as it targets terrorists and is proportional to the threat to its civilians. But to the outside world, it looks—or is made to look—like a "cycle" with no beginning or end point. Indeed, it is part of the plan of the terrorist to create what can then be described as a cycle, with equal blame on both sides. This "symmetry of blame," so common in the media today, rewards those who initiate the violence and punishes those who merely respond to it.

The cycle could, of course, be broken by the democracy, if it were simply to choose not to respond to the terrorism. Israel has tried that approach on several occasions. Following the bombing of a Tel Aviv nightclub in late February 2005, in which four young Israelis were killed and more than fifty injured, Israel honored a cease-fire agreement by refraining from taking any retaliatory measures.[4] This restraint was made somewhat easier by Prime Minister Abbas's sharp words against the bombing, and by the fact that the bombing was apparently the work of the Syrian-led Islamic Jihad, rather than of a terrorist organization located in the West Bank or Gaza. In early June 2005, Israel also chose not to respond to rocket attacks on Gush Kativ and Sderot in which three people were killed and several injured. Israeli officials explained that it would withhold any military action at this time to give the Palestinian Authority an opportunity to act against the terrorists.

But no democratically elected government can continue to ignore repeated acts of terrorism against civilians when it has a military option. It can, perhaps, absorb one, two, or even three serious attacks, but after a while, opposition candidates will begin to make an issue of the government's "softness" on terrorism and this issue will begin to resonate with the electorate. For example, despite polls in early 1996 showing overwhelming support for the Labor Party, Benjamin Netanyahu capitalized on what historian Benny Morris described as an "unprecedentedly savage, concentrated Muslim fundamentalist terrorist offensive" in late February through early March of that year.[5] "[T]he

Right devastatingly used" this "fundamentalist offensive" to "smear [Prime Minister] Peres personally and to undermine the public's confidence in the peace process."[6] As Morris continued, "By election day, May 29, most Jewish Israelis remembered only the dozens of bloodied shirts of the bomb victims and linked them to the Oslo agreements that had facilitated the terrorists' campaign."[7]

Some of the past terrorism against Israel was orchestrated by Yasser Arafat and the Palestinian Authority as part of their negotiating strategy. The communications minister of the PLO acknowledged this after the start of the second intifada:

> The PA had begun to prepare for the outbreak of the current Intifada since the return from the Camp David negotiations, by request of President Yasser Arafat, who predicted the outbreak of the Intifada as a complementary stage to the Palestinian steadfastness in the negotiations, and not as a specific protest against [Ariel] Sharon's visit to the Al-Haram Al-Qudsi [Temple Mount]. . . . The Intifada was no surprise from the Palestinian leadership . . . the PA instructed the political forces and factions to run all materials of the Intifada.[8]

On other occasions terrorism has been employed by groups seeking to embarrass and weaken the Palestinian Authority. These sorts of incidents happen, as in the Tel Aviv bombing case. Factions will sometimes try to use this so-called "terrorists' veto" to curtail peace talks or cease-fire agreements. The June 2005 rocket attacks against Israel were seen as part of an "internal dialogue" between radical terrorist groups and the Palestinian Authority and as a challenge to those seeking to make peace.

Israeli opponents of peace can likewise try to scuttle particular peace initiatives, as evidenced by plans to provoke violence in order to prevent the Israeli withdrawal from Gaza.[9] The difference is that the Israeli government has both the capacity and the willingness to employ force against its own citizens who threaten unlawful violence.

Those who favor peace must develop a strategy for responding to terrorist attacks that are designed to thwart the peace process. It is not enough to argue that Israel must simply absorb the attacks in the greater interest of making peace. Even if that were the morally correct position for Israel to take—and reasonable people can disagree over this—it simply will not work in the context of Israel's deeply divided and fragmented democracy and its volatile political system that makes even stable governments vulnerable to no-confidence votes and cabinet resignations. It is a mistake to think Israel's political system is comparable to the far more stable system in the United States. The dynamics are simply too different to draw meaningful comparisons. In any event, how many acts of terrorism against Americans would it take before a U.S. administration would have no choice but to retaliate?

What then should Israel do, and what should the United States and the international community encourage Israel to do, if it were to face, as it has in the past, a wave of terrorist attacks calculated to thwart the peace process?

Obviously, it should depend, at least in part, on who the source of the attacks turns out to be. If it is an external source—say, Iran or Syria—that might create a different dynamic than if the source were Hamas, the Al-Aqsa Martyrs Brigades, or even the PLO itself.

On one occasion, Israel did retaliate against Syria for an attack for which it concluded Syria bore some responsibility. The retaliation was largely symbolic, directed as it was against a deserted terrorist camp fourteen miles northwest of Damascus.[10] The attack was probably intended as a warning that Israel would hold Syria responsible for attacks planned on its soil and/or with the help of its intelligence or its surrogates. Despite the relatively mild nature of the retaliation—and the brutal nature of the terrorist attack led by Syrian Islamic Jihad against Israeli teenagers in a nightclub that provoked the retaliation—the international community, with the exception of the United States, condemned Israel.[11]

What if Israel were to respond to a Syrian-instigated terrorist attack by more sustained, targeted, and deadly bombings directed against Syrian military or intelligence targets? Would such a military response, with its inevitable casualties, damage the peace process with the Palestinians? (On a much larger scale, would an Israeli attack against Iranian nuclear targets damage the Israeli-Palestinian peace process? More on this in chapter 13.)

There is no question that Israel's relationship with the Palestinians cannot be completely separated from its relationship with other Arab and Muslim nations, regimes, and groups. For years, Arab and Muslim nations and groups have seized on the Palestinian conflict as the primary excuse for their negative attitudes and actions toward Israel. But at the same time, Israel has managed to de-link the Palestinian conflict from its conflicts with Egypt and Jordan. Both countries were eventually willing to make peace—a cold peace, to be sure, but a peace nonetheless—with Israel *before* Israel made peace with the Palestinians. This was especially difficult for Jordan to do, because a majority of its population is Palestinian and it had controlled the West Bank for two decades before the 1967 war. Syria too seemed willing—at least for a time—to make peace with Israel in exchange for the Golan Heights and other considerations, but without any assurance of a settlement of the Palestinian issue. Certainly, Yasser Arafat made it clear that he would not make peace with Israel unless Saudi Arabia signed off on any deal, especially with regard to Jerusalem, but that may have been a ploy (a ploy that backfired when Saudi Arabia did agree and Arafat backed out nonetheless).

All this is by way of background to the question of whether Israel can make peace with the Palestinians while preserving military options against non-Palestinian states that continue to sponsor, encourage, or tolerate the targeting of Israeli civilians by terrorist groups over which they have some control.

The even more daunting question is whether Israel can continue to make peace with the Palestinian Authority while taking military action against *Palestinian* terrorists who are seeking to scuttle the peace process. On April 14, 2005, for example, Israeli troops engaged in a gun battle with a Palestinian man who was "responsible for several shooting attacks against Israeli civilians and attempted suicide bombings." Israeli authorities alleged that "his activities were being directed by the Lebanese guerrilla group Hezbollah." Israeli troops entered the Balata refugee camp to arrest him, and he fired on the soldiers, "hitting one in his bulletproof vest." The troops returned fire, wounding him. They then took him to a hospital, but he died. Palestinian president Abbas called this a "serious violation" of the truce between Israel and the Palestinians, despite an agreement that Israel "reserves the right to pursue 'ticking bombs'—militants who are plotting attacks."[12] On May 19, 2005, Israel announced that it would employ "restraint" in responding to rocket attacks against Israeli cities from Gaza. It recognized that Hamas was trying to break the cease-fire and "expressed continuing desire to coordinate the evacuation of Israel's Gaza settlements with the Palestinian Authority."[13]

The final question in this series is whether an Israeli government that absorbs repeated terrorist attacks without taking firm military action against the terrorists—whoever they may be—can be strong enough domestically to make the kind of peace the Palestinians would accept.

No one can know the answers to these daunting questions with any certainty until and unless the various scenarios are played out on the ground. But even before more entirely predictable terrorist acts occur, there should be careful advance planning. The Israeli government and the Palestinian Authority should discuss the likely scenarios—small terrorist attacks, large attacks with multiple victims, Palestinian attacks, Hezbollah attacks, and so on. Agreed-upon general parameters should be negotiated, so that there are no real surprises—or excuses. Having said that, it must be added that since all possibilities can never be anticipated, there will necessarily have to be some improvisation and even some surprises. But cooperation is essential, even if it only minimizes the inevitable conflicts.

The United States and the international community—in theory, even the United Nations—could perhaps play some positive role in reducing the friction that will inevitably result from a renewal of terrorist attacks. The United States, either alone or multilaterally, could assume responsibility, during the delicate course of the peace process, for responding to terrorist attacks, so as to keep Israel out of any "cycle of violence" that could endanger the process. The problem, of course, is that Israel has far more experience in controlling terrorism in the Palestinian areas than the United States and its allies do. This is evidenced by the much greater success Israel has had in preventing terrorism in its occupied territories than the United States has had in occupied Iraq. The United States could work together with Israeli intelligence to send a powerful message to potential terrorists that they will not be allowed to derail the peace process, that any terrorist act will be answered by an international or multinational response, and that they will not be able to drag Israel into participating in a "cycle of violence" destructive of peace. By negotiating under fire, Israel is perceived as making concessions to terrorists. But by waiting until there is an end to terrorism, Israel may never make it to the peace table.

Israel alone cannot make peace with the Palestinians and combat terrorists who are seeking to destroy any prospects for peace. It needs the assistance of other nations, especially the United States, and if that assistance is provided, it will become far more difficult for terrorists to thwart peace. Otherwise, terrorists will retain the veto they have long used so effectively every time Israel and the Palestinians have made any progress toward peace.

Nor should the world become too encouraged by the recent apparent reduction in terrorist attacks against Israelis. Many attacks have been attempted by Palestinian terrorists and thwarted by Israeli intelligence. Some preventive measures were probably helped by cooperation from the Palestinian Authority and thus must be credited to the ongoing peace process, but many were simply thwarted by old-fashioned intelligence-gathering and others by the security fence. All that needs to happen for the peace process to become greatly endangered, however, is one mass-casualty attack or several smaller attacks in close proximity to one another. It would be remarkable indeed if this did not occur at some critical point in the peace process. That is why all who seek peace must do everything in their power to prevent terrorist attacks, and if they do occur, to take action that will salvage the delicate peace process.

Over the years, several proposals have been offered to end the veto terrorists currently hold over any enduring peace. They all involve some outside presence in the area whose role it would be to prevent or respond to terrorism. The influential *New York Times* columnist Thomas Friedman has suggested stationing a U.S.-led NATO force in the West Bank, Gaza, and East Jerusalem in order to secure Israel's borders.[14] Friedman is vague about NATO's specific role in the region. At one point, he suggests that "30,000 NATO troops" could serve in lieu of a Palestinian military. They would have responsibility for "controlling all borders and entry points, . . . ensur[ing] that no heavy weapons come in," and they could "work with the Palestinian police force . . . on internal security."[15]

Friedman acknowledges the Israeli concern that "such an international force would block Israel from hot pursuit of Palestinian terrorists, who would kill Jews and then run behind NATO, and NATO itself would become a target." He argues, however, that the Israeli policy of "hot pursuit" has not worked: "It has resulted in the Palestinian Authority's being destroyed and more Israelis being killed and feeling insecure than ever. The only way Israel is going to have security is if Palestinians provide it by restraining their own, which will happen only when they have a responsible state, which can emerge only under NATO supervision—not Israeli occupation."[16]

President Clinton's ambassador to Israel and Middle East adviser Martin Indyk wrote an important article for *Foreign Affairs* magazine, calling for a NATO "trusteeship" in the occupied territories that would ensure both military and political stability in an emerging Palestinian state.[17] Indyk modeled his proposal after trusteeships in East Timor and Kosovo. In form, NATO would seize control of the occupied territories from the Palestinian Authority and hold them "in trust of the Palestinian people." NATO would oversee the building of democratic institutions, help draft a constitution, create an independent judiciary, and install the mechanism for free elections.

NATO would enable withdrawal by Israeli forces from the territories by deploying special counterterrorism forces. "These [forces] would not be peacekeepers or monitors; rather, they would be tasked with maintaining order, suppressing terrorism, and restructuring and retraining the Palestinian security services," just as the United States is currently doing in Afghanistan.[18] This U.S.-led force would be "composed of small, experienced units capable of the kinds of operations that Israeli Special Forces now carry out in the Palestinian territories." It would also include British Special Forces experienced in combating IRA terrorists.[19]

As Indyk recognized, "[T]he notion that a U.S.-led fighting force would take responsibility for combating Palestinian terrorism and rebuilding Palestinian security capabilities is perhaps the most controversial element in the trusteeship proposal." Palestinians would "try to portray it as part of a Western, imperialist occupation," while "Israelis would be concerned that the international force would not have the IDF's [Israeli Defense Forces] motivation to confront the terrorists, and would be deeply frustrated when the IDF were not permitted to engage in hot pursuit of terrorists on trusteeship territory." Also, Israelis would fear that the American people would blame Israel for American casualties, and that U.S. support for Israel would wane. Finally, Indyk acknowledges that "acceptance of such a force would breach a fundamental tenet of Israel's national security doctrine that requires Israel to defend its own citizens by itself."[20]

Following Friedman's and Indyk's call for NATO peacekeepers in the region, Senator Richard Lugar (R-IN), chairman of the Senate Foreign Relations Committee, expressed his desire to see a more muscular U.S. presence in the region:

> If we're serious about having a situation of stability, a very direct action, I think is going to be required. We ought to involve our NATO allies. We ought to involve others in the Middle East. The Terrorists have to be routed out because they will ruin any possibility for peace.[21]

Specifically, Lugar said that U.S. forces might actively pursue Hamas forces. "It may not be just Hamas, but clearly Hamas is right in the gun sights."[22] Lugar cautioned, however: "I would just say this is down the trail," and that the United States must be "very, very careful" about any U.S. military commitment.[23] He further conditioned his support for U.S. deployment on the successful completion of peace talks.

Even Lugar's tepid proposal brought immediate rebuke from the White House. Press Secretary Ari Fleischer insisted, "The president's message is that the best security comes from the Israelis and Palestinians working together to fight terror."[24] The State Department concurred. According to spokesman Richard Boucher, U.S. troop involvement in the Middle East is "above and beyond" America's policy of sending only monitors to the region.

Finally, the informal Geneva proposals included the following: "A Multinational Force (MF) shall be established to provide security guarantees to the Parties, act as a deterrent, and oversee the implementation of the relevant provisions of this Agreement." They would, among other tasks, "help in the enforcement of anti-terrorism measures."[25]

None of these proposals is without serious potential downside risks. But they all reflect the concern that if *only* Israel responds to the entirely predicable terrorist "veto," it will indeed become an effective veto, because Israel's response will be blamed for generating a "cycle of violence" that is incompatible with a peace process. If it becomes clear that any such cycle will be broken by the firm responses of others—and with the approval of the international community—this may serve as a disincentive to even trying to invoke the terrorist veto.

8 Are Israeli Counterterrorism Measures the Cause of Suicide Bombings and a Barrier to Peace?

What Israel is doing [targeted killing], it's a systemic criminal act. They are opening the door in front of more radical, extreme, fanatic leadership. If this is the kind of partners they want, I'm sure that they are wrong.

> —*Zaid Abu-Zayyad, senior Fatah official, former Palestinian minister for Jerusalem affairs*[1]

We had a consistent view of it, that this kind of response [targeted killing] is too aggressive and it just serves to increase the level of tension and violence in the region.

> —*Former secretary of state Colin Powell*[2]

[T]argeted killings of this kind are unlawful [and] unjustified.

> —*British foreign minister Jack Straw*[3]

British Foreign Secretary Jack Straw was simply wrong when he declared that targeted assassinations of this kind—specifically referring to the killing of Yassin and Rantisi—are unlawful and in violation of international law. And he knows it because his own government has authorized the killing of terrorist leaders who threaten British interests.

I challenge Straw to distinguish Israel's killing of Yassin and Rantisi from the coalition's targeting of Al-Sadr, Saddam Hussein and his sons, Osama bin Laden, and Mullah Omar Mohammed.

—*Alan Dershowitz*[4]

When intelligence information says that the only way to prevent an attack is to take preventative action, then we have no choice but to stop the terrorists before they enter the country. This is the way to prevent the escalation that everyone wants to avoid. Every nation would do the same. It doesn't look nice, but it's a question of stopping them right there or suffering the consequences.

—*Israeli prime minister's spokesman Ra'anan Gissin*[5]

Communists, when faced with ideology and survival, chose survival, but Islamic militants, when faced with the same choice, often choose ideology, making them a culture of death.

—*Former Israeli prime minister Benjamin Netanyahu*[6]

Israel reserves the right to defend its citizens, just like the U.S.

—*Israeli prime minister Ariel Sharon*[7]

Even before Israel came into existence—and certainly before there was any "occupation"—the Jewish population of the area was subjected to well-organized terrorist attacks by Islamic extremists. Understandably, the Jewish community developed countermeasures designed to prevent or minimize these unlawful and immoral acts. During the most recent campaign of suicide bombings and rocket attacks, the nature of the Israeli responses has changed. The Israeli military has employed extremely sophisticated techniques to ferret out potential terrorist threats. These efforts have succeeded in preventing thousands of planned terrorist attacks and have saved tens of thousands of innocent lives. Yet some have argued that these measures are responsible, in whole or in part, for the continuing "cycle of violence." The evidence is strongly to the contrary.

One particularly controversial technique used by Israel has been the targeted killings of terrorist leaders and operatives. Although Israel has agreed to suspend such targeting, except in "ticking bomb" cases involving imminent threats, it is likely that if terrorism persists, the Israeli army will again use this tactic because it has been extremely effective. Two fundamental questions are raised by this practice: Is this tactic legal under international law? Even if legal, is it wise as a matter of policy?

As to the first question, there can be absolutely no doubt of the legality of Israel's policy of targeting Hamas leaders for assassination. Hamas has declared war against Israel. All of its leaders are combatants, whether they wear military uniforms, three-piece suits, or religious garb. There is no realistic distinction between the political and military wings of Hamas, any more than there is a distinction between the political and military wings of al-Qaeda. The official policy of Hamas, like that of al-Qaeda, is the mass murder of civilians. The decision to employ that policy was made by its so-called "political" leaders.

The United States properly targeted Osama bin Laden and his associates, as well as Saddam Hussein and his sons. Under international law, combatants are appropriate military targets until they surrender. They may be killed in their sleep, while preparing military actions, or while participating in any other activity. Nor need they be arrested or even given a chance to surrender. Only if they come out with their hands up, or waving a white flag, or affirmatively manifesting surrender by some other means, may they avoid the ultimate sanction of a war they started, namely death.

Military law does of course require that purely civilian casualties be minimized, even in the pursuit of legitimate military targets. Both the United States and Israel seek to minimize civilian deaths, in part because neither has any incentive to kill innocent civilians. When Israel first went after the head of Hamas, it deliberately used a relatively small bomb in order to minimize collateral damage. As a result, its legitimate target escaped with minor injuries. Had it not cared about collateral damage, Israel easily could have used a multiton bomb, which would have assured the death of the target but also increased the likelihood of killing more innocent bystanders.

Precisely how much collateral damage is too much is a matter of degree, but international law does not condemn the targeting of combatants unless the number of innocents killed in the process is completely out of proportion to the importance of the military objective.

In June 2005, I interviewed the commander of the Israeli Air Force, General Elyezer Shkedy, about targeted killings and civilian casualties. He told me that until the beginning of 2004, the ratio of terrorists to civilians killed by targeted bombings was approximately 1:1. But as a result of sophisticated technological improvements, that ratio changed dramatically between early 2004 and 2005 to twelve terrorists killed for every civilian killed. Preventing terrorist leaders from planning, approving, or carrying out acts of terrorism against innocent civilians is an important and appropriate military objective.

Having concluded that Israel's (and America's) policy of targeting terrorist leaders is entirely lawful, it does not necessarily follow that it is always wise as a matter of policy. Reasonable people can differ as to the wisdom not only of the policy, but also of its particular application to individual cases. For example, prior to the actual commencement of the war against Iraq, the United States tried to take out Saddam Hussein but failed. Had it succeeded in killing Saddam, it might have avoided a war that has proved very costly in terms of human life. The targeted assassination of Saddam Hussein would have been good policy, especially if it succeeded without the killing of large numbers of innocent civilians. Likewise with the targeting of bin Laden and some of his chief deputies. The early deaths of these combatants might have saved many Afghani and American lives.

Hamas rejects any two-state solution. Occasionally it agrees to a temporary cease-fire, but it generally uses that period of Israeli inaction to rearm and prepare for a recommencement of terrorism. If Israel could actually end the so-called cycle of violence by stopping its targeting of Hamas leaders, it would be wise to do so. But the historical record suggests that when Israel eases up in its preventive attacks on terrorist leaders, the terrorism eventually persists, sometimes even increases. It is not a cycle of violence; it is a Hamas policy of terrorism against innocent civilians to which Israel responds by targeting guilty murderers it is unable to arrest. Nor are these actions in any way morally (or legally) equivalent, as the International Red Cross has mistakenly stated.

I believe that targeted assassination should be used only as a last recourse, when there is no opportunity to arrest or apprehend the murderer, when the terrorist leader is involved in planning or approving ongoing murderous activities, and when the assassination can be done without undue risk to innocent bystanders. Proportionality is the key to any military action, and targeted assassination should be judged under that rubric.

Under any reasonable standard, Israeli policy with regard to the targeted assassinations of "ticking-bomb" terrorists does not deserve the kind of condemnation it is receiving, especially in comparison with other nations and groups whose legal actions are far less proportionate to the dangers they face.

Any democracy confronting threats to its civilian population comparable to those faced by Israel would respond in much the same way Israel is now responding to the terrorism being conducted by Hamas and other terrorist groups. Whatever else may be said about targeted killings or other controversial antiterrorism tactics employed by Israel, they are simply not the cause of the terrorism, but rather a response to it.

As suicide bombings increase—in Iraq, in Saudi Arabia, in Spain, in Bali, and in Russia—more and more people have come to believe that this tactic is a result of desperation. They see a direct link between oppression, occupation, poverty, and humiliation, on the one hand, and a willingness to blow oneself up for "the cause," on the other hand. It follows from this premise that the obvious remedy for suicide bombing is to address its root cause—namely, *our* oppression of the terrorists.

But the underlying premise is demonstrably false: there is no such link as a matter of fact or history. Islamic terrorism against Jews—even Jews whose families had lived in Jewish cities like Hebron and Safed for centuries—preceded any occupation or oppression. Further, during the period between 1948 and 1967 when Gaza was brutally occupied by Egyptian military forces and the West Bank was occupied by Jordan, there was no terrorism directed against the occupiers, even though the conditions were worse in many respects than they became under the Israeli occupation. Terrorism in general, and suicide bombing in particular, is a tactic, selected by privileged, educated, and wealthy elitists because it has proven successful. Moreover, even some of the suicide bombers themselves defy the stereotype of the impoverished victims of occupation driven to desperate measures by American or Israeli oppression. Remember the September 11 bombers, several of whom were university students and none of whom were "oppressed" by the United States; they were dispatched by a Saudi millionaire named Osama bin Laden.

Bin Laden has now become the hero of many other upper-class Saudis who are volunteering to become *shahids* (martyrs) in Iraq, Israel, Russia, and other parts of the globe. Majid al-Enezi, a Saudi student training to become a computer technician, recently changed career plans and decided to become a martyr; he crossed over to Iraq, where he died. His brother Abdullah celebrated that decision: "People are calling all the time to congratulate us—crying from happiness and envy. . . . There are many young men who wish they could cross over into Iraq, but they can't. Thank God he was blessed with the ability to go."[8] These rich kids glorify the culture of suicide, even in distant places. As Tufful al-Oqbi, a student at the elite King Saud University, described this situation, "Young people are wearing t-shirts with Laden's picture on them just the way people used to wear pictures of Che Guevara," the Cuban revolutionary. According to a recent news account, wealthy women students "sport Osama bin Laden t-shirts under their enveloping abayas to show their approval for his calls to resist the United States."[9]

Why do these overprivileged and well-educated young men and women support this culture of death, while impoverished and oppressed Tibetans continue to celebrate life, despite their brutal occupation by China for half a century? Why have other oppressed people throughout history not resorted to suicide bombings and terrorism? The answer lies not in the degree of oppression but rather in differences among the elite leadership of various groups and causes. The leaders of Islamic radical causes, especially the Wahhabis, advocate and incite suicide terrorism, while the leaders of other causes advocate different means. Recall Mahatma Gandhi and Martin Luther King Jr., whose people were truly oppressed but who employed nonviolent means of resistance. It is the leaders who send suicide bombers to blow themselves up. No suicide bomber ever sent himself to be blown up.

The bombers accept death because they have been incited into a frenzy of hatred by imams preaching "kill the infidels." Sheikh Muhammed Sayed Tantawi, the leading Islamic scholar at the elite Al-Azhar University in Cairo (which is not "occupied") has declared that "martyrdom operations"—which means suicide bombings—are the "highest form of jihad"[10] and an Islamic commandment. An even more mainstream role model, Yasser Arafat's widow, who lives in a multimillion-dollar residence in Paris, has said that if she had a son, she would want him to become a suicide bomber because there is no "greater honor" than to become a martyr.[11]

Young children, some as young as twelve and thirteen, are incited and seduced into strapping bombs onto themselves by these older and better-educated elitist leaders. The children are promised virgins in heaven, praise and money for their families here on earth, and posters portraying them as rock stars. It is an irresistible combination for some, and the blame lies squarely at the feet of the elitists who exploit them, use them, and eventually kill them.

There is absolutely no evidence to support the claim of a direct relationship between occupation and suicide bombing. If anything, occupation makes it more difficult to launch successful terrorist attacks. This is not to argue for occupation; it is to separate the arguments regarding occupation from the claim that it is the fact of occupation, and the oppression it brings, that *causes* suicide bombing. Indeed, were Israel to end its occupation of Gaza (as it is doing) and most of the West Bank (as I have long believed it should), it is likely that terrorism would actually increase, as terrorist commanders secure more freedom to plan and implement terrorist actions. The same might well be true in Iraq, were the United States to pick up and leave.

The time has come to address the real root cause of suicide bombing: elitist incitement by certain religious and political leaders who are creating a culture of death and exploiting the ambiguous teachings of an important religion. Abu Hamza, the cleric who tutored the convicted shoe bomber Richard Reid, urged a large crowd in 2004 to embrace death.[12] "Islamic young people are in love with death," claim some influential imams, but it is these leaders who are arranging the marriages between the children and the bomb belts.

Palestinian terrorism reached its nadir of immorality in 2004 when terrorist leaders paid an eleven-year-old Palestinian child one dollar to carry an innocent-looking package through Israeli security. The child agreed to do the job without knowing that the package contained a deadly bomb attached to a cell phone detonator. The terrorists' Plan A was to have the bomb delivered to another terrorist inside Israel so that it could be detonated in the middle of a large city, killing as many civilians as possible. Their Plan B—to be implemented if the boy were stopped by Israeli security—was to detonate the bomb, along with its innocent eleven-year-old Palestinian courier, at the checkpoint, so as to kill as many Israeli security guards as possible. Fortunately, an Israeli guard found the bomb and it was safely disarmed, despite an effort by terrorists watching from a distance to call the cell phone and blow up the boy and the security guards.[13]

The child was questioned briefly and released, as soon as the Israeli authorities were convinced that he did not know what he was carrying. Instead of praising the Israelis for saving her son's life and criticizing the terrorists for trying to murder her child, the mother of the boy attacked the Israelis for "beating" her son and said she could not believe he had been given a bomb because "our religion does not allow using children for such acts."[14]

Whether or not a proper interpretation of Islam allows the use of children as suicide bombers, it is patently clear that some Islamic leaders directly encourage, even incite, children to become martyrs. Salah Shehadeh, a former leader of Hamas in Gaza, said in a May 26, 2002, interview that children were being recruited into a special branch of Hamas. In an interview on Al-Jazeera television, a prominent Muslim professor defended the use of what he called callously "the children bomb."[15]

There is evidence that this recruitment is working. A poll conducted by Islamic University of one thousand youngsters between the ages of nine and sixteen showed that 49 percent said they had participated in anti-Israel violence and 73 percent expressed a desire to die as martyrs. Not surprisingly, some children have been blown up in the process of detonating or planting bombs.[16]

The 2004 case did not even involve a child "volunteer"—as if that concept were not itself an oxymoron. It involved using a child who was tricked into becoming a potential human bomb. This is child abuse at its worst, and yet we have heard little criticism of Palestinian terrorists from international organizations dedicated to protecting children from abuse and exploitation. In addition to using children as unknowing couriers of death, Palestinian terrorists have also used people pretending to be sick in Red Crescent ambulances to carry bombs.[17] (This tactic has been emulated by terrorists in Iraq as well.)

The terrorists' use of children and medical ploys is cruel and cynical, because it exploits the sympathy of decent security guards toward youngsters and sick civilians. Equally cruel and cynical is that the terrorists deliberately seek to increase the suffering of their own people by having innocent children and ambulances subjected to cumbersome security checks.

If terrorists did not use children and ambulances, democracies would not need to delay them. But terrorists have learned that this tactic works, because some human rights groups and international organizations play into their hands by condemning the democracies for violating international law whenever they detain children or delay ambulances. It is a deliberate tactic by the terrorists to provoke the democracies into taking self-protective measures that the terrorists know will anger the terrorists' own people and provoke international condemnation. The terrorists thus deliberately increase the suffering of their own people and then exploit it to encourage more terrorists and more condemnation of the victims of terrorism.

Some who sympathize with the terrorists will be outraged at the suggestion that terrorist leaders would deliberately devise a strategy that subjects their own people—especially sick people and children—to delays and searches. But that is the reality of terrorism.

Why then do the democracies fall into this well-designed trap? What else could they do but subject suspicious children and ambulances to self-protective searches? Even when the net is cast narrowly, it will inevitably catch some innocent people. In 2002, the Supreme Court of Israel confronted the issue of how a democracy could deal with terrorists who use ambulances to facilitate terrorism. It ruled that despite the reality that Palestinian terrorists exploit human rights law by using it as a sword to facilitate terrorism, the Israeli military must abide by the letter of the law, even though it will increase Israel's civilian casualties.

Terrorist leaders have exploited this humane ruling by increasing their use of ambulances and children. This exploitation will end only when human rights groups focus their criticism on terrorists who improperly *use* children and ambulances, rather than on democracies that properly *stop* children and ambulances that may well be carrying explosives.

Perhaps, now that suicide bombers have targeted Saudi Arabia, responsible Islamic leaders will better understand that it is their people who will be the ultimate victims of this tactically imposed culture of death, just as the UN took a somewhat tougher line against terrorism after a UN enclave in Iraq was targeted and a senior UN diplomat was killed.

Russia as well, which routinely condemned Israel for its counterterrorism, is now seeking Israeli cooperation in its fight against Chechen terrorism. President Vladimir Putin, during a visit to Israel in April 2005, described Russia as Israel's "strategic ally."[18]

A Palestinian state will itself likely become a target of terrorists seeking to destabilize it. Then it too will have a stake in preventing the kinds of incitements by elite leaders that are the most direct causes of terrorism. The question remains: will a new Palestinian state take steps to reduce or eliminate the religiously and nationalistically inspired hate speech that contributes so greatly to an atmosphere in which so many Palestinians would rather die killing Israelis than live in peace with them?

Peace cannot be built on a foundation of hate. For more than three-quarters of a century, beginning with the anti-Jewish massacres incited by the grand mufti of Jerusalem in 1929, hatred has fueled violence, and violence has begotten counterviolence. Several generations of Palestinians have been raised on hatred of Israel and Jews and Judaism. This hatred has been conveyed in the schools, in the mosques, and in the officially controlled media. It is expressly incorporated in the Hamas Charter and in other influential documents. In Israel too there has been hatred toward Palestinians, Arabs, and Muslims, but on a much smaller scale and without state sponsorship. A small number of anti-Palestinian terrorist acts can be attributed to this hate speech. Even if formal peace is finally achieved between the Palestinians and the Israelis, violence—in the form of terrorism—will persist unless steps are taken to stem the systematic dissemination of hate speech, especially that directed against the Jewish state. This will not be an easy task, especially if the Palestinian state adopts genuine democratic and civil libertarian principles, including freedom of speech, religion, and association. With these freedoms comes the license to express hateful views, as the world has witnessed in post-Soviet Russia and some other former communist nations. (The Soviet Union itself promoted hate speech, but it tightly controlled its dissemination and could therefore be pressured into turning off, or at least turning down, the spigot. Since the demise of the Soviet Union, former Soviet-controlled governments have had more difficulty controlling indigenous hate speech. It is clearly a work in progress.)

Israel, which is a democracy with freedom of speech, religion, and assembly, has also been troubled by its own brand of hate speech directed against Arabs and Muslims. It has had to compromise some freedoms in the interest of controlling hate. For example, its election law precludes a political party from running for the Knesset

if its objects or actions, expressly or by implication, include one of the following:
   (1) negation of the existence of the State of Israel as the state of the Jewish people;
   (2) negation of the democratic character of the State;
   (3) incitement to racism.[19]

Its criminal law also prohibits several other forms of what we call "hate speech" against Arabs, Muslims, or others.

In 1988, the Kach Party, which endorses violence in the pursuit of the expansion of the Israeli state and the denial of citizenship rights to Israeli Arabs, was banned from the Knesset elections based on this provision. The decision was upheld by the Israeli Supreme Court.[20] The Kach Party was completely outlawed in 1994 after Baruch Goldstein, a supporter of the party and a candidate for Knesset, entered a West Bank mosque and murdered twenty-nine Muslims. Kach members have carried out attacks against Arabs and expressed support for anti-Arab actions initiated by other groups.

In addition to outlawing a racist and violent political party, the Knesset adopted a law in 1986 "which specified 'incitement to racism' as a criminal offence."[21] This law subjects anyone who publishes anything that tends to provoke racism to five years in prison and anyone who possesses such material to one year in prison.[22]

While anti-Arab sentiment is still a reality in some sectors of Israeli society, the measures taken by the Knesset have stripped this racist element of political clout and influence. Similar measures adopted in a future Palestinian state would ultimately diminish the authority of the anti-Israel hate speech that threatens peace.

Israel also employs preventive detention against suspected terrorists. While most such detentions have involved Arabs, a significant number have involved suspected Jewish terrorists or inciters of violence against Arabs.[23]

Nor is Israel the only democracy that has limited hate speech because of a unique history of racial or religious violence. Modern-day Germany has criminalized Holocaust denial, as have several other democracies.[24] The United States stands as an exception to the rule of placing any restraints on specific genres of dangerous hate speech. I would not want to see the United States change its more absolute approach to protecting nearly all speech, but what is right for the United States—especially near the edges of absolute freedoms—may not necessarily be right for every other democracy facing different problems.

Even if the Palestinian government were to adopt the most absolute prohibition against the censorship of all speech—which it almost certainly will not to do—it could take steps, consistent with the full protection of freedom of speech, to reduce the impact of hate speech. It could begin by deleting anti-Jewish hate material from state-sponsored outlets, such as official textbooks, state-run media, and governmentally sponsored religious exercises. (The Palestinian constitution was amended in 2003 to ensure that Islam would be the only official religion of the Palestinian state.)[25] A good rule of thumb might be that the kinds of statements that could not be made about Muslims, the Muslim religion, or the Muslim state of Palestine should not be able to be said about Jews, Judaism, or the Jewish state of Israel. This "ism equity" would provide some symmetrical control over anti-Jewish hate speech. There is some evidence of a reduction in anti-Jewish and anti-Israel rhetoric by some Palestinian outlets since the death of Arafat, but there is still a great deal of incitement of hate speech both from among Palestinian Arabs and from Syria, Egypt, Saudi Arabia, and other Islamic centers. Even within the Palestinian Authority, incitement continues. Consider, for example, the following speech delivered on May 13, 2005, by Sheik Ibrahim Mudeiris, "a paid employee of the Palestinian Authority":

> Israel is a cancer spreading through the body of the Islamic nation, and because the Jews are a virus resembling AIDS, from which the entire world suffers. . . . You will find that the Jews were behind all the civil strife in this world. The Jews are behind the suffering of the nations. . . . It was the Jews who provoked Nazism to wage war against the entire world, when the Jews, using the Zionist movement, got other countries to wage an economic war on Germany and to boycott German merchandise. . . . But they are committing worse deeds than those done to them in the Nazi war. Yes, perhaps some of them were killed and some burned, but they are inflating this in order to win over the media and gain the world's sympathy. . . . . The day will come when we will rule America. The day will come when we will rule Britain and the entire world—except for the Jews. The Jews will not enjoy a life of tranquility under our rule, because they are treacherous by nature, as they have been throughout history. The day will come when everything will be relieved of the Jews—even the stones and trees which were harmed by them. Listen to the Prophet Muhammad, who tells you about the evil end that awaits Jews.[26]

The Palestinian information minister requested that the Religious Affairs Ministry, which employs Mudeiris, "suspend him, investigate him, and prevent him from delivering further sermons on Fridays." The Palestinian Authority also withdrew an Arabic translation of the notorious anti-Semitic forgery *The Protocols of the Elders of Zion* from its Web site.[27] But much hate speech persists. So long as this incitement, whatever its source, continues, there will be some willing and anxious to die as martyrs. And so long as there are suicide martyrs, peace will be difficult to achieve.

9 What If a Palestinian State Became a Launching Pad for Terrorism?

Our agreements with the Israelis are like the Trojan horse. I explain to our people that this is the only way to get into the walls of Jerusalem, like the wooden horse the Greeks used against the Trojans.

—*Faisal al-Husseini, former rector of Al-Quds University and PLO representative in Jerusalem*[1]

We distinguish the strategic, long-term goals from the political phased goals, which we are compelled to temporarily accept due to international pressure. If you are asking me as a Pan-Arab nationalist what are the Palestinian borders according to the higher strategy, I will immediately reply: "From the river to the sea." Palestine in its entirety is an Arab land, the land of the Arab nation, a land no one can sell or buy, and it is impossible to remain silent while someone is stealing it, even if this requires time and even [if it means paying] a high price.

If you are asking me, as a man who belongs to the Islamic faith, my answer is also "From the river to the sea," the entire land is an Islamic Waqf which can not be bought or sold, and it is impossible to remain silent while someone is stealing it. . . .

If you are asking me as an ordinary Palestinian, from the "inside" or from the Diaspora, you will get the same answer and without any hesitations.

—*Faisal al-Husseini*[2]

What if Israel were to accede to every demand being made by the Palestinian Authority, the UN, the European Community, the Saudis, the Egyptians, and the Jordanians? What if Israel were to abandon the settlements, agree to the creation of a Palestinian state with its capital in Jerusalem, compensate the refugees, and remove its soldiers from the West Bank and Gaza? What if it were even willing to sign off on the Geneva initiative? What if, after taking all of these steps, terrorism against its civilians continued, even escalated? What would the international community then expect Israel to do? What would the United States do? What would the international community do?

These are the very questions being asked by moderate Israelis, and their American supporters, who crave peace. They are particularly troubling questions in light of how the international community responded after Ehud Barak offered the Palestinians not all, but nearly all, of the above wish list and the Palestinians responded by escalating the terrorism.

The standard answer being offered today is that any peace would, of course, be conditional on good-faith efforts by the newly created Palestinian state to end the terrorism. But public opinion polls taken by Palestinians themselves show that a large proportion of Palestinians favor a continuation of terrorism until all of Palestine—which includes Israel—is liberated. A poll conducted in the middle of 2002 by a Palestinian research organization showed a majority of Palestinians approving of the goal of liberating "all of historic Palestine"—which includes all of Israel.[3] It is possible, to be sure, that those figures were inflated by the then current violence and would diminish if real peace were achieved.[4] But it is possible that the opposite may be true: if a Palestinian state is achieved by terrorism—or if that perception exists among most Palestinians—then many will urge an escalation of terrorism to achieve the ultimate goal of many of the Palestinian groups, including Hamas, Hezbollah, Islamic Jihad, and even elements within the Fatah movement. There is even precedent for this latter scenario: when Israel was forced out of southern Lebanon by Hezbollah terrorism, several Palestinian groups called for an increase in terrorism. Thomas Friedman summarized this perspective as follows:

> Ever since the unilateral Israeli withdrawal from Lebanon, Palestinians have watched too much Hezbollah TV from Lebanon, which had

peddled the notion that Israel had become just a big, soft Silicon Valley, and that therefore, with enough suicide bombs, the Jews could be forced from Palestine, just as they had been from South Lebanon.[5]

Given the expressed goal of these increasingly popular radical groups, those of us who urge the creation of a Palestinian state cannot ignore the realistic possibility that such a state might well continue to support, encourage, or at the very least tolerate continuing terrorism against Israeli civilians. Arafat's personal involvement in (and denial of) the shipment of terrorist weapons on the ship *Karine A* from Iran in 2002—after promising to end terrorism—certainly raised questions about his reliability in ending terrorism. Abbas seems more trustworthy, in the sense of not lying, but he has refused to agree to use force against terrorist groups to disarm them.

Any objective observer of the Mideast situation must acknowledge the significant probability that a Palestinian state—or, at the very least, certain enclaves within such a state—could serve as a launching pad for renewed terrorism. Until and unless that frightening scenario is addressed, with concrete guarantees from the international community, it is likely that distrust among some moderate Israelis will persist. It is not enough to say that Israel retains the right to defend itself and to retaliate against terrorism. When Israel had done so in the past, it had been condemned by the international community and the United Nations. Such condemnation would only grow stronger if Israel were to attack a newly formed Palestinian state that was giving lip service to stopping terrorism but was secretly supporting it, or even just closing its eyes to it. The United Nations could not be counted on, as evidenced by UNRWA's refusal to do anything about terrorism that is sometimes openly planned in its refugee camps. Only the United States, with the cooperation of European nations, could provide the needed guarantees. But little thought is currently being given to eliminating this pressing "what if" barrier to peace.

10 Will Civil Wars Be Necessary to Bring About Peace?

Palestinians are near civil war to establish democratic rule—their own terrorists more a threat to the newly elected [Mahmoud] Abbas than are Israeli tanks.

—Victor Davis Hanson, senior fellow and historian
at the Hoover Institution at Stanford University[1]

And now? On the Palestine side, a ferocious struggle for power and maybe civil war. In fact, the conflict between the modernists and the jihadists has been going on for some time now, but Israeli military actions and the veneer of Palestinian comity provided by Arafat somewhat obscured it. Now the Palestinians will finally have to decide if they will allow Hamas to wreck their prospects for a normal life. Israeli policy will depend significantly on the outcome of this nasty process of Palestinian self-definition. But time is not altogether on Israel's side.

—Editorial, the New Republic[2]

President Mahmud Abbas reiterated, while chairing the Palestinian national dialogue sessions yesterday, that he would not take any practical step that would lead to a civil war, alluding to disarming the factions.

—BBC Worldwide Monitoring[3]

There are signs that the new Palestinian leader is preparing to carry out the security reforms that Arafat repeatedly promised but failed to enact. Nevertheless, Mr Abbas has insisted that it is unrealistic for Israel to demand that the PA's forces confront and disarm the militant groups: such an aggressive approach would only lead to a civil war, he says. Instead, Mr Abbas is trying to use his powers of persuasion—and his mandate from the Palestinian people—to persuade and co-opt the militants.

—Economist.com[4]

In a separate development, Mr. Abbas warned Wednesday in a speech to Palestinian police officers that he would use "an iron fist" against any Palestinians who violate the truce with Israel that was declared in February.

—New York Times[5]

In a destructive manner, the prime minister blocked today the chance to bring the [Gaza] disengagement plan to a vote by the people and thus prevent a civil war.

—*The Council of Jewish Settlements, statement following the Knesset vote rejecting a referendum on unilateral Gaza and northern West Bank withdrawal*[6]

Though Mr. Sharon spoke of an "atmosphere of a civil war" within Israel over the withdrawal, he said he was confident the departure of nearly 9,000 settlers from Gaza could be completed "quietly and peacefully."

—New York Times[7]

Shortly after the establishment of Israel as an independent nation in 1948, the new government had to employ force to disarm Jewish militia groups. The most dramatic confrontation took place off the coast of Tel Aviv, when Prime Minister David Ben-Gurion ordered Israel's army to sink a ship, the *Altalena*, that was bringing arms to Menachem Begin's Etzel (or Irgun), the militia group that was responsible for blowing up a wing of the King David Hotel, which had been the headquarters for the British occupation.

Ben-Gurion's actions were extraordinarily controversial—and remain so to this day. I know old Israelis who cannot utter the name of Ben-Gurion without adding a strong epithet. "His first action as prime minister was to kill Jews," a former member of Etzel, now a retired diplomat, seethed during a discussion of the *Altalena* affair. But history has vindicated Ben-Gurion's actions. By disarming the paramilitary groups and demanding a monopoly of arms by the official Israeli military organization under the civilian control of the government, he assured that democratic principles and governmental accountability would govern the use of all military force.

Over the years since the *Altalena* affair, various Jewish underground groups have employed sporadic violence against perceived enemies. One such group, calling itself "TNT"—"Terror Neged Terror," or "Terror Against Terror"—attacked several Palestinian officials whom it regarded as complicit in terrorism. Several Jewish terrorists were arrested and imprisoned. Even more important was the banning of the Kach Party, founded by Rabbi Meir Kahane, from Knesset elections for inciting racism.

Despite these sporadic outbursts of underground violence, no one can doubt Israel's commitment to preventing "private armies" from fighting the war against terrorism. Israeli governments of all political stripes have regarded these "gangs" as part of the problem, rather than part of the solution. They have fought them, using many of the same means, including administrative detention, employed against Palestinian terrorists. This has angered some Israelis. I know, because several disgruntled Israelis asked me to look into the tough treatment these "Jewish freedom fighters" were receiving at the hand of the Israeli legal system. Other Israelis believed that the "Jewish terrorists" were not being treated harshly enough. The important point, however, is that there are no private armies in Israel that operate outside the democratic chain of command. That is the legacy of the swift, decisive, and painful actions Ben-Gurion took at the very beginning of Israeli statehood.

Another legacy is that despite threats of a "civil war" by settlers who are unwilling to leave their homes in the Gaza Strip or West Bank if ordered to do so, there is little support among the general population for civil disobedience or civil war. There will be some unrest, perhaps even some violence, but Israel will be able to carry out its side of any agreement to disband settlements without a civil war.

The question remains whether the new Palestinian leadership can promise the same. Will it take decisive and painful action to disarm terrorist groups that are committed to Israel's destruction, and if it does will there be a civil war? To date, president Mahmoud Abbas has adamantly refused to try to disarm terrorist groups, even those that operate within the structure of the PLO. His excuse has been that so long as Israel continues to occupy Palestinian areas, he lacks the political, military, and moral power to take such a divisive step. The issue is further complicated by the shifting tactics of some of the terrorist groups as they seek to defeat the new president in elections by discrediting him as too harsh on his own people:

> Hamas has decided to participate for the first time in upcoming Palestinian legislative elections, and both it and Islamic Jihad are seeking a role in the Palestine Liberation Organization. . . .
>
> "This is a turning point for the region," said Nabil Aburdeina, a top adviser to Abbas. "There is a truce. . . . There is a unanimous Palestinian agreement on the Cairo Declaration."[8]

Moreover, the "Cairo Agreement" is itself unclear:

> The reason is that Abbas gave an undertaking in Sharm e-Sheikh last month that he had achieved a cease-fire agreement with the terrorist organizations. In Arabic, he used the words *"wakf itlak nur"*— loosely translated as "opening fire is forbidden." However, these words were totally absent from the agreement reached by the Palestinian terrorist factions in Cairo last week. Abbas, backed by the head of the Egyptian Intelligence Services, General Omar Suleiman, did in fact announce that Hamas, Islamic Jihad and other terrorist leaders had made a commitment to maintain quiet, but here they used a different Arabic expression, *"tahdiah,"* meaning quiet. Nowhere was the original expression, *"wakf itlak nur,"* used, nor even *"hudna,"* a cease-fire undertaken by Muslims when fighting a non-Muslim enemy.
>
> As Jews we must continue to think in Hebrew when the Palestinians attempt to confuse us with their Arabic vocabulary. At first they threatened us with a Jihad—a holy war. They then promised a hudna, which exploded in a Jerusalem bus bombing in the summer of 2003.
>
> Abbas then appeared on the scene and first promised a hudna, and later in Sharm e-Sheikh a "wakf itlak nur."
>
> And what came of this? "Tahdiah," quiet.

According to its real meaning this expression permits the Palestinian organizations to perpetrate a terrorist attack from time to time, just as in the Yasser Arafat era, from the first years after the Oslo Accord until he started an all-out war on September 29, 2000.

Moreover, according to last week's Cairo decision, this "quiet" is conditional on further Israeli concessions and the meeting of Palestinian demands, first and foremost "the return of the Palestinian refugees to their property and homes."[9]

It remains to be seen whether Palestinian terrorist groups, especially Hamas and Islamic Jihad, will renounce terrorism in favor of democratic participation, and if so, what level of political influence they will achieve. The most likely scenario is a mixed one in which these groups try to accomplish by democratic means what they have thus far failed to accomplish by violence, but without giving up the terrorist option. Full-scale civil war is a possibility but not a probability. Whatever the eventual outcome, Israel must remain prepared for a renewal of terrorism and the possibility of civil strife and armed conflict both within the Palestinian state and between it and Palestinian terrorists.

11 Is the Security Fence a Barrier to Peace?

So, this is not about security. This is about land annexation. It is an apartheid wall. It is a wall that is designed to turn the Palestinian territory into a prison and at the same time, make us live in separatist, isolated enclaves . . . or ghettos that are totally disconnected and, therefore, preempting the outcome of negotiations and preventing the possibility of a territorial contiguous and viable Palestinian state.

—*Hanan Ashrawi, member of the Palestinian Legislative Council*[1]

But it's not coming down in the short run, because it's defensive. As long as the Palestinians send terrorists onto school buses and to night-clubs to blow up people, Israel has no choice but to build the fence. And it's sort of *1984* doublespeak that some say the wall is aggressive. [A] wall, by its nature, is defensive.

—*New York senator Charles Schumer*[2]

I couldn't continue reaching out when Palestinian society was being directed, by its mainstream political and religious leadership, into jihad. The wall that we are building now is only the concrete expression of the wall of hatred that Palestinian society built first.

99

And so I support the barrier, with regret but no apology. And I expect the Arab world to ask itself why Israelis like myself, who despise barriers and once hoped for a different Middle East, now seek solace in barbed wire and concrete slabs.

—*Yossi Klein Halevi, author and journalist*[3]

But in the ICJ's [International Court of Justice] view, that has overwhelming international support, the wall's construction cannot just be ignored by giving it a political colour. The network of electric fencing, barbed wire and concrete walls that Israel vows to go ahead with "constitutes breaches by Israel of various of its obligations under the applicable international humanitarian law and human rights instruments." It has resulted in "de facto annexation" of some occupied areas and "cannot be justified by military exigencies or by the requirement of security or public order." The barrier, in fact, is a means of economic strangulation, shutting out Palestinians from their jobs and barring their access to their fields and orchards.

—The Nation[4]

We accept that the military commander cannot order the construction of the Separation Fence if his reasons are political. The Separation Fence cannot be motivated by a desire to "annex" territories to the state of Israel. The purpose of the Separation Fence cannot be to draw a political border. . . . Of course, regarding all of these acts, the military commander must consider the needs of the local population. Assuming that this condition is met, there is no doubt that the military commander is authorized to take possession of land in areas under his control. . . . To the extent that construction of the Fence is a military necessity, it is permitted, therefore, by international law.

—*Israeli Supreme Court president Aharon Barak,*
security fence judgment[5]

It is often said that one man's terrorist is another man's freedom fighter. By extension, is not one man's "Berlin Wall" another man's "peace line"? Israel's controversial construction of a security fence between Jewish and Palestinian areas, which has landed the government of Ariel Sharon in the International Court of Justice in the Hague, is widely condemned in this country and elsewhere as a unilateral repartition of the Holy Land. But few of those who have loudly denounced Israel, including Jack Straw and the Foreign Office, seem to remember that similar barriers exist in a part of the United Kingdom. We refer, of course, to the "peace lines" of Belfast, first erected in the early 1970s at the behest of the British Army.

—*London* Daily Telegraph[6]

Israel will soon have two security fences (or "barriers," as Israel prefers to call the West Bank fence, while rejectionists have labeled the existing wall an "apartheid wall," despite the reality that only about 5 percent of the West Bank barrier and none of the Gaza barrier is a wall).[7] The first such fence (I am using the most accurately descriptive word) was erected on the border separating Israel from the Gaza Strip. It was completed in 1995, and since that time has been nearly 100 percent effective in preventing terrorists from entering Israel from the Gaza Strip, though it has not prevented rocket attacks on Israel from Gaza. This fence has not been particularly controversial because it is located on the border and does not involve the "taking" of Palestinian land. Moreover, the final border between Israel and Gaza is settled, since Israel has renounced all claims to land in Gaza and there is no disputed territory. Nor will there remain any Israeli settlements in the Gaza Strip.

This is in sharp contrast with the situation on the West Bank, where the final borders with Israel are in considerable dispute. Although the Palestinians claim that they want a "return" of all the territory Israel captured from Jordan after Jordan attacked Israel in June 1967, neither the United Nations nor the United States recognizes this absolute claim. As previously documented, the UN Security Council explicitly and resoundingly rejected the Arab and Soviet demand that Israel return "all" territories or even "the" territories it captured from Jordan in the course of defending itself from an unjustified attack. The Security Council resolution contemplated some territorial adjustments so as to achieve "secure and reorganized boundaries" that would allow "every state in the area" to live "in peace." This resolution did not even recognize the rights of Palestinians or the need for Israel to "return" land that did not belong to any Palestinian state.[8]

The United States has recognized that any peace will require territorial adjustments. President George W. Bush announced in a letter to Prime Minister Ariel Sharon dated April 14, 2004:

As part of a final peace settlement, Israel must have secure and recognized borders, which should emerge from negotiations between the parties in accordance with UNSC Resolutions 242 and 338. In light of new realities on the ground, including already existing major Israeli population centers, it is unrealistic to expect that the outcome of final status negotiations will be a full and complete return to the armistice lines of 1949, and all previous efforts to negotiate a two-state solution have reached the same conclusion. It is realistic to expect that any final status agreement will only be achieved on the basis of mutually agreed changes that reflect these realities.[9]

President Bill Clinton, as well, in his offers made at Camp David and Taba, recognized the need for territorial adjustments, as did the Palestinians who worked on the Geneva proposals. There is no absolute certainty at this writing about the precise nature of the final borders, although their general parameters are fairly clear. The only absolute certainty is that the final borders will be different from the pre-1967 borders, but that they will not be greatly different.

It is this uncertainty that creates the problem regarding the security fence, and most particularly its appropriate location. Two courts have addressed this difficult issue: the Supreme Court of Israel and the International Court of Justice.

The Israeli government has both a legal and a moral obligation to comply with the Israeli Supreme Court's decision regarding the security fence. After all, the Israeli Supreme Court is a creation of the Israeli legislature and is therefore representative of all of its people—Jews, Muslims, and Christians alike. Moreover, the Israeli Supreme Court has a real stake in both sides of the fence dispute. Its job is to balance the security needs of its citizens against the humanitarian concerns of West Bank Palestinians. It tried to strike that balance by upholding the concept of a security fence while insisting that the Israeli military authorities give due weight to the needs of the Palestinians, even if that requires some compromise with the security of Israelis.

Contrast this with the questionable status of the International Court of Justice at The Hague. No Israeli judge may serve on that court as a permanent member, while sworn enemies of Israel serve among its judges, several of whom represent countries that do not themselves abide by the rule of law. Virtually every democracy voted against that court's taking jurisdiction over the fence case, while nearly every country that voted to take jurisdiction was a tyranny. Israel owes the International Court absolutely no deference. It is under neither a moral nor a legal obligation to give any weight to its predetermined decision.

The Supreme Court of Israel recognized the unquestionable reality that the security fence has saved numerous lives and promises to save more, but it also recognized that this benefit must be weighed against the material disadvantages to West Bank Palestinians. The International Court, on the other hand, discounted the saving of lives and focused only on the Palestinian interests. By showing its preference for Palestinian property rights over the lives of Jews, the International Court displayed its one-sidedness.

The International Court of Justice is much like a Mississippi court in the 1930s. The all-white Mississippi court, which excluded blacks from serving on it, could do justice in disputes between whites, but it was incapable of doing justice in cases between a white and a black. It would always favor white litigants. So too the International Court. It is perfectly capable of resolving disputes between Sweden and Norway, but it is incapable of doing justice where Israel is involved, because Israel is the excluded black when it comes to that court—indeed, when it comes to most United Nations organs. A judicial decision can have no legitimacy when rendered against a nation that is willfully excluded from the court's membership by bigotry.

Just as the world should have disregarded any decision against blacks rendered by a Mississippi court in the 1930s, so too should all decent people contemptuously disregard the biased decisions of the International Court of Justice when it comes to Israel. To give any credence to the decisions of that court is to legitimate bigotry.

The International Court of Justice should be a court of last resort to which aggrieved litigants can appeal when their own country's domestic courts are closed to them. The Israeli Supreme Court is open not only to all Israeli Arabs, but also to all West Bank and Gaza Arabs. The Israeli Supreme Court is the only court in the Mideast where an Arab can actually win a case against his government. The Israeli government will comply with the rule of law by following the decision of its own highly respected Supreme Court rather than that of a biased court from which its judges are excluded.

Anyone looking at the facts will quickly understand why the International Court of Justice deserves no deference. Consider its chief justice. Andrew McCarthy, a former U.S. federal prosecutor, focused on the chief justice in analyzing the court's "fence" decision:

> The ICJ began by announcing its awareness that "developing friendly relations among nations based on respect for the principle of equal rights and self-determination of peoples is among the purposes and principles of the Charter of the United Nations." These words, uttered as a foretaste to a condemnation of Israel for exercising its right of self-determination, were expressed by the ICJ's chief justice, Shi Jiuvong, of China—a Communist regime that denies civil rights, specializes in show trials, terrorizes dissenters, and colonizes Tibet. According to his biography on the ICJ's own website, Shi was a prominent government legal adviser in 1989, when the regime infamously crushed a popular uprising seeking exactly such "equal rights and self-determination" on behalf of the Chinese people.[10]

Professor Eric Posner, writing in the *New York Times*, employed a statistical analysis to explain, "Why have countries abandoned the [International Court of Justice]?" His conclusion:

> The most plausible answer is that they do not trust the judges to rule impartially, but expect them to vote the interests of the states of which they are citizens. Statistics bear out this conjecture. When their home countries are parties to litigation, judges vote in favor of them about 90 percent of the time. When their states are not parties, judges tend to vote for states that are more like their home states. Judges from wealthy states tend to vote in favor of wealthy states, and judges from poor states tend to vote in favor of poor states. In addition, judges from democracies appear to favor democracies; judges from authoritarian states appear to favor authoritarian states. This is not to say that the judges pay no attention to the law. But there is no question that politics matter.[11]

When international politics matter, they tend to matter disproportionately against Israel. Israel should continue to ignore the decision of the ICJ and to obey the rulings of its own far less political Supreme Court. It should also remind the world that "security fences have been built throughout the world, often in disputed territories,"[12] and that none has ever been subjected to the criticism directed at Israel.

The precise location of the fence will not be important if a negotiated peace is achieved, because a fence can be moved, as it is being moved in response to the decision of the Supreme Court of Israel. But if peace talks fail and Israel applies its policy of unilateral withdrawal to the West Bank, the fence may well become the default boundary. This is a powerful incentive for the Palestinians to negotiate more favorable borders.

In the meantime, the fence will continue to be built and will continue to prevent the deaths of numerous civilians at the hands of terrorists who are determined to "wreck the peace process" (in the words of one terrorist leader).

On May 27, 2005, CNN broadcast a report on terrorist groups that are determined to prevent peace between Israel and the Palestinians. It included a slickly produced video that "shows a suicide bomber where to stand on a bus" so as to maximize civilian deaths and injuries. The video also provides instructions on how to make suicide bombs and belts. One of the groups' bombers blew himself up at a Tel Aviv nightclub for teenagers, killing twenty-three Israelis and injuring more than one hundred. Several other terrorists were caught trying to infiltrate Israel in an effort to blow themselves up. These terrorist groups have been escalating their recruitment efforts as the peace process seems to be moving forward.

On June 10, 2005, I drove to various points along the fence, including some portions that are made of large concrete slabs to prevent the shooting of Israeli civilians driving on adjacent roads. I went through a checkpoint and observed Arab men, women, and children doing the same. I spent a considerable period of time at a newly constructed transit center designed to facilitate passage. It was air-conditioned and had comfortable bathrooms, and the guards used electronic gizmos that promise quicker checks. It also contained "bomb rooms," for the safe detonation of explosives that terrorists will surely try to smuggle through or explode on the spot. The guard who showed me around wore a bulletproof vest and kept his gun drawn at all times.

The security fence represents a trade-off between the prevention of terrorism on the one hand and significant inconvenience to Palestinians on the other hand. Much can be done by Israel to reduce this inconvenience and to eliminate any humiliation or gratuitous hurt inflicted on innocent Palestinians.

But in the end the fence is a necessary evil—made necessary by the persistence of the greater evil of terrorism. When terrorism stops, the fence will come down. In the meantime, there will be inconvenience to innocent Palestinians. Israel is entitled to strike the balance in favor of preventing terrorism, but it should do everything reasonable to reduce the consequences to Palestinians.

12 Is a Militarized Palestine a Barrier to Peace?

In the Israeli-Palestinian conflict, weapons can in no way help find the solution. . . . We don't need arms. A Palestinian state should be demilitarized—not because that's what Israel demands, but in our own interest.

—*Sari Nusseibeh, former PLO Jerusalem Commissioner*[1]

The character of the provisional Palestinian state will be determined through negotiations between the Palestinian Authority and Israel. The provisional state will have provisional borders and certain aspects of sovereignty, be fully demilitarized with no military forces, but only with police and internal security forces of limited scope and armaments, be without the authority to undertake defense alliances or military cooperation, and Israeli control over the entry and exit of all persons and cargo, as well as of its air space and electromagnetic spectrum.

—*"Israeli Cabinet Statement on Road Map and 14 Reservations"*[2]

Tikkun continues to stress that the Palestinian state we would support could only be created on conditions similar to those imposed on Austria after World War II—total demilitarization and political neutrality enforced by the Great Powers. . . . Israel would have to have treaty rights to invade the moment there was an introduction of tanks, planes, or heavy weapons. We have no illusions about the PLO itself and would never agree to a Palestinian state that significantly threatened Israel's security.

—Michael Lerner, editor of Tikkun *magazine*[3]

A lasting peace will require a demilitarized Palestine, with only a domestic police force capable of keeping the peace and preventing terrorism, but without an army, navy, or air force capable of waging aggressive war against Israel (or Jordan, for that matter). Palestinian negotiators at Camp David in 2000 seemed to accept this limitation and have not insisted on the full sovereign right to build a large-scale armed force. As Dennis Ross recounts the negotiations over this issue:

> Palestinians had more of a problem with the symbolism of not having an army than with the practicality of limiting their forces and the weapons they could possess. . . . On security, I said the Palestinians would accept a nonmilitarized state, provided they were permitted levels and categories of weapons that would provide them with credible means to deal with any internal threats to Arafat.[4]

It is unlikely that the need for an essentially demilitarized Palestine will now become a barrier to peace and a reasonable two-state solution.

The only guarantee of peace in the region is a qualitatively superior Israeli military deterrent. Whenever an Arab nation, or a combination of Arab nations, had believed itself capable of destroying Israel militarily, there had been war. Whenever Israel's military superiority has been clear, there has been no war. Israel's military actions have all been taken in self-defense or in anticipatory self-defense. Most, though not all, of these protective actions have been justified.[5] Even when they have been unjustified, they were taken for reasons of self-defense, not for aggressive or expansionist reasons. If a final peace is reached between Israel and the Palestinians—and eventually between the other Arab and Muslim nations and Israel—there will be no reason to fear the Israeli military. Those few Israelis who might still favor aggressive war to "recapture" parts of biblical Israel will constitute an even tinier proportion of the population than they do now. Because the Israeli government holds a monopoly on the use of arms, these extremists will have no access to weapons of warfare. Some could surely obtain guns and explosives, but the Israeli government has demonstrated an ability and willingness to control Jewish terrorists.

A Palestinian state, on the other hand, will not soon secure a monopoly on the use of arms. Terrorist organizations and militias—such as Hamas, the Al-Aqsa Martyrs Brigades, Islamic Jihad, and others—will continue to have access to weapons of all kinds. Even if the Palestinian state renounced all support of terrorism, other states, most particularly Iran and Syria, will likely continue to arm terrorist groups dedicated to Israel's destruction. Nor is it out of the question that someday Hamas might gain control over the Palestinian government, either by means of a coup, an election, or some such combination. Israel cannot be asked to accept a fully militarized Hamas state on its vulnerable borders. Even today, rockets rain down on Israeli towns and cities from the Gaza Strip, and their precise sources are difficult to target because of their mobility.

Nations that have started and lost wars have generally agreed to disarm and remain essentially demilitarized for at least some considerable period of time. Some, like Germany following its defeat in World War I, have broken their agreements, with disastrous consequences. The Palestinians, unlike the Germans, have never been armed to the degree that they could wage aggressive war, as distinguished from terrorist attacks. Nor is there anyone rushing to arm them. Jordan and Egypt have a stake in keeping their arms limited, as do the United States and, of course, Israel. The Israeli demand that a Palestinian state remain essentially demilitarized, while retaining the capacity to control terrorists in its midst, will not serve as a barrier to peace if the Palestinians truly want a peaceful two-state solution.

13 Is the Iranian Nuclear Threat a Barrier to Peace?

The Zionist regime possesses stockpiles of nuclear warheads and no concerns are expressed on this matter. But, there are objections to Iran's peaceful nuclear activities.

—Iranian foreign minister Kamal Kharrazi[1]

Iran will not sit idly by awaiting a strike against it, and would resort to using the preemptive strike option against Israel and the U.S. . . . The principle of preemption strike is not exclusive to the U.S.

—Iranian defense minister Ali Shamkhani[2]

The sharp increase in focus on Iran's alleged threat (nuclear weapons, connections to terror, etc.) is very clear. . . . Perhaps the purpose of all of these initiatives [to put pressure on Iran] is to evoke some action by Iran or Syria that can be interpreted by Washington-media as justification for military action, or perhaps just to rattle the leadership to contribute to internal repression, disaffection, disruption.

—Noam Chomsky, MIT professor of linguistics[3]

Beyond the imbalances in territory and population, the most important differences are related to core values and objectives. The leaders

111

of Iran's Islamic Republic (including the unelected "supreme leader") routinely deny the legitimacy of Jewish sovereignty and threaten genocide, but there is no Israeli equivalent.

Iran parades Shahab missiles with signs saying "Wipe Israel Off the Map," and former President Akbar Hashemi Rafsanjani speaks about the destruction of Israel. In this closed and radical environment, international commitment and treaty pledges are meaningless and readily ignored.

—*Gerald M. Steinberg, columnist*[4]

The idea that this tyranny of Iran will hold a nuclear bomb is a nightmare not only for us but for the whole world.

—*Israeli foreign minister Silvan Shalom*[5]

Clearly, if I was the leader of Israel and I'd listened to some of the statements by the Iranian ayatollahs that regarded the security of my country, I'd be concerned about Iran having a nuclear weapon as well. And in that Israel is our ally, and in that we've made a very strong commitment to support Israel, we will support Israel if her security is threatened.

—*President George W. Bush*[6]

The Palestinians do not pose a strategic threat to Israel—at least at present. Conventional terrorism cannot destroy Israel, though it can make life miserable for its people. Were Palestinian terrorism to escalate to include the use of weapons of mass destruction, especially nuclear weapons, then Israel would face an existential threat. But in the absence of such an escalation, the Palestinians do not pose an immediate strategic threat to Israel. Of course, the very existence of a conflict between the Palestinians and Israel may contribute to the existential dangers posed by well-armed nations capable of marshaling a significant military threat against Israel. Before the destruction of Saddam Hussein's regime, Iraq posed such a threat, especially since it was actively seeking—especially during the 1970s and 1980s—to develop weapons of mass destruction and delivery systems capable of reaching Israel (as Iraqi Scuds did during the first Gulf war). Today Iran poses such a threat. It already has a rocket capable of reaching every part of Israel, and no reasonable person doubts the desire of its leaders to develop a nuclear warhead. Suzanne Fields wrote for the *Washington Times*:

> In 2001 Hashemi Rafsanjani, the former president of Iran, speculated that in a nuclear exchange with Israel his country might lose 15 million people, which would amount to a small "sacrifice" from among the billion Muslims worldwide in exchange for the lives of 5 million Israeli Jews. He seemed pleased with his formulation.[7]

Several years later, Rafsanjani said the following to a crowd at a Friday prayer gathering in Tehran:

> If a day comes when the world of Islam is duly equipped with the arms Israel has in possession, the strategy of colonialism would face a stalemate because application of an atomic bomb would not leave any thing in Israel but the same thing would just produce damages in the Muslim world.[8]

Even more recently, Hassan Abbassi, a Revolutionary Guards intelligence theoretician teaching at Al-Hussein University, threatened to use Iran's missiles against Jewish and Christian targets: "Our missiles are now ready to strike at their civilization, and as soon as the instructions arrive from Leader [Ali Khamenei], we will launch our missiles at their cities and installations."[9] These repeated threats must be taken seriously.

It is possible, but highly unlikely in the view of many experts, that peace between Israel and the Palestinians will end Iran's nuclear threat against Israel. Iran *purports* to be threatening Israel on behalf of the Palestinians, and if that were Iran's only grievance against Israel, it might follow that Palestinian satisfaction with Israeli peace offerings would eliminate the grievance and thus the threat. But Iran does not accept the two-state solution, the Palestinian authority, or the elected leaders of the Palestinian people. It supports Hezbollah and other rejectionist groups that will never be satisfied unless Israel is wiped off the map. And since Israel will never commit politicide, it is unlikely that Iran will ever give up its belligerent and threatening posture toward the Jewish state.

Both Israel and the United States have taken the position that in light of Iran's history and avowed threats to use nuclear weapons against Israel, that nation will not be permitted to develop a nuclear weapon. How this policy will be translated into action remains to be seen. The United States has apparently let it be known that it will not prevent Israel from taking unilateral military action, if that becomes necessary to destroy an impending Iranian nuclear weapon. Whether Israel has the military capacity, working alone, to carry out this dangerous option is unclear. Iran has learned from Israel's preventive airstrike in 1981 against Iraq's nuclear facility. It has spread its nuclear facilities around the country, placing some smack in the middle of large cities such as Tehran. It has also encased its nuclear facilities within thick protective walls and roofs. The United States, in a very public gesture, sold bunker-busting bombs to Israel, perhaps to enhance the deterrent threat against Iran's further development of nuclear weapons.

Objectors to Israel's possession of nuclear weapons cite a double standard: the United States is focusing on preventing the development of nuclear weapons in Iran while failing to condemn Israel for already possessing these weapons and continuing to expand its nuclear arsenal.[10] Israel Shahak, a strident anti-Zionist, has claimed that "Israel is preparing for a war, nuclear if need be, for the sake of averting domestic change not to its liking, if it occurs in some or any Middle Eastern states. . . . Israel clearly prepares . . . to use for the purpose all means available, including nuclear ones."[11] Israel's history, however, has demonstrated that it harbors no such aggressive intentions and that the deterrent power of a defensive nuclear arsenal is necessary for its survival and security. In fact, during his U.S. trip in April 2005, Ariel Sharon said that his government does not plan to attack Iran.[12]

As Shimon Peres, the dovish father of Israel's nuclear capacity, told the *Jordan Times* in 1998, "We have built a nuclear option, not in order to have a Hiroshima, but to have an Oslo."[13] Israel has never inflicted destruction with its nuclear weapons that it has possessed for decades. (It has never even bombed an enemy city with conventional weapons, even after its own cities were bombed by Egypt, Jordan, and Iraq.)[14] Rather, Israel's nuclear arsenal is an essential tool of deterrence for a tiny country surrounded by hostile enemies. Israel has been engaged in multiple wars while already in possession of nuclear weapons and has refrained from using them. Even while under surprise attack in the 1973 war, and in a position of great weakness, Israel continued to use its nuclear capabilities solely as a deterrent and a bargaining tool.[15]

So long as any well-armed nation threatens Israel's existence, there can never be real and full peace in the Mideast. Today, Iran poses the greatest threat to peace in the region, but tomorrow it could be another Islamic fundamentalist regime, or a terrorist group that owns weapons of mass destruction. Nor is there anything Israel can do—politically, diplomatically, or in any other peaceful way—to eliminate the threat, since the threat grows out of the categorical refusal of so many Islamic fundamentalists to accept Israel's existence. No nation can be asked to accept its own demise as a condition to peace. Yet there are those who place the blame exclusively on Israel for merely existing. The columnist Barbara Amiel recounted how "the ambassador of a major EU country"—later revealed to be French ambassador to Britain Daniel Bernard—"politely told a gathering at my home that the current troubles in the world were all because of 'that shitty little country Israel.'"[16] "Why," he asked, "should the world be in danger of World War Three because of those people?"

Israel's continued existence as a Jewish democracy must become the unquestioned *constant* in any international equation for peace in the Mideast. Those who cannot accept Israel's existence—even after the occupation is ended and the Palestinians accept peace and establish their own state—must be the ones treated as international pariahs, rather than Israel. There will be some who will never accept Israel, and so long as they continue to be treated as "respected" members of the international community, "respected" academics, and "respected" religious leaders, Israel will feel threatened. This threat must end if peace is to be achieved. These rejectionists must be recognized for what they are: barriers to peace and bigots who accept every other kind of state except a democratic Jewish state.

A major reason why some cannot accept Israel is their unwillingness to accept normalcy for Jews. They can accept Jews as victims. That is why the Holocaust resonates so strongly for so many, even including some who cannot accept Israel. The fact that the United Nations was willing to sponsor a day of commemoration for the Holocaust, while so many of its members continue to refuse to recognize Israel's legitimacy, speaks volumes. Jews as noble *victims*, yes! Jews, as strong, independent, and proud *victors*, never! The image of the Jewish warrior, defending Jews aggressively against their enemies, is an alien image for many. For some, it is even a cause, if not a justification for, anti-Semitism.[17]

Unless and until the entire world comes to accept normalcy for the Jewish state—treats it like *any* other state, stops excluding it from *any* international organizations or groups, recognizes its right to exist and thrive as a Jewish democracy, welcomes it with open arms into the family of nations—Israel cannot be expected to lower its guard. It cannot be expected to reduce its defensive or deterrent arsenal, to alter its policy of proactive self-defense, or to place its trust in the United Nations. If and when the world comes to accept Israel—really accept it—then and only then can there be any realistic discussions of disarmament or submission to the authority of international organizations. Normalcy is the minimal prerequisite for a full and real peace.

Normalcy with regard to Israel will also benefit the rest of the world, because the unique focus on Israel—often to the exclusion of the world's real problems—distorts priorities and provides an excuse for inaction. For example, when the South American and Arab nations of the world convened in May 2005 at a summit designed to address their common economic problems, the first issue on which they focused was Israel, and the first resolution they agreed upon was one critical of the Jewish nation.[18] Both the South American and Arab countries have bigger problems, but the focus on Israel provides an excuse to avoid confronting them. Similarly at other conferences dealing with issues as diverse as sexism, slavery, racism, the environment, poverty, and genocide, the focus has been on Israel and the real problems escaped critical attention and condemnation. On many university campuses, there is more criticism directed at Israel than at nations engaged in real genocide, real apartheid, real slavery, and real discrimination against women. The world will become a better place when Israel becomes normalized by the international community and the world's most serious problems are addressed in the order of their real priorities and the real human suffering being inflicted by so many nations and groups.

Some religious fundamentalists reject Israel on theological grounds: the nation that rejected Jesus as their messiah and Mohammad as their prophet cannot be allowed to succeed, to thrive, to defeat its enemies— to be rewarded for its sin! Others reject the image of the strong and righteous Jewish warrior out of guilt over the Holocaust: they must see the Jew as "Nazi" perpetrator and the Palestinian as "Jewish" victim in order to expiate their own, their family's, their nation's, their church's guilt over the Holocaust.

More than a century ago, in *Der Judenstaat* [The Jewish state], Theodore Herzl argued that establishing a Jewish state would finally "normalize" the Jewish people. He wrote, "We shall live at last as free men on our own soil, and die peacefully in our own homes."[19]

The Six-Day War was a test of that premise. Prior to the war, when it looked as if the Jews of Israel might be slaughtered by a genocidal attack from its Arab neighbors, much of the world showed sympathy for Israel. But following Israel's decisive victory against several Arab armies, its image quickly changed from victim to victor, from wimp to warrior.

It was *not* the occupation that changed attitudes; it was the victory. After all, Israel immediately accepted Security Council Resolution 242 calling for an exchange of land for peace. It was willing to end the occupation in exchange for normal relationships with the Arab world and secure and recognized boundaries and states. The Arabs issued their notorious "three no's": no peace, no negotiation, no recognition. Israeli defense minister Moshe Dayan repeatedly told audiences and journalists, "I'm waiting for the phone to ring," suggesting that he would trade land for peace as soon as there was a willing peace partner.[20]

The hard left began to demonize Israel before "the occupation" was perceived as "an occupation"; recall that prior to Israel's capturing the Gaza Strip and the West Bank, these "Palestinian" areas were "occupied" for twenty years by Egypt and Jordan respectively without any international criticism. They were not even deemed occupations by the international community. It took some years following 1967 for the concept of "occupation" to become the standard word for Israel's continued presence in these areas. Changes in attitude toward Israel could be seen, however, in the immediate aftermath of its 1967 victory.

The question remains: will there be another change in attitude if Israel makes peace with the Palestinians? Perhaps among some. But certainly not among those who reject Israel's right to exist as a Jewish democracy.

Israel certainly cannot count on any change by the Iranian government. Indeed, the Iranian mullahs may be deliberately trying to sabotage peace by drawing Israel into a conflict over its developing nuclear weapons capacity. Were Israel to attack Iran's nuclear facilities—either alone or together with the United States—it would become more difficult for the Palestinians to make peace with Israel. Yet Israel may, quite understandably, regard Iran's nuclear threat as far more dangerous than any threat posed by the Palestinians. It is imperative therefore for the international community—and most especially for France, Russia, China, and the UN—to address the continuing Iranian threat, because it constitutes a potentially significant barrier to peace between Israel and the Palestinians.

I do not want to overstate my case. Peace is possible even in the face of pervasive hatred, but it is considerably more difficult. Moderate Israelis will be less willing to offer compromises that are perceived as weakening their security if they see a future world even more virulent in its anti-Israel hatred than it is today. Several moderate Israelis have told me that they have been increasingly reluctant to support ending the military occupation, especially since it appears as if anti-Israel rhetoric has been escalating, rather than diminishing, as the Israeli government offers concessions in the interests of peace. "I used to think that it didn't matter what we did," an Israeli moderate told me. "They will hate us just as much even if we give back the whole West Bank as well as the Gaza." He paused and then continued: "I was wrong. It does make a difference. They hate us even more when we give more, because it confuses their image of us as totally evil. And our enemies see it as a sign of our weakness and their strength."

It certainly seems true that petitions for divestment, boycott, and other forms of singular demonization of Israel are not diminishing, certainly not in Europe or at the United Nations, as Israel offers concession after concession. In some quarters, these one-sided attacks may be increasing both in frequency and vituperation. As we shall see in chapter 14, the largest British professors' union rejected a petition to boycott Israeli universities back in 2003, during the height of the bloodshed. Then, after Israel announced its decision to withdraw from the Gaza Strip and parts of the West Bank—and when it looked like peace was really possible—that same group voted to boycott two Israeli universities. The Presbyterian Church too escalated its divestment campaign against Israel, just as Israel was making difficult sacrifices for peace. Susan Blackwell, a Birmingham University lecturer and an advocate of the boycott by the British professors' union, declared that the purpose of the boycott was to condemn the "illegitimate state of Israel."[21] Despite the subsequent reversal of the boycott decision—at least for now—this continuing threat of sanctions sends a terrible and dangerous message both to Israelis and Palestinians: it tells the Israelis that they will earn no international support from their concessions, and it tells the Palestinians that they will continue to have international support even if the peace process fails because of renewed terrorism or their unwillingness to compromise. That message is similar to the one sent after Israel made momentous concessions at Camp David and Taba and Arafat rejected those concessions and opened the floodgates of suicide terrorism. Despite Israel's willingness to offer peace and Arafat's refusal to accept it, the Israelis were vilified throughout Europe and Arafat was given a pass. That message contributed to the continuing violence that bloodied the region between 2000 and 2004. A similar message now will decrease the prospects for peace and increase the likelihood of renewed violence.

In chapter 8, I discussed incitements to violence from Palestinians themselves—Hamas leaders, imams preaching on Palestinian-run radio and television, official textbooks—and how it could be eliminated or reduced by a Palestinian state. But there are sources of hate speech outside of Palestine that pose significant barriers to peace. Some of these come from the UN, European diplomats, university campuses, religious leaders, and individual political leaders. The Palestinian leadership sometimes uses this external incitement and hate speech to further its cause and strengthen its bargaining position. Though the Palestinian leadership cannot completely control these sources of hate, it can influence them. If the Palestinian leadership were to make it unambiguously clear that *it* regards this hatred as a barrier to peace and that *it* wants it to stop, this would have a positive and powerful influence on its purported allies.

With these considerations in mind, let us now turn to the problem of hatred in general, and hate speech in particular, as significant barriers to peace.

PART II

Overcoming the Hatred Barriers to Peace

E verybody understands the geopolitical barriers to peace—disputed borders, continuing terrorism, division of religious holy places, the nuclear threat from Iran, and other such issues discussed in part I of this book. But there are more subtle, though quite important, barriers that do not fit easily into these more familiar categories. Primary among them are the atmospherics that make peace difficult. These include the hatred deliberately directed against each side by extremists on the other side.

Some might assume—incorrectly, in my view—that hatred itself cannot be a barrier to peace so long as it is not converted into injurious actions. When I was a kid we used to say, "Sticks and stones may break your bones, but names can never hurt you." That was wrong back then—names can certainly cause pain and damage. But it is even more incorrect now, especially in the context of trying to bring about peace between Israel and the Palestinians. Terms such as "Nazi," "racist," "genocide," and "apartheid," directed at the Mideast's only democracy that operates under the rule of law, serve to encourage the view that this is an unresolvable conflict between good and evil, and that any compromise with evil would be wrong. On the other side, words like "dogs," "two-legged animals," and "terrorists" directed against all Muslims or Arabs[1] also discourage compromise and engender suspicion that "those people" don't really want peace but only temporary tactical advantage.

There is a difference, however, between the hate coming from the two sides: much of the most hateful language directed against Israel

121

comes from mainstream academics, politicians, religious leaders, state-controlled media, diplomats, and others in positions of authority and influence. Most of the hateful language directed against Palestinians, on the other hand, comes from marginalized extremists who have little authority or influence over mainstream supporters of Israel. There is a clear asymmetry in the hate speech that is in no way correlated with the underlying actions of each side.

In the chapters that follow, I will focus on hate speech from academics, from political and diplomatic leaders, and from religious sources. I will demonstrate that there is an explicit campaign of vilification against Israel as part of a larger strategy designed to thwart the peace process. I will also show that the vilification is escalating just as Israel and the Palestinians are moving closer to peace, thus demonstrating that its goal is not to influence Israeli policy in a positive way. Instead the goal of this well-coordinated campaign is entirely negative: namely, to produce a generation of future leaders—political, economic, religious, academic—who are virtually programmed to be stridently anti-Israel. In chapter 16, I will present a case study of one such coordinated effort that has been under way for more than twenty years by Professor Noam Chomsky of MIT, the columnist Alexander Cockburn of the *Nation*, an itinerant academic named Norman Finkelstein who is currently teaching at DePaul University, and a large group of followers and sycophants who flood the Internet with attacks against the Jewish state and its supporters.

I do not mean to suggest, of course, that there exists an overarching "conspiracy" of which all vilifiers of Israel are knowing members. Simpleminded "conspiracy theories" of that kind rarely bear much of a relationship to the complexity of the real world. What I am suggesting is that some of this hate speech is, in fact, coordinated. The Chomsky-Cockburn-Finkelstein conspiracy is real and acknowledged by the conspirators themselves. Other groupings are merely loosely knit. Some have no connection with each other except for a common goal. Many are simply isolated instances of hate speech that may contribute to the goal. Taken together or separately, they constitute significant barriers to peace, by emboldening the rejectionists and the terrorists, as well as by encouraging Arab moderates who are somewhat skeptical of the peace process to delay any resolution until Israel becomes much weaker as a result of generational changes in its sources of support.

14 More Palestinian Than the Palestinians

So first of all, let's call the [Oslo] agreement by its real name: an instrument of Palestinian surrender, a Palestinian Versailles.

—*Edward Said, late Columbia University professor of*
English and comparative literature[1]

The details of the Camp David talks remain officially secret but Arafat's concessions—for which read, capitulation—are obvious.

—*Robert Fisk, Middle East correspondent, London* Independent[2]

Academia

It is fortunate that Israel must make peace with the Palestinians and not with the professors. The current Palestinian leadership includes many pragmatists who understand the need to compromise. Many professors, on the other hand—especially in Europe but also in the United States—have become so polemical, so extreme, and so opposed to Israel's very existence that they themselves have become significant barriers to peace. They are, in a word, more Palestinian than the Palestinians.

The role model for this destructive stance was Professor Edward Said of Columbia University. Said was not only a believer in violence and bloodshed, he was himself a practitioner of violence. On one occasion, he and his son threw rocks at Israelis along the Lebanese border.[3] He refused to condemn far more lethal acts of violence directed against innocent Israeli civilians.

In light of this background, it is significant that Said was widely regarded as a moderate among advocates for the Palestinian cause. Were he a Jewish supporter of Israel who expressed comparable views on the Israeli side, he would be regarded as an unreconstructed hardliner, well to the right of the most hawkish members of the current Israeli government. The closest comparison would be to the late Meir Kahane, the assassinated leader of the widely reviled Kach Party, who was banned from running for office in Israel. Like Kahane, Said opposed the two-state solution. Like Kahane, Said believed that those seeking peace were too soft on their enemies. And like Kahane, Said refused to condemn terrorism and himself demonstrated symbolic support for terrorists.

It speaks volumes about the different attitudes toward peace on both sides of the conflict that one of these mirror-image ideologues is regarded as a respected moderate by his side, while the other is regarded as a reviled reactionary by his. A leading German newspaper, *Frankfurter Allgemeine Zeitung*, exemplified this double standard when it described Said—who opposed the Oslo Accords, the Clinton-Barak peace proposal, and the two-state solution—as an "intellectual [who] pleaded constantly for a peaceful coexistence of Jews, Muslims, Christians";[4] whereas the same paper characterized me—who has always favored peace and each of the above proposals—as a "militant."[5] This is the same word often used in the European press to characterize terrorists who kill innocent civilians, thus suggesting a moral equivalence between pro-Israel advocates of a two-state compromise on the one hand and anti-Israel murderers on the other.

The very idea that a man who regarded Yasser Arafat as *too* willing to compromise in order make peace is a "moderate" powerfully demonstrates the double standard applied to Israel, on the one hand, and the Palestinian cause on the other. Both former president Bill Clinton and President George W. Bush understand that Arafat was the major barrier to peace in the Middle East. Arafat's rejection of the generous offer made by Ehud Barak at Camp David and Taba—statehood on 95 percent of the West Bank and all of Gaza—was condemned by true moderates such as Prince Bandar of Saudi Arabia but praised by opponents of peace such as Edward Said and the leaders of "rejectionist" groups like Hamas and Hezbollah. Said has always been in very bad company with his anti-Israel, anti-peace views.

In his rejection of the two-state solution, of the Oslo Accords, and even of Arafat's all too feeble efforts at peacemaking, Said showed himself to be the Meir Kahane of the Palestinian cause. Those who condemned Kahane's extremism and methodology should also have condemned Said's extremism and that of his current followers. Both men were barriers to peace, though Said was far more influential on his side than Kahane ever was on his. Both men raised difficult and provocative questions about the future of the Middle East. Both men offered destructive and wrongheaded solutions that assured a continuation of violence rather than offering a realistic hope for peace based on two states living side by side.

In other words, the compromise sought by indigenous Palestinians on the ground—Palestinians whose children were killing and being killed—was not good enough for a fancy academic living in New York, far removed from the strife of daily life in Ramallah, Hebron, and Gaza. Said was content to observe and comment on the violence, even to throw rocks from behind the safety of a fence in Lebanon, but not to try to reduce or prevent it. He was typical of a genre of "Palestinian" diaspora intellectuals who made it more difficult for Palestinians on the ground to make peace. He grossly exaggerated his own Palestinianism, falsely claiming to have spent his childhood in Jerusalem before Israelis expelled his entire family to Egypt immediately prior to the Independence War. As he wrote in 1999, "I was born in Jerusalem and had spent most of my formative years there and, after 1948, when my entire family became refugees, in Egypt."

Following an exposé by the Israeli academic Justin Weiner,[6] Said told the *New York Times*, "I have never said I am a refugee,"[7] which, of course, he had.[8]

Said's anti-peace legacy persists at the Department of Middle East and Asian Languages and Cultures (MEALAC) of Columbia University and at dozens of other Middle East departments in this country and around the world.

Among the statements allegedly made by Columbia faculty in recent years are the following:

- Chairman Hamid Debashi: "Half a century of systematic maiming and murdering of another people has left . . . its deep marks on the faces of the Israeli Jews, the way they talk, walk, the way they greet each other. . . . There is a vulgarity of character that is bone-deep and structural to the skeletal vertebrae of its culture."[9]

- Professor Joseph Massad: "The Jews are not a nation. . . . The Jewish state is a racist state that does not have a right to exist."[10]

- Professor Massad, to a student in his class who asked whether Israelis give advance warning before they demolish houses: "I will not have anyone sit through this class and deny Israeli atrocities."[11]

- Professor Massad: "Israeli demands that Palestinians recognize the holocaust are not about the holocaust at all, but rather about the other part of the package, namely recognizing and submitting to Israel's 'right to exist' as a colonial-settler racist state. . . . The Palestinian people should continue to resist this Zionist package deal."[12]

- Professor Massad Al-Ahram: "The ultimate achievement of Israel: the transformation of the Jew into the anti-Semite and the Palestinian into the Jew."[13]

- Professor Nicholas De Genova: "The heritage of the victims of the Holocaust belongs to the Palestinian people. . . . Israel has no claim to the heritage of the Holocaust."[14]

Other universities have experienced similar hate speech against Israel, Israelis, and Jews. In April 2002, fliers appeared around the campus of San Francisco State University depicting a dead baby accompanied by the words "canned Palestinian children meat slaughtered according to Jewish rites under American license."[15] A month later, on May 7, pro-Palestinian activists surrounded a group of students holding a pro-Israel peace rally at SFSU's Malcom X Plaza. The activists shouted at the Jewish students, "Go back to Russia," "Hitler didn't finish the job," "Fuck the Jews," and "Die, racist pigs."[16] According to bioethics professor Laurie Zoloth, "The police could do nothing more than surround the Jewish students and community members who were now trapped in a corner of the plaza, grouped under the flags of Israel, while an angry, out of control mob, literally chanting for our deaths, surrounded us. . . . This was neither free speech nor discourse, but raw, physical assault."[17] She later remarked, "The Jewish students here are absolutely people who stand in the peace camp. These are students who have steadfastly called for a two-state solution and tried desperately to work with the pro-Palestinian groups. . . . But at San Francisco State to say that I believe in a two-state solution and the right of Israel to exist becomes a right-wing position."[18] Professor Zoloth soon left SFSU in disgust, accepting a position at Northwestern University.

Also in the Bay Area, a Berkeley instructor offered an English class in the school's course catalog that read:

> The brutal Israeli military occupation of Palestine, an occupation that has been ongoing since 1948, has systematically displaced, killed, and maimed millions of Palestinian people. And yet, from under the brutal weight of the occupation, Palestinians have produced their own culture and poetry of resistance. . . . Conservative thinkers are encouraged to seek other sections.[19]

The university's chancellor directed the English department to remove the last line of the course blurb, issuing no further sanctions. On Holocaust Remembrance Day at Berkeley in 2002, fifteen hundred demonstrators disrupted a Jewish memorial ceremony in order to demand divestment from Israel.[20]

In a matter of months, Concordia University in Montreal twice demonstrated its hostility toward Israel and its own Jewish students. In September 2002, hundreds of protesters rioted at the site of former Israeli prime minister Benjamin Netanyahu's scheduled speech. "[P]rotesters punched and kicked prospective listeners . . . shattered windows, upended newspaper boxes, and hurled furniture." The university responded by canceling the speech.[21] Lest anyone think that it was Netanyahu's conservative views that resulted in his being censored, the same thing happened to former prime minister Ehud Barak two years later.[22]

With tensions high, in January 2003, Concordia's student union *banned* the school's Hillel, a Jewish campus organization, and froze all Student Activity Fund contributions to the group.[23] The Concordia Student Union's pretext for banning Hillel—and pretext is the only way to describe it—was that a recent Concordia graduate had placed a one-page flyer advertising Israel's Mahal Web site on a Hillel flier distribution table, thereby allegedly violating Canada's Foreign Enlistment Act, a never-enforced prohibition against recruiting for foreign militaries (instituted during World War II to prevent Nazi recruiting).

According to Hillel co-president Noah Joseph, "The general impression I get is that fewer Jewish students want to come here."[24] I have refused to speak at Concordia until they invite Netanyahu and Barak back and assure their safety and ability to deliver their speeches, no matter how much security is required. No university that deserves that title should ever permit the threat of violence to prevent a speech. Those who threaten the violence should be punished, rather than those who peacefully want to speak or listen.

An incident at Yale was less dramatic, but perhaps is more representative of campuses that apply a double standard to anti-Semitic utterances as opposed to other genres of bigoted speech. It also shows what often happens when Jews speak out—*if* they speak out—in response to anti-Semitism: they find themselves accused of disproportionate media control and a censorious attitude toward academic freedom.

The Af-Am Cultural Center invited the poet and playwright Amiri Baraka to speak shortly after the release of his poem "Somebody Blew Up America." In the poem, Baraka accuses four thousand Jewish employees in the World Trade Center of staying home from work on September 11, and suggests possible Israeli involvement in the attacks. Baraka's audience gave him a standing ovation[25] following a lecture in which he read a portion of his poem, which includes the stanzas:

> Who know why Five Israelis was filming the explosion
> And cracking they sides at the notion?
> . . .
> Who knew the World Trade Center was gonna get bombed?
> Who told 4,000 Israeli workers at the Twin Towers
> To stay home that day.
> Why did Sharon stay away?[26]

In defense of her organization's invitation to Baraka, Yale's assistant dean, Pamela George, compared a well-documented anti-Semite's lecture to a talk given a month earlier by a former Israeli general.[27] Student columnist Sahm Adrangi wrote:

> Yet the Baraka controversy isn't really about free speech. It's about how special interests manipulate the public discourse to advance their agendas.
> See here's the thing: Baraka has always been provocative, but his

status as a virulent hatemonger really began last October. That's when he criticized Israel. . . .

Then came the Anti-Defamation League, the Zionist group who ought to stick "Israeli" in front of its name (when was the last time it condemned defamation of Muslims and Arab-Americans?). Spotting an anti-Israel stanza in Baraka's "Somebody blew up America," the ADL launched a publicity campaign to punish Baraka for his critical views on Israel. . . .

Why should this conspiracy theory usher in the most vitriolic attacks on Baraka's reputation in his 40-year career? Because Israeli sympathizers tend to occupy prominent positions in the American media. . . .

But does the prevalence of Jews in American media, business and politics help explain America's steadfast support for Israel, whose 35-year occupation of Palestinian lands is an affront to human decency? Of course.[28]

Adrangi's bigotry is exceeded only by his ignorance. In fact, the Anti-Defamation League is among the most active organizations "condemn[ing] defamation of Muslims and Arab-Americans."[29] To take just one example, when the Reverend Jerry Falwell called the Prophet Mohammed "a terrorist" in a television interview, ADL national director Abraham Foxman immediately issued a statement strongly condemning the remark. "The Rev. Jerry Falwell has once again demonstrated his intolerance by his outrageous charge about the Prophet Mohammed. He owes an apology to the millions of good people who follow the Muslim faith."[30] If any Yale student ever uttered bigoted generalizations about blacks, gays, or women comparable to the ones about Jews uttered by Adrangi, he would never be able to show his face at Yale again. Nor would the *Yale Daily News* publish such views.

In Europe the situation is even worse. I'm now referring not to Muslim-generated anti-Israel and anti-Jewish hate speech, but rather to bigotry among the most elite groups.

Many British academics and scholastic organizations have threatened or imposed boycotts on Israeli educators and academic institutions. Oxford professor of pathology Andrew Wilkie refused to accept an Israeli as a Ph.D. student because of Israel's treatment of the Palestinians. As he wrote to Amit Duvshani, a master's student in molecular biology at Tel Aviv University:

Thank you for contacting me, but I don't think this would work. I have a huge problem with the way that the Israelis take the moral high ground for their appalling treatment in the Holocaust and then inflict gross human rights abuses on the Palestinians because they wish to live in their own country. I am sure that you are perfectly nice on a personal level, but no way would I take somebody who has served in the Israeli Army.

After his e-mail was made public, Professor Wilkie apologized, and Oxford suspended him for two months for violating its antidiscrimination policy.[31]

Mona Baker, an Egyptian-born professor at the University of Manchester Institute of Science and Technology (UMIST) fired a pair of Israeli nationals from the two scholarly journals she owns and edits. Both Israelis had worked for the journals for three years. One, Dr. Miriam Schlesinger, is a former chairman of Amnesty International's Israel chapter. It was not for the content of her work, however, that she and her conational were fired. It was simply because they were Israelis. By Baker's own admission, they had to go "because of the current situation."[32] (Ironically, the two journals bill their specialty as "cross-cultural communication.") In the face of an international—but not much of a domestic—outcry, spearheaded by Harvard professor Stephen Greenblatt, Baker remained unrepentant. In an interview with the *Sunday Telegraph*, she announced, "Israel has gone beyond just war crimes. It is horrific what is going on there. Many of us would like to talk about it as some kind of Holocaust which the world will eventually wake up to, much too late, of course, as they did with the last one."[33] Following a brief investigation, UMIST elected not to take disciplinary action against Professor Baker.[34]

In May 2003, the Association of University Teachers (AUT), Britain's largest university professionals' union, voted *against* a proposed academic boycott of Israel. The ban would have directed members to "sever academic links with Israeli institutions and funding agencies, boycott conferences in Israel, and refuse to participate as referees in hiring or promotions by the country's universities." The proposal failed by a ratio of around two to one; the members feared that a boycott would "harm progressive Israeli academics campaigning against the Sharon government."[35] Then on April 22, 2005—after Israel took significant actions toward peace—the very same association reversed itself and voted to boycott Israeli Jewish professors at two lead-ing Israeli universities.[36] In a telling moment just prior to the associa-tion's approval of the boycott, Susan Blackwell, the principal anti-Israel leader within the union, "draped [herself] in a Palestine flag."[37] Ms. Blackwell has noted that the boycott's true objective is to strike a blow at the "illegitimate state" of Israel.[38] So much for the two-state solution that the Palestinian leadership is trying to negotiate! Blackwell is satis-fied to drape herself in the Palestinian flag while Palestinian children continue to die. Nor is the goal of the British blacklist to influence Israel to take positive steps toward peace. That is clear from its timing, as well as from the acknowledgment of its prime sponsor that it was intended merely to hurt that "illegitimate state." Moreover, according to Amnon Rubinstein—a leading Israeli peace advocate—one of the pro-boycott Web sites links to anti-Semitic sites. Rubinstein calls the leaders of the boycott effort "academic skinheads."

Even the Palestinian Al-Quds University in Jerusalem released a statement against the British association blacklist, saying, "We are informed by the principle that we should seek to win Israelis over to our side, not to win against them. . . . Therefore, informed by this national duty, we believe it is in our interest to build bridges, not walls; to reach out to the Israeli academic institutions, not to impose another restric-tion or dialogue-block on ourselves."[39] Instead of heeding the moder-ate words of those they claim to support, British university teachers voted to collectively punish Israeli academics in a manner that leading Palestinian academics did not support. They've become more Palestin-ian than the Palestinians, and at precisely the time when Israel is taking more risks and making more sacrifices for peace than it has since Camp David in 2000. A spokesman for the Union of Jewish Students got it exactly right when he said, "Things in the Middle East are moving for-ward while in the UK they are moving backwards. These boycotts have struck a blow at talks between Israel and Palestine."[40] As Israel's ambas-sador to London Zvi Ravner noted, "The last time that Jews were boy-cotted in universities was in 1930s Germany."[41] Professor Efraim Karsh, the head of the Mediterranean Studies department at King's College in London, elaborated on this theme, pointing out that the British action "resonates of darker periods in European history in which Jews were ostracized and denied free access to institutions of higher learning. Only now it is the Jewish State of Israel, rather than individ-ual Jews, that is singled out for ostracism."[42]

Not only would an academic blacklist be harmful and wrong, it might also be illegal. According to Jocelyn Prudence, head of the Universities and Colleges Employers Association, "This would appear to run contrary to contractual law, race and religious discrimination law, and academic freedom obligations."[43] In reality, the boycott is a form of loyalty oath; more accurately, a *dis*loyalty oath. Jewish professors must vocalize their opposition to their government in order to evade blacklisting. Dr. Emanuele Ottolenghi of the Middle East Center at St. Anthony's College at Oxford University wrote, "Oaths of political loyalty do not belong to academia. They belong to illiberal minds and repressive regimes. . . . Based on this . . . the AUT's definition of academic freedom is the freedom to agree with its views only."[44]

Susan Blackwell, of course, denies that there is any academic freedom in Israel:

You cannot talk about academic freedom and free debate in Israel in the same way you can talk about it in the UK or in almost any other country in the world. It is poisoned by the occupation. It is corrupted by it. There is no academic freedom. . . . Those people who do stick their head above the parapet and speak out are subject to witch-hunts and victimisation.[45]

Anyone who has ever spent any time at an Israeli university, as I have, will recognize the complete mendacity of this statement. There is more academic freedom in Israel than almost anywhere in the world, as even many of Israel's most strident critics acknowledge.[46] A recent article in the journal *Political Science and Politics* found that academic freedom is perceived by professors as being more robustly protected in Israel than any other country surveyed, including Japan, the Netherlands, Sweden, and the United States. Freedom House has reported that there is "widespread academic freedom in Israel," even "growing polarization between right and left academics," including "ad hominem attacks on both sides."[47] Anti-Zionist and anti-Israel professors and students—Israeli, Arab, European—have complete freedom to criticize Israel and its policies. But now some members of the AUT are trying to curtail academic freedom in Israel by imposing its perverse blacklist and disloyalty oath.

On May 26, 2005, following an international outcry and threats of counter-boycotts, the union voted to rescind its earlier decision, but several members promised to reintroduce the measure at future meetings. Unfortunately, the preference of those who support the boycott for anti-Israel bigotry over academic freedom is all too typical of many academics—in the United States as well as in Great Britain—who have become more Palestinian than the Palestinians. A personal note: shortly after the British publication of my book *The Case for Israel,* Dame Ruth Deech, a governor of the British Broadcasting Corporation, asked for a copy at an Oxford branch of Blackwell's, one of Britain's leading bookstore chains. The salesperson responded, "There is no case for Israel."[48]

Europe

The columnist Barbara Amiel wrote the story that would come to stand for the proposition that anti-Semitism has become fashionable once again in Europe. As previously recounted, she reported that "the ambassador of a major EU country"—later revealed to be French ambassador to Britain Daniel Bernard—"politely told a gathering at my home that the current troubles in the world were all because of 'that shitty little country Israel.'"[49] "Why," he asked, "should the world be in danger of World War Three because of those people?" Then Amiel reported an incident in which the host of a private lunch "made a remark to the effect that she couldn't stand Jews and everything happening to them was their own fault." When faced with a shocked silence, the hostess snapped, "Oh come on . . . you all feel like that."[50]

On January 30, 2005, the *Washington Post* published an article titled "In Europe, an Unhealthy Fixation on Israel," which reported the following:

> Go to a dinner party in Paris, London, or any other European capital and watch how things develop. The topic of conversation may be Iraq, it may be George Bush, it may be Islam, terrorism or weapons of mass destruction. However it starts out, you can be sure of where it will inevitably, and often irrationally, end—with a dissection of the Middle East situation and a condemnation of Israeli actions in the occupied territories.[51]

Synagogue firebombings, cemetery vandalism, and ubiquitous graffitied swastikas in major cities testify eloquently to an increasing hostility toward Jews—apologists would say it is a reaction to Israeli policies—throughout Europe. Watchdog groups across the continent confirm sharp increases in anti-Jewish vandalism, assaults, and threats over the last several years. An anti-Israel activist at London University has defended the torching of synagogues as a "rational" protest against Israeli policies. As Amos Oz summarized the environment, "[T]he graffiti in Europe have also changed from wall to wall. When my father was a young man in Vilna, every wall in Europe said, 'Jews go home to Palestine.' Fifty years later, when he went back to Europe on a visit, the walls all screamed, 'Jews get out of Palestine.'"[52]

Political cartoons in newspapers throughout Europe have seized on centuries-old Jewish stereotypes for their anti-Israeli drawings. Manfred Gerstenfeld documented a few of the more notorious:

> In April 2002, the Italian quality daily La Stampa published a cartoon about the IDF's siege on the Church of the Nativity in Bethlehem. It showed an Israeli tank turning on the infant Jesus, who asks: "Surely they don't want to kill me again?"
>
> In the same month the Greek daily Ethnos, close to the Socialist Party, depicted two IDF soldiers (with stars of David on their helmets) dressed as Nazis stabbing helpless Arabs. The caption: "Do not feel guilty, my brother. We were not in Auschwitz and Dachau to suffer, but to learn."
>
> In 2003 the British Independent daily printed a Dave Brown cartoon showing Ariel Sharon as a child-eater. This fits neatly into the anti-Semitic libel that Jewish ritual required the use of the blood of Gentile children. Perhaps it is no coincidence that this accusation originated in England during the Middle Ages.[53]

Particularly troubling and antagonistic to the peace process is the increasing tendency for those who hate Israel in Europe to compare Israeli Jews to Nazis. The June 2, 2005, issue of the Wall Street Journal Europe carried an article by Tom Gross entitled "J'Accuse," documenting numerous political cartoons in mainstream European newspapers that portray Israel and its leaders as Nazis. Such portrayals are not, however, limited to cartoons.

On a 2002 visit to Ramallah, the Portuguese Nobel laureate in literature José Saramago said, "though there are differences of time and place, what is happening here is a crime that may be compared to

Auschwitz. They are turning this place into a concentration camp." When pressed by an Israeli reporter to point out the gas chambers, Saramago cryptically replied, "There aren't any yet."[54] Another Nobel Prize winner, Mairead Corrigan Maguire, traveled to Israel and called its nuclear weapons arsenal "gas chambers perfected."[55] The Oxford poet Tom Paulin published a poem about "another little Palestinian boy" "gunned down by the Zionist SS." He recommended that Brooklyn-born Jewish settlers in the West Bank "should be shot dead. I think they are Nazis, racists. I have nothing but hatred for them." Paulin accused Tony Blair's administration of being "a Zionist government." Further, "I never believed that Israel had the right to exist at all," Paulin said. "It is an artificial state."[56]

During the Jenin battle, the Irish writer Tom McGurk penned a column in the *Sunday Business Post* entitled "Israeli Holocaust in Palestine." In it he wrote, "The scenes in Jenin last week looked uncannily like the attack on the Warsaw Jewish ghetto in 1944." Only the brave few may speak out, however, because "[t]he Holocaust version of history has become an indispensable ideological weapon" for Israel. Citing the "leading Jewish intellectual" Norman Finkelstein, McGurk concluded, "How extraordinary that so many in the liberal democratic West should feel so strangely muted, so emotionally strangled in the face of Nazi-style barbarism toward the Palestinians by the state of Israel."[57]

Notice that Israel is never compared to Stalin's Soviet Union, to Mussolini's Italy, to Franco's Spain, to Castro's Cuba, to Pinochet's Chile, to Pol Pot's Cambodia, or even to Hirohito's Japan. It is always and only compared to Hitler's Nazi Germany. I have often wondered what could possibly motivate any person of presumed decency to compare Israel's treatment of Palestinians to what the Nazis did to the Jews during the Holocaust. Israel's goal is to protect its civilians from Palestinian terrorism, whereas the Nazi goal was to genocidally murder every Jewish baby, child, woman, and man so as to eliminate the Jewish race. The analogy is obscene, and yet it is repeated daily on college campuses by mainstream European political activists, and even by writers and intellectuals. Its target audience is the current generation of college students too young to remember the Holocaust and too caught up in the passions of the day to bother to research the history. When a lie is repeated often enough, it risks becoming conventional wisdom. Comparing Israel to Nazi Germany is anti-Semitism, pure and simple. There is no other explanation for it, especially in light of the reality that there is no actual similarity between Hitler's systematic genocide against the Jews and Israel's effort to defend itself from genocidal threats against its Jewish population. In Europe especially, it seems important for the children and grandchildren of Hitler's "willing executioners" and those who stood idly by to turn the Jews into Nazis, so as to be able to say "you are as bad as you claim our parents and grandparents were." As Israeli psychiatrist Zvi Rex put it, "The Germans will never forgive the Jews for Auschwitz."[58]

A poll conducted by Germany's University of Bielefeld found "more than 50% of respondents equating Israel's policies toward the Palestinians with Nazi treatment of the Jews. Sixty-eight percent of those surveyed specifically believed that Israel is waging a 'war of extermination' against the Palestinian people."[59]

Another false and pernicious analogy is South African apartheid. This absurd analogy demeans and insults those black Africans who really suffered from true apartheid. Naive people will come to think, "If what Israel is doing is apartheid, maybe South African apartheid wasn't that awful after all." It is in this way that powerful words lose their meanings.

The slander that portrays Israel as a "racist colonialist apartheid state" is already so widespread as to be part of the international community's ordinary parlance. The security barrier is an "apartheid wall." The Law of Return is "just another instrument of a 'racist apartheid state.'"[60] The West Bank and Gaza, when offered to Palestinians for a future state, become "Bantustans." Approximately four thousand Non-Governmental Organizations (NGOs) from around the world (many from repressive countries that practice real apartheid, racism, and slavery) signed a declaration demanding "complete and total isolation of Israel as an apartheid state."[61] The United Nations Durban conference NGO resolution condemned "Israel's brand of apartheid and ethnic cleansing."[62] Far-left professors invoke the campaign against apartheid South Africa as the model for divestiture and boycott against Israel. Noam Chomsky wrote the forward to a book titled *The New Intifada: Resisting Israel's Apartheid*. Student organizations hold workshops on "Apartheid, Israel Style."[63] Indeed, as Jay Nordlinger wrote, "That Israel, like the old Boer Republic, is an 'apartheid state' is almost an article of faith on many campuses today."[64]

The apartheid allegation, like the Bantustan charge discussed in chapter 3, is an attempt by Israel's enemies to vilify and delegitimize the

Jewish state. It is the most recent manifestation of the UN's infamous "Zionism is racism" resolution in 1975. Those who make the charge don't want Israelis and Palestinians to negotiate a peace; they want an end to Israel. As the South African journalist and anti-apartheid activist Benjamin Pogrund put it, "[C]lear purpose can be discerned in the efforts to make the apartheid stigma stick—to have Israel viewed as and declared illegitimate, as was done with apartheid South Africa. That is, to challenge its right to existence."[65]

Tellingly (and predictably), nations whose laws *do* discriminate based on race, ethnicity, and religion are never subjected to the apartheid comparison. Even Jordan—that paragon of "moderate" Arab nationhood—does not permit Jews to become citizens. But no one is interested in drawing parallels between Jordan and South Africa. That is because no one is interested in isolating, dismantling, boycotting, or demonizing Jordan.

On the other side of the Jordan River, Israeli Arabs have full citizenship and the same rights to political participation as Jews enjoy, including representation in the Knesset and the Supreme Court. The international law scholar Anne Bayefsky writes that those who make the analogy ignore "the fact that Arab states have virtually purged themselves of Jews, while in Israel the 20 percent Arab population enjoys more democratic rights than anywhere in the Arab world."[66]

Richard Cohen summarized the situation as follows: "The word 'apartheid'—used by those urging the boycott—is flung in Israel's face. Yet Israel is nothing like the South Africa of old. Ethiopian Jews, who are black, are not deprived of the vote or forced to live in townships. Arab Israelis elect representatives to the parliament. This is hardly apartheid. In fact, the people who label it so trivialize the loathsome practice."[67]

The *Jerusalem Post* editorialized that those who compare Israel to apartheid South Africa ignore the facts that "Israeli Arabs, unlike apartheid-era blacks, participate actively in political life; that Palestinians spurned the offer of a state because it failed to meet their maximalist demands; and that Palestinian groups such as Hamas wage war against Israeli civilians with the express purpose of destroying the Jewish state."[68]

Omer Bartov, writing in the *New Republic*, mocked the kind of thinking that produces an apartheid comparison:

So some may think that destroying Israel is legitimate and some may think otherwise. Some may think that Israel is an apartheid colonial settler state based on a racist ideology, and some may have a different opinion. There are two sides to the question. Through such a "free exchange of ideas" we will all prosper intellectually. This brings to mind Hannah Arendt's observation, when she visited Germany in 1950, for the first time since she fled the Nazis, that the Germans viewed the extermination of the Jews as a matter of opinion: some said it happened, some said it had not happened. Who could tell? The average German, she wrote, considered this "nihilistic relativism" about the facts as an essential expression of democracy.[69]

Finally, the core of apartheid was white minority rule over a black majority. Throughout the history and prehistory of Israel, Jews have never wanted to rule over a majority Arab population. The division of land contemplated by the Peel Commission and implemented by the United Nations had a Jewish majority in the Jewish state and an Arab majority in the Arab state. Moreover, Israel has repeatedly offered to end the occupation in exchange for peace, recognition, and secure boundaries. This is not apartheid. It is democracy. If only the Arabs and Muslim states of the world would be as democratic. Yet the apartheid label persists among so many academics and media pundits, especially in Europe.

It should not be surprising, in light of this academic and media one-sidedness, that another recent poll showed that more Europeans (59 percent) regard Israel as more of a threat to world peace than any other country in the world.[70] Among the runners-up were the United States, North Korea, Iran, and Iraq. Syria, Libya, Saudi Arabia, and China were not even in the running.

How then to explain this afactual, ahistoric, and immoral attitude among so many Europeans? At one level it is simply the latest manifestation of millennia-old efforts to blame the Jews for all the evils in the world. When plagues broke out in Europe, it was the Jews' fault. When wells were poisoned, obviously the Jews did it. When Christian children were found murdered, who else but the Jews? Most recently the cardinal of Honduras blamed the recent sex scandal in the Catholic Church on—you guessed it—the Jews.

There is more at issue here than primitive anti-Semitism, though surely that phenomenon plays a role in some of the polling results. A generation of Europeans has been miseducated by its own media and leaders about Israel. The United Nations has contributed to this miseducation by condemning Israel more frequently than any other nation, well out of proportion to its faults. Criticism of Israeli policies is certainly fair game, but criticism of Israel is rarely comparative, contextual, or constructive throughout Europe. Instead Israel is singled out for demonization and delegitimization.[71]

Several commentators have sought to distinguish illegitimate anti-Semitism from legitimate criticism of Israeli policies. Among them have been Professor Irwin Cotler, the minister of justice and the attorney general of Canada;[72] Natan Sharansky, the former Soviet dissident and current political dissident in Israel;[73] President Lawrence Summers of Harvard University;[74] and columnist Thomas Friedman of the *New York Times*.[75] They all agree that criticism of Israel, as well as of any other nation, is desirable, but they all also agree that some of what passes as criticism of Israel is really anti-Semitism. The line is difficult to define, and most people employ variations on the famous test articulated by Justice Potter Stewart in determining what constitutes hardcore pornography: "I shall not today attempt further to define the kinds of material I understand to be embraced within that shorthand description [of hard-core pornography], and perhaps I could never succeed in intelligibly doing so. But I know it when I see it."[76]

In order to avoid the inevitable subjectivity of any such test, I have tried to articulate several criteria that distinguish anti-Semitism from legitimate criticism. The following are my checklists:

A. A Checklist of Factors That Tend to Indicate Anti-Semitism

1. Employing stereotypes against Israel that have traditionally been directed against "the Jews." For example, portraying Israel as devouring the blood of children or characterizing Israeli leaders with long hook noses or rapacious looks.[77]

2. Comparing Israel to the Nazis or its leaders to Hitler, the German army, or the Gestapo.[78]

3. Characterizing Israel as "the worst," when it is clear that this is not an accurate comparative assessment.[79]

4. Invoking anti-Jewish religious symbols or caricaturing Jewish religious symbols.[80]

5. Singling out only Israel for sanctions for policies that are widespread among other nations, or demanding that Jews be better or more moral than others because of their history as victims.[81]

6. Discriminating against individuals only because they are Jewish Israelis, without regard to their individual views or actions.[82]

7. Emphasizing and stereotyping certain characteristics among supporters of Israel that have traditionally been used in anti-Semitic attacks, for example, "pushy" American Jews, Jews "who control the media," and Jews "who control financial markets."[83]

8. Blaming all Jews or "the Jews" for Israel's policies or imperfections.[84]

9. Physically or verbally attacking Jewish institutions, such as synagogues or cemeteries, as a means of protesting against Israel.[85]

10. Stereotyping all Jews as fitting into a particular political configuration (such as "neo-conservatives," Zionists, or supporters of Sharon).[86]

11. Accusing Jews and only Jews of having dual loyalty.[87]

12. Blaming Israel for the problems of the world and exaggerating the influence of the Jewish state on world affairs.[88]

13. Denying, minimizing, or trivializing the Holocaust as part of a campaign against Israel.[89]

14. Discriminating against only Israel in its qualification for certain positions or statuses, such as on the Security Council, the International Court of Justice, and the International Red Cross.[90]

15. Blaming the Jews or Israel, rather than the anti-Semites, for anti-Semitism or for increases in anti-Jewish attitudes.[91]

16. Taking extreme pleasure from Israeli failures, imperfections, or troubles.

17. Falsely claiming that all legitimate criticism of Israeli policies is immediately and widely condemned by Jewish leaders as anti-Semitic, despite any evidence to support this accusation.[92]

18. Denying that even core anti-Semitism—racial stereotypes, Nazi comparisons, desecration of synagogues, Holocaust denial—qualifies as anti-Semitic.[93]

19. Seeking to delegitimate Israel precisely as it moves toward peace.[94]

20. Circulating wild charges against Israel and Jews, such as that they were responsible for the September 11 attacks, the anthrax attacks, and the 2005 tsunami.[95]

B. A Checklist of Factors That Tend to Indicate Legitimate Criticism of Israel

1. The criticism is directed at specific policies of Israel, rather than at the very legitimacy of the state.

2. The degree and level of criticism vary with changes in Israel's policies.

3. The criticism is comparative and contextual.

4. The criticism is political, military, economic, and so forth, rather than ethnic or religious.

5. The criticism is similar to criticism being raised by mainstream Israeli dissidents.

6. The criticism is leveled by people who have a history of leveling comparable criticisms at other nations with comparable or worse records.

7. The criticism is designed to bring about positive changes in Israeli policies.

8. The criticism is part of a more general and comparative criticism of all other nations.

9. The criticism is based on objective facts rather than name calling or polemics.

10. The critic subjects his favorite nation to comparable criticism for comparable faults.

Much of the current attack against Israel—especially in Europe, in the Arab world, and among hard-left academics—falls squarely on the side of anti-Semitism. Some virulent statements do not, but they are still part of a systematic effort by extremist groups to win by propaganda what they have not been able to win by terrorism. These polls show it is succeeding. This very success contributes to a lack of progress toward peace. It will be more difficult for the Palestinian leadership to take the difficult steps needed to achieve peace so long as it believes it is winning the propaganda war. Among the greatest threats to world peace, therefore, is not Israel, but European bigotry against the Jewish nation.

As I travel around the United States speaking to audiences about the war on terrorism, the question I am asked most frequently is how to explain the divergence of opinion between most Americans and most

Europeans regarding the Israeli-Arab conflict. Most Americans see Israel as a bastion of democracy, surrounded by tyrannical and oppressive regimes bent on the destruction of the nation and the elimination of any Jewish presence in the region. They see Israel as a strong American ally with a deep commitment to basic human rights, struggling against terrorists who target innocent women, children, students, and other civilians. They focus on the freedom of speech and press in Israel, the independent judiciary, the commitment to the equality of women, gays, and others who are discriminated against in Arab countries. They note that Israeli Arabs serve on the Supreme Court and the Knesset, on university faculties, and in businesses, while Jews are imprisoned and even executed in some Arab countries. They point to the fact that the Palestinians were twice offered a state—first by the United Nations in 1948 and then by Israel and the United States in Camp David in 2000—and instead of accepting these offers, they resorted to terrorism and bloodshed.

On balance, most Americans favor Palestinian statehood, not as a reward for terrorism, but rather as a reward for ending terrorism if the Palestinian Authority were seriously to crack down on terrorists, rather than encouraging and supporting them. American support for Israel remains strong among Christian Americans as well as among the tiny population of Jewish Americans (less than 2 percent).

The contrast with Europe is striking. Most Europeans seem instinctively to be suspicious of Israel and Israelis. They support the Palestinian cause, while often ignoring or opposing the equally justified claims of other disenfranchised groups such as the Kurds, the Armenians, the Tibetans, the Basques, the Catholics in Northern Ireland, the Chechens, and others. Virulent anti-Zionism sometimes crosses over to subtle anti-Semitism. This should come as no surprise on a continent where open anti-Semitism was rampant until quite recently.

Though there are two sides (or more) to the complex issues surrounding the Arab-Israeli conflict, many Europeans seem to enjoy singling out Israel for criticism. The impression among some Europeans seems to be that Israel is not only at fault for all the problems in the Middle East, but is also the worst human rights violator in the world. How else can one explain the attempts to boycott only Israeli scholars and scientists and to divest from companies that have investments only in Israel?

A good working definition of anti-Semitism is taking a trait that is common to many groups and singling out Jews for criticism for exhibiting that trait. That's what Hitler did in the 1930s. That's what Harvard's President A. Lawrence Lowell did in the 1920s when he tried to keep Jews out of Harvard because "they cheat." And that is what advocates of divestment and boycott against Israel alone are doing. The proper way to approach divestment and boycott is to list every country in the world in order of total human rights record and then to divest from or boycott the most serious offenders first. If that approach were followed, Israel would be among the last countries subject to these sanctions. Most Arab countries and the Palestinian Authority would be among the first. Some European countries would be higher on the list than Israel.

The time has come for European intellectuals and public figures— from Nobel laureates to members of the British Association of University Teachers, to the mayor of London, to ordinary decent people—to look at themselves in the mirror and ask whether this unique focus on the only Jewish nation reflects some deep, lingering pathology, rather than the comparative merits of Israeli and Arab actions in the Middle East. Honest Europeans should come away from such an exercise deeply disturbed. Bigotry against a nation, especially the Jewish nation, by so many Europeans is a particularly ugly phenomenon in light of the last century's history.

The United Nations

The United Nations' disdain for Israel is long-standing and beyond dispute as Israel moves closer to making peace with the Palestinians. From its "Zionism equals racism" resolution in 1975 through Kofi Annan's lame rhetorical defense of the UN's Israel-specific resolutions—"Can the whole world be wrong?"—it has consistently treated Israel as the "Jew" among nations.

UN hate has actually accelerated in recent years. After voting for the creation of the Jewish state and admitting it to the General Assembly, the UN, especially following Israel's victory in the Six-Day War of 1967, has turned against that nation. Professor Irwin Cotler, now the minister of justice and attorney general of Canada, pointed to the reconvening of the Geneva Convention on December 5, 2001, as a prime example of discriminatory treatment. Fifty-two years after its adoption in 1949, the contracting parties of the Geneva Convention met again in Geneva to put Israel in the dock for violating the convention. Until that time, not one country in the international community was ever brought before the contracting parties of the Geneva Convention—not Cambodia with regard to genocide, not the Balkan states with regard to ethnic cleansing, not Rwanda with regard to genocide, not Sudan or Sierra Leone with regard to the killing fields in those countries. When politics overruns the law, the result is prejudice to the Geneva Convention and to the universality of its principles. Regrettably, in the Middle East, and particularly with regard to the Israeli-Palestinian conflict, this government-sanctioned hate speech has not been given the importance it deserves. It is this state-sanctioned culture of incitement that is the most proximate cause of violence and terror. The assault on terrorism should, in fact, begin with efforts to end this state-sanctioned incitement.[96]

According to Columbia law professor Anne Bayefsky, in just the first four months of 2004, the UN Human Rights Commission passed nine country-specific condemnation resolutions. *Five* were directed at Israel, and only four at the rest of the world (Belarus, Cuba, North Korea, and Turkmenistan).[97] If the United Nations is to be believed, 56 percent of all the worldwide human rights violations worthy of country-specific condemnation are committed by a nation with 0.1 percent of the world's population. As Professor Cotler summarized the situation:

> Israel has systematically been denied equality before the law in the international arena. Human rights standards should certainly be applied to Israel, but they must be applied equally to every state. Human rights must be respected, but the rights of Israel deserve equal respect. While major human rights violators enjoyed complete immunity, one particular state was singled out for differential and discriminatory treatment.[98]

Perhaps the worst example was the UN World Conference Against Racism, Racial Discrimination, Xenophobia and Related Intolerance, held in Durban, South Africa, in 2001. The Durban conference singled out Israel for rebuke. It was the only nation whose very existence was ridiculed, and at a conference attended by Saudi Arabia, Iran, China, and Sudan, no less! At a planning session held in Geneva, the confederation of nongovernmental organizations (NGOs) that attended the UN conference drafted a declaration calling Israel "an apartheid, racist, and fascist state."[99] The conference's final, adopted NGO resolution identified Israel as a "racist, apartheid" state, and one that practices "genocide" and "ethnic cleansing." The resolution called for "the full cessation of all links (diplomatic, economic, social, aid, military cooperation and training) between all states and Israel."[100] It labeled Israel's law of return—a law similar to those in many UN member states and in the Palestinian Authority—an apartheid instrument and recommended the creation of a special UN committee charged with prosecuting Israeli war crimes.[101]

The official conference draft proposal was only slightly more moderate, expressing "deep concern" over "the racist practices of Zionism . . . as well as the emergence of racism and discriminatory ideas, in particular the Zionist movement, which is based on racial superiority."[102] It denounced Zionism as "a new kind of apartheid, a crime against humanity."[103] This language was excised from the final draft, but only after the United States and Israel left the conference in protest.

Conference documents are only half the story. The surrounding atmosphere at the conference, in the streets of Durban, turned into a carnival of anti-Semitic vitriol. The Arab Lawyers' Union handed out cartoons to delegates showing a Star of David equaling a swastika.[104] Another leaflet showed Hitler announcing, "If I had not lost, Israel would not exist today."[105] Protesters held up signs reading "Hitler Should Have Finished the Job" and "Kill the Jews."[106] A group of Iranian women heckled a Jewish Caucus press conference to a halt, one woman yelling, "Six million dead and you're holding the world hostage!"[107]

By the close of the conference, Representative Tom Lantos (D-CA) announced, "What you have here is the paradox of an anti-racism conference that is itself racist."[108] Secretary of State Colin Powell denounced the "hateful language" on display, which he accused of subjecting "only one country in the world, Israel, [to] censure and abuse."[109] Senator Charles Schumer begged Kofi Annan to "do more to remove the UN from the taint of anti-Semitism."[110] And Elie Wiesel dubbed Durban "a conference of racism."[111] Professor Cotler, who was there, summarized it as follows:

Yet what was supposed to be a conference *against racism* turned into a conference of *racism against Israel and the Jewish people*. A conference to commemorate the dismantling of South Africa as an apartheid state called for the dismantling of Israel as an apartheid state. A conference that was supposed to be dedicated to the protection and promotion of human rights increasingly spoke about Israel as being a meta-violator of human rights and as the new anti-Christ of our time.[112]

After the Durban conference and several similar orgies of hate, I received a phone call from a Brazilian journalist who asked me to respond to the charge being made in her home country that Israel was at least indirectly to blame for the deadly truck bombing of the UN headquarters hotel in Baghdad that killed, among others, a prominent Brazilian diplomat, Sergio Vieira de Mello. I was not surprised at the question, considering its source. Among many South Americans, as among many Eastern Europeans, the knee-jerk response to nearly every evil is "blame it on the Jews." For example, Cardinal Oscar Andrés Rodríguez Maradiaga, the archbishop of Tegucigalpa, Honduras—an apparent runner-up in the recent balloting for a new pope—has blamed the "Jewish media" for the scandal involving Catholic priests having sex with young parishioners. In his bigoted words:

> It certainly makes me think that in a moment in which all the attention of the mass media was focused on the Middle East, all the many injustices done against the Palestinian people, the print media and the TV in the United States became obsessed with sexual scandals that happened 40 years ago, 30 years ago. Why? I think it's also for these motives: What is the church that has received Arafat the most times and has most often confirmed the necessity of the creation of a Palestinian state? What is the church that does not accept that Jerusalem should be the indivisible capital of the State of Israel, but that it should be the capital of the three great monotheistic religions?[113]

The question by the Brazilian journalist got me to thinking: who does really share the blame with the terrorists themselves for the horrific explosion that killed and injured so many innocent people? Although the primary culprit is clearly the terrorist group that planned and executed the mass murder, the secondary culprit is the UN itself. For more than a quarter of a century the UN has actively encouraged terrorism by rewarding its primary practitioners, legitimating it as a tactic, condemning its victims when they try to defend themselves, and describing as "freedom fighters" the murderers of innocent children. No organization in the world today has accorded so much legitimacy to terrorism as has the UN. (The Nobel Prize committee, various church groups, and some universities rank a strong second, third, and fourth.) The historical facts are a matter of indisputable record.

Consider the following:

- There are numerous occupied people around the world seeking statehood or national liberation, including the Tibetans, the Kurds, the Turkish Armenians, and the Palestinians. Only one of these groups has received official recognition by the UN, including observer status and invitations to speak and participate in committee work. That group is the one that invented and perfected international terrorism—namely, the Palestinians. The UN has made it clear that to ensure that your cause is leapfrogged ahead of others', adopt terrorism as your primary means of protest. The Tibetans, whose land has been occupied more brutally and for a longer period of time than the Palestinians', but who have never practiced terrorism, cannot even receive a hearing from the UN. This has sent the message to aggrieved groups that terrorism works.

- The UN has for years refused to condemn terrorism unequivocally, while at the same time encouraging and upholding "the legitimacy of the struggle for national liberation movements" against "occupation"—in other words, the use of terrorism against innocent civilians to resist occupation. This has sent the message to aggrieved groups that terrorism is legitimate.

- The UN has allowed terrorists to use UN-sponsored "refugee camps" as terrorist bases. This has sent the message to the world that the UN closes its eyes to terrorism.

- The UN has repeatedly condemned efforts by Israel to prevent and respond to terrorism. This has sent a message to the victims of terrorism that if they fight back they risk sanctions. It has also sent a message to terrorists that if they kill and maim innocent people, they can provoke a reaction that will result in the condemnation of other countries.

- The UN has allowed states that sponsor terrorism to sit on the Security Council and to chair various important committees, while denying Israel these same rights. This has sent the message that the UN applies a double standard when it comes to terrorism.

The bottom line is that it has been the UN that has served as an international megaphone for the perverse message that any people who feel that they are occupied have the right to resist occupation by randomly murdering innocent civilians anywhere in the world. Now the chickens have come home to roost. Some Iraqis, who feel that they are now occupied, have taken the UN's message to heart and are now engaged in a "national liberation movement" of the kind long praised by the UN, and are now using the tactics rewarded by the UN against that very organization.

Now that the victims of "national liberation terrorism" are UN employees instead of Jewish babies, maybe the UN will finally come to its senses and understand that by legitimating and rewarding terrorism, it has created a Frankenstein monster that can be turned against any nation, organization, or group. But the UN has not shown an ability to learn from its mistakes, and so I doubt we will see much of a change in its historic double standard with regard to terrorism. Unless we do, no one will be safe from this UN-created, -fed, and -rewarded monster that now threatens the entire world.

The Arab World

The worst hatred, of course, comes from the Arab and Muslim world, and sometimes even Israel's "peace partners." Susan Sachs opened her exposé of anti-Semitism in the Arab world[114] with the following anecdotes: "Stay in any five-star hotel anywhere from Jordan to Iran, and you can buy the infamous forgery 'Protocols of the Elders of Zion.' Pick up a newspaper in any part of the Arab world and you regularly see a swastika superimposed on the Israeli flag."[115] She cites an official Jordanian textbook that "describes Jews as innately deceitful and corrupt. 'Up to the present . . . they are the masters of usury and leaders of sexual exhibitionism and prostitution.'"[116]

To demonstrate Sachs's point, I have divided examples of the proliferation of anti-Semitism in the Arab world into four subdivisions, quoting from a few representative dispatches issued by the indispensable

Arabic and Hebrew translation company, the Middle East Media Research Institute.

The Blood Libel

In March 2002 the Saudi government-sponsored daily *Al-Riyadh* published a column by Dr. Umayma Ahmad al-Jalahma, professor at King Faysal University, outlining the "special ingredient" Jews use in their Purim pastries. First, al-Jalahma laid the historical foundation:

> Before I go into the details, I would like to clarify that the Jews' spilling human blood to prepare pastry for their holidays is a well-established fact, historically and legally, all throughout history. This was one of the main reasons for the persecution and exile that were their lot in Europe and Asia at various times.[117]

Then he described the Purim celebration: "during the holiday, the Jews wear carnival-style masks and costumes and overindulge in drinking alcohol, prostitution, and adultery. . . . For this holiday, the victim must be a mature adolescent who is, of course, a non-Jew—that is, a Christian or a Muslim."[118] (In contrast, children *under ten* are drained of their blood for Passover.[119]) As for the precise extraction procedure:

> These needles do the job, and the victim's blood drips from him very slowly. Thus, the victim suffers dreadful torments—torment that affords the Jewish vampires great delight as they carefully monitor every detail of the blood-shedding with pleasure and love that are difficult to comprehend.[120]

In an Egyptian paper, Hussam Wahba described the textual origins of the blood libel: "One need only point out that they are "blood suckers" according to the Talmudic dictates, which urge them to murder and draw blood of Muslims in particular, and Christians even more so, and to use this blood in religious Israeli rituals."[121]

The Talmud was completed and closed years before the advent of Islam. Mr. Wahba also reports, "Whoever visits the Israeli parliament known as 'The Knesset' will notice at the main entrance a sentence written on the wall saying: 'Compassion towards a non-Jew is forbidden.'"[122] (I guess I left my glasses at home during my many visits to the Knesset, because I missed that particular sign.)

The Protocols of the Elders of Zion

In November 2002, Egyptian state television began broadcasting a forty-one-part series, *A Knight without a Horse*, based on *The Protocols of the Elders of Zion*. Defending the decision to air the programs over U.S. State Department objections, Galal Duweidar, editor of the Egyptian government daily *Al-Akhbar*, expressed disgust at "the new Zionists" who "deny, as did their fathers and grandfathers [before them], the principles calling for freedom of expression when they conflict with their own goals and conspiracies." Duweidar continued his defense:

> Thomas Friedman, the Zionist agent with the Israeli identity and the American citizenship, continued his hostile, filthy attack against Egypt and on behalf of the goals of the aggressive Israel. . . . He attacked the program, but ignored the fact that at issue was scientific literature based on legitimate history.[123]

As the shows aired, and the debate heated, a masthead editorial in *Al-Akhbar* suggested that whether or not the *Protocols* are a forgery, "The most important question is: in practice, doesn't Zionism seek to take over the world with money, murder, sex, and the [other] most despicable of means, primarily in our generation?"[124] The Saudi newspaper *Al-Riyadh* published an op-ed expressing the opinion that

> Arab publishers throughout the world have a religious and national obligation to print, without considerations of profit or loss, the Protocols of the Elders of Zion, in inexpensive popular editions. . . . The Protocols of the Elders of Zion is true, and anyone who doubts this is invited to read them and see which of them have come true and in what way.[125]

The Holocaust

Many in the Arab world suffer a split personality when it comes to the Holocaust. On the one hand, they claim the gas chambers are a Jewish fabrication. On the other, they praise Hitler for his valiant deeds and bemoan the fact that he was not entirely successful. Seif 'Ali Al-Jarwan wrote in a Palestinian Authority daily, "What Hitler did to the Jews actually exposed the Jewish plot." In the very next paragraph, though, he asserted, "The truth is that such persecution was a malicious fabrication by the Jews. It is a myth which they named 'The Holocaust' in order to rouse empathy."[126]

In "The Lie About the Burning of the Jews," Dr. Rif'at Sayyed Ahmad, director of the Jaffa Research Center in Cairo, explained:

> What interests us here is that this lie [about] the burning of the Jews in the Nazi crematoria has been disseminated throughout the world until our time in order to extort the West and make it easier for the Jews of Europe to hunt Palestine [sic] and establish a state on it, in disregard of the most basic principles of international law and the right of peoples to independent life without occupation.[127]

Fatma Abdallah Mahmoud wrote in the Egyptian government daily Al-Akhbar that Jews are "accursed, fundamentally, because they are the plague of the generation and the bacterium of all time. Their history always was and always will be stained with treachery, falseness and lying. Historical documents prove it." The Holocaust is a "fraud . . . carefully tailored, using several faked photos completely unconnected to the truth."

> The entire matter, as many French and British scientists and researchers have proven, is nothing more than a huge Israeli plot aimed at extorting the German government in particular and the European countries in general. But I, personally and in light of this imaginary tale, complain to Hitler, even saying to him from the bottom of my heart, "If only you had done it, brother, if only it had really happened, so that the world could sigh in relief [without] their evil and sin."[128]

In the same paper, the daily columnist Ahmad Ragab wrote: "Thanks to Hitler, of blessed memory, who on behalf of the Palestinians, revenged in advance, against the most vile criminals on the face of the earth. Although we do have a complaint against him for his revenge on them was not enough."[129]

The late Hamas leader Dr. 'Abd al-'Aziz Al-Rantisi concocted a more creative Holocaust hypothesis. He suggested that Zionists collaborated with Hitler to persecute Europe's Jews so that the Jews would immigrate to Palestine. "The Nazis received tremendous financial aid from the Zionist banks and monopolies. . . . The German researcher Prof. Frederick Toben believes there was no animosity between the Nazis and the Jews, whether politically, ideologically, or philosophically." He concluded his column by saying, "When we compare the Zionists to the Nazis, we insult the Nazis. . . . While disagreement proliferates about the veracity of the Zionist charges regarding the Nazis' deeds, no one denies the abhorrent Zionist crimes, some of which camera lenses have managed to document."[130]

On the other side of the ledger, there are some Arabs who are seeking a better understanding of the Holocaust and its impact on Jewish consciousness. In May 2005 the *Boston Globe* reported on the opening of the first Arabic-language Holocaust museum, developed by Khaled Kasab Mahameed, a Muslim Israeli lawyer in Nazareth. The *Globe* reported that "it is part of the cutting edge new thinking among some Palestinians that it is vital to understand the Holocaust if Arab-Israeli conflicts are ever to be resolved." Another resident of Nazareth, Nazzir Majili, traveled to the Auschwitz death camp two years ago with a group of 260 Israelis—half Arab, half Jews—in an attempt to foster better understanding between Arab and Jewish citizens of Israel. "We are living together and we want to make peace. But how, if we don't know who they are, and from where they came, and what is the source of their pain?" Majili asked rhetorically. Mahameed has been widely ostracized and criticized among Arabs, especially those living outside Israel, for his efforts, but he is persisting. It takes courage to make peace through truth. It is much easier to continue the hatred with Holocaust denial lies.

September 11

As with the Holocaust, a considerable portion of the Arab media is of a mixed mind about the September 11 attacks. Some journalists are delighted at fellow Arab terrorists' accomplishments, while others accuse Jews/Israelis/the Mossad/Americans or some combination of the four of perpetrating the hijackings.

According to Ahmad al-Muslih of Jordan's *Al-Dustour*, "What happened is, in my opinion, the product of Jewish, Israeli, and American Zionism, and the act of the great Jewish Zionist mastermind that controls the world's economy, media, and politics."[131] Another Jordanian columnist, Rakan al-Majali, explained on the day after the attacks, "it is clear that Israel is the one to benefit greatly from the bloody, loathsome terror operation that occurred yesterday, and that it seems to benefit still more by accusing the Arabs and Muslims of perpetrating this loathsome attack."[132]

In an interview for an Egyptian university's Web site, the former imam of New York's Islamic Center and the Mosque of New York City squarely identified Jews as the responsible party. "[Jews] are the only ones capable of planning such acts." When asked why the Americans have been kept in the dark, Sheikh Al-Gamei'a replied that Americans *suspect* Jews' guilt, but they don't have the courage to speak out, for fear of Jewish reprisals. "We know that they [the Jews] have always broken agreements, unjustly murdered the prophets, and betrayed the faith." He ended on a somewhat hopeful note: "The Jews who control the media acted to hush it up so that the American people would not know. If it became known to the American people, they would have done to the Jews what Hitler did!"[133]

Several American Jew-haters have also tried to give credence to the lunacy that it was Israel that perpetrated the attacks of September 11. As we have seen, Amiri Baraka said as much in his "poem" that received a standing ovation at Yale. And as we shall see in chapter 16, the radical columnist Alexander Cockburn refused to discredit this absurd blood libel against the Jewish state, claiming that he lacks sufficient evidence "to determine whether they [the claims that Israel perpetrated both September 11 and the anthrax attacks] are true or not."

The Jews even received blame for the December 2004 tsunami triggered by a massive earthquake in the Indian Ocean that claimed more than two hundred thousand lives. *Al-Osboa*, an Egyptian weekly magazine, reported that the tsunami "'was possibly' caused by an Indian nuclear experiment in which 'Israeli and American nuclear experts participated.'"[134]

Other Religious Groups

Several major religious groups have become significant barriers to peace, some on theological grounds, some for opportunistic reasons, and others on what appears to be simple bigotry harking back to old prejudices. There are also some religious groups that have facilitated peace and seem genuinely interested in seeing it achieved. The latter is what should be expected of all religions, which loudly proclaim a love of peace. But too often these proclamations are drowned out by parochial attitudes and actions that make peace difficult, if not impossible, to achieve. It is important that, just as academics, diplomats, politicians, and others who get in the way of peace not be given a pass because of their status, religions and religious leaders as well be held accountable for the misuses of their theologies.

The General Assembly of the Presbyterian Church (USA) voted to divest from only one country in the world. No, it was not China, which has occupied Tibet for half a century and continues to deny basic human rights to its own citizens. No, it was not Iran, which threatens nuclear holocaust, executes dissenters, and denies religious freedom to Christians and Jews. No, it was not Saudi Arabia, which executes women for adultery and publishes *The Protocols of the Elders of Zion*. No, it was not North Korea, Libya, Russia, Sudan, Cuba, or Belarus. It was—you guessed it—Israel, the only democracy in the Middle East and America's most reliable ally in a troubled part of the world.

The way the Presbyterian divestment will work is simple: a blacklist will be prepared for the church's leaders, listing multinational corporations that in any way support Israel's policies with regard to the Palestinians with which the Presbyterians disagree. The Presbyterians would divest from any company on the Israel list, while continuing to invest in corporations that support Saudi Arabian apartheid, Chinese repression, Russian aggression in Chechnya, Cuban dictatorial actions, and other horrible policies throughout the world.

How did the church come to such a ludicrous, wrongheaded position? Just look at the text of the original resolution itself, which bursts with bigotry and ignorance. It effectively blames the Israelis for Palestinian slaughter of civilians by asserting that the occupation is the "root" of terrorism. This canard ignores the reality that the Palestinian leadership opted for murder and violence as the tactic of choice well before there was any occupation, and that the leaders of Hamas, Hezbollah, and Islamic Jihad have vowed to continue murdering Jews after the occupation ends, as long as the Jewish state exists.

The Presbyterian resolution effectively calls for the end of Israel by insisting on "the right of [Palestinian] refugees to return to their homeland." This is a well-known euphemism for turning Israel from a Jewish state into another state with a Palestinian majority. (Jordan is the other.)

The resolution also condemns Israel's military actions taken in defense of its civilians. It claims, without an iota of proof and against all the available evidence, that Israel commits "horrific acts of violence and deadly attacks on innocent people," when the truth is that Israel, like the United States, goes to extraordinary lengths to avoid killing innocent people. It equates Israel's targeting of terrorists with Palestinian targeting of civilians.

The president of Harvard University, Lawrence Summers, in a speech delivered in Harvard's Memorial Church in 2002, included the singling out of Israel for divestment as the sort of "actions that are anti-Semitic in their effect if not their intent." The one-sided actions of the Presbyterian Church fit into this category. Lest there be any doubt about the motivations of at least some of its leaders, it should be recalled that a delegation from the U.S. Presbyterian Church met with the terrorist group Hezbollah in October 2004. An elder of the church, Ronald Stone, praised the group—"We treasure the precious words of Hezbollah and your expression of goodwill towards the American people"—and contrasted it favorably to Jewish leaders: "As an elder of our church, I'd like to say that according to my recent experience, relations and conversations with Islamic leaders are a lot easier than dealings and dialogue with Jewish leaders."[135] This is the same Hezbollah that produces videos instructing suicide bombers how to maximize civilian deaths in order to kill any prospects of peace.

Praise of Hezbollah, coupled with divestment from Israel, encourages the continued use of terrorism by Palestinian extremists, who see that when Israel responds to their terrorism, it causes an important church to punish Israel. I do not believe that a majority of the 2.5 million Presbyterians in the United States want their church used to support terrorism. But they are now on notice that their church has been hijacked and its name misused in the service of an immoral tactic.

Balanced criticism of Israel and of specific policies of its government is proper and essential to democratic governance. But the Presbyterian resolution is so one-sided, so anti-Zionist in its rhetoric, and so ignorant of the realities on the ground that it can only be explained by the kind of bigotry that the Presbyterian Church itself condemned in 1987 when it promised "never again to participate in, to contribute to, or (insofar as we are able) to allow the persecution or denigration of Jews." Unless the church rescinds this immoral, sinful, and bigoted denigration of the Jewish state, it will be "participating in" and "contributing to" anti-Jewish bigotry and the encouragement of terrorism.

But Rabbi Michael Lerner of *Tikkun* magazine supports this targeted divestment campaign against "specific firms that actively contribute to the enforcement of the Occupation."[136] Which occupation? Not the occupation of Tibet by China. Not the occupation of Kurdistan by Syria, Iraq, and Turkey. Not the occupation of Chechnya by Russia. No, only The Occupation—the one by Israel, which it offered to end in 2000 and 2001 and which it is in the process of ending now. Lerner has urged "local Tikkun Communities" (his self-aggrandizing capitalization) to initiate "targeted divestment campaigns" against Israel and *only* Israel.[137] He has also urged his "followers"—he styles himself something of a guru with a cult following—to support and "join with the Presbyterians" in their malevolent divestment campaign.[138] The reason given by Lerner for supporting the Presbyterian divestment campaign is even more sinister and troubling: "to counter the false and misleading charges that these targeted campaigns [against Israel alone] are anti-Semitic."[139] Lerner's thinking, such as it is, seems to go something like this: if Jews like him support sanction directed against only Israel, then it can't possibly be anti-Semitic. That is about as logical as the discredited argument made by some Arab representatives to the UN who supported the "Zionism equals racism" resolution that they could not be anti-Semites because they too are Semites. As we will see in chapter 16, Norman Finkelstein has shown that even a Jew can be an anti-Semite, and now Michael Lerner has shown that even a rabbi can support anti-Semitic actions.

All of this anti-Israel and anti-Semitic hate speech by those who regard themselves as more Palestinian than the Palestinians makes it far more difficult for moderate Palestinians and moderate Israelis to do the work of making peace through compromise. Externally generated hatred and distrust is a true enemy of peace.

The time has come for all who purport to favor peace to stop being more Palestinian than the Palestinian leaders who are actively seeking a compromise resolution of this bloody conflict. The continued demonization of Israel is a barrier to peace, and those who persist in their anti-peace rhetoric and actions—whether in academia, at the UN, in Europe, in the Arab world, or in religious groups—will have blood on their hands if their hate speech and hateful actions contribute to a breakdown of the peace process and a continuation of the bloodshed.

15 More Israeli Than the Israelis

We will never give up the Golan. *We* will never divide Jerusalem.
—American evangelical radio host Janet Parshall (emphasis added)[1]

We are here in force until the people of Israel understand that *we* are opposed to the division of Jerusalem.
—Dr. Joseph Frager, president of American Friends of Ateret Cohanim (a yeshiva in the Muslim Quarter of Jerusalem's Old City)[2]

You cannot be a rational human being and surrender this [Gaza].
—Dr. Joseph Frager[3]

I think the day will come when the secret service and the government will look for Jews who are willing to risk their lives and go into Arab villages and kick them out, kill them . . . and we have thousands of civilians with the military know-how to instigate a mega-attack against Arabs.

—Mike Guzofsky, a follower of Meir Kahane's philosophy[4]

They (the Palestinians) are animals and it's about time the world understood that.

—*Shoshana Gal-Or, member of the religious moshav Mevo Modi'im*[5]

Arabs Are Sand Niggers.

—*Written across the door of a Palestinian shop in Hebron*[6]

On the other side of the ledger—though far smaller in numbers and influence—are some Jews and American evangelical Protestants who oppose the sorts of pragmatic compromises that elected Israeli leaders are prepared to make in the interests of peace. Many of these opponents to compromise are motivated by religious or other ideological considerations. Those who base their claims on the Bible believe that God gave all of Israel—they call it Eretz Yisrael Hashlima (the Complete Land of Israel)—to the Jews and that it would violate God's will to surrender any of "Eretz Israel," especially those portions of the West Bank (which they call by their biblical and historical names "Yehuda" or Judah and "Shomron" or Samaria) that carry biblical significance.

Some of the extremists use language that parallels the hate speech used by anti-Israel zealots. Take Rabbi David Samson, who said, "Their [the Arabs'] children are born with Molotov cocktails in their hands. These are a people as unfeeling as jackals."[7] Or Effie Eitam, leader of the National Religious Party: "I don't call these people animals. These are creatures who came out of the depths of darkness. It is not by chance that the State of Israel got the mission to pave the way for the rest of the world, to militarily get rid of these dark forces."[8] These horrible words have no place in the debate and must end if there is to be real peace. Jewish law forbids *loshon harah*—evil words—and these Jewish hatemongers who often claim the mantle of Jewish law should abide at least by that precept.

Some ultra-Orthodox Jewish rabbis mis-cite theology in support of their political preferences, claiming that the Halachah, the Jewish rabbinic common law, absolutely forbids Israel from giving up the Gaza Strip or any part of the West Bank. In one instance, the Jerusalem rabbi Avigdor Neventzal said that any Jew who cedes any part of Israel to a non-Jew would rightfully be subject to a *din rodef*—"a religious license to kill a fellow Jew particularly dangerous for society." Benjamin Netanyahu, who is himself hawkish on territorial compromise, promptly contradicted Rabbi Neventzal's proclamation. "We are a state based on the rule of law, and if we have to make a difficult and painful choice, we must submit to it, as it is customary in lawful democratic society."[9]

It doesn't take a rabbi or religious scholar to see that Rabbi Neventzal's view is preposterous and has no basis in Jewish law. It is a manipulation of Jewish law in the interests of politics, just as it was a manipulation of Jewish law to claim, as some did, that the murder of Yitzhak Rabin was justified by the Maimonidean principle of *rodef*—a variant on the universal principle of self-defense. What these narrow-minded religious warmongers don't seem to understand is that if their dangerous misinterpretation of Jewish law were correct—which it is not—that would be the strongest argument for rejecting Jewish law itself. A religious law that forbids territorial compromise in the interests of peace, or that justifies the murder of an elected leader who is seeking peace, is not a law worth following or even studying. Their baseless interpretation is, in the end, a self-defeating argument against the relevance and eternal validity of Jewish law. Their most vocal critics should be those who believe that Jewish law remains a guide to all contemporary actions and attitudes, even those involving war and peace.

There *is* an eternal principle of Jewish law that is worth preserving. It is the principle of *pikuach nefesh*, the transcendence of life over nearly every other value. The Bible says, "I call heaven and earth to record this day against you, that I have set before you life and death, blessing and cursing: therefore choose life, that both thou and thy seed may live."[10] The leader of American Modern Orthodox Judaism Rabbi Joseph Soloveitchik once reportedly said that even the finger of a single Jew was holier than the entire Western Wall.[11] This is simply a dramatic variation on the Talmudic dictum that "Whoever destroys a soul, it is considered as if he destroyed an entire world. And whoever saves a life, it is considered as if he saved an entire world."[12] Jewish law does not praise those who save an acre of land at the cost of human lives.

How dare a rabbi from Brooklyn or New Jersey, or even a rabbi in a safe neighborhood of Israel whose children and followers do not serve in the army, choose land over life—and then blame that immoral choice on Jewish law, whose life-affirming morality looks squarely in the opposite direction. These rabbis should be relegated to the dustbin of history, along with parochial religious leaders from other faiths who distort the moral teachings of their faiths into immoral recipes for continuous warfare and persistent hate.

Some who defend these rabbis claim they *are* choosing life because they believe that giving up land will in fact be dangerous to the lives of Israelis. But these rabbis, often uneducated in, and abysmally ignorant of, secular subjects such as military history and politics, lack the expertise to make cost-benefit calculations about land-for-peace efforts. Nor have they been elected to make these difficult choices. As Theodore Herzl insisted, "We shall keep our priests within the confines of their temples in the same way as we shall keep our professional army within the confines of their barracks."[13]

Many evangelical Christians have an additional religiously based opposition to compromise. They believe that the land of Israel was promised to Jews by a covenant between God and Abraham, and that Jews must recover all of their ancient homeland—that is, Israel proper and the occupied territories—as a prerequisite to the Second Coming. Oklahoma senator James Inhofe gave a speech in which he said, "God appeared to Abram and said, 'I am giving you this land'—the West Bank. This is not a political battle at all. It is a contest over whether or not the word of God is true."[14] And at the National Rally in Solidarity with Israel in April 2002 on the Mall in Washington, D.C., the evangelical radio host Janet Parshall declared, "*We* will never give up the Golan. *We* will never divide Jerusalem."[15] Former Christian Coalition executive director Ralph Reed, along with Rabbi Yechiel Eckstein, recently founded Stand for Israel, an organization devoted to mobilizing evangelical Christian support for Israel.[16] Reed insisted, in a talk given to the Anti-Defamation League and excerpted in ads in the *New York Times* and the *Los Angeles Times*, that conservative Christian support for Israel is more a matter of shared values between the United States and Israel, as well as a belief in the inviolability of Abraham's covenant, than an attempt to usher in the End of Times.[17]

Several conservative Christian public figures have proved unamenable to land-for-peace compromise in the Middle East. As former House Majority Leader Dick Armey said, "I'm perfectly content to have a Palestinian state. I am not content to give up any part of Israel for that purpose of that Palestinian state."[18] In 2003 the Reverend Pat Robertson showed that he would even undercut President George W. Bush over Israel. When the president, along with the EU, the UN, and Russia, issued the Middle East Road Map, Robertson announced that the Road Map "imperil[s] the state of Israel" and violates the "clear mandate of the Bible."[19] Joseph Farah, an Arab-American evangelical

Christian, goes even further, advocating Palestinian transfer in the name of a biblically mandated Greater Israel, as described by a Canadian journalist:

> The 50-year-old founder, editor and chief executive officer of World-NetDaily.com, a politically and socially conservative news site, advised Israel to annex the West Bank and Gaza and "transfer" its 3.5 million inhabitants to neighbouring Arab states.
>
> "Population transfers are not pretty and not without problems," said Farah, an evangelical Christian who cites biblical passages in his writings to buttress his views.[20]

As explained in the *Atlanta Journal-Constitution*:

> "One area where many evangelical Christians see no room for compromise is the conflict between Israel and the Palestinians," said Paul Boyer, an emeritus professor of history at the University of Wisconsin whose works include "When Time Shall Be No More: Prophecy Belief in Modern American Culture."
>
> In their view, Boyer said, Israel has a divine right to the West Bank because it is part of the land that God promised to Abraham, as stated in Genesis. Palestinians want the West Bank, a territory captured by Israel in the 1967 Middle East War, as part of a Palestinian state.
>
> "Matters of ultimate destiny ordained by God are not matters to be negotiated around the table," he said.[21]

Some Israelis are suspicious that some Zionist Christians have ulterior motives. They are particularly anxious over continued support by American evangelicals for an Israel that must make difficult and inevitable land compromises. Will evangelicals abandon Israel once it cedes dominion over Bethlehem and Hebron? In other words, do evangelical Christians love Israel for its citizens or for its size? Will Tom DeLay allow "good" to compromise with "evil"?: "'Standing up for good against evil is very hard work; it costs money and blood,' DeLay told a crowded hall in the Israeli parliament building. 'But we're willing to pay.'"[22]

Further, Israelis worry that evangelicals see Israel only as a means to the End of Days, at which time Jews must embrace Jesus. As reported by Zev Nagel of the *Jerusalem Report*:

But Dr. Brenda E. Brasher, an expert on fundamentalist Christianity, is not so sanguine about ties with evangelical groups in general, and the [Knesset Christian Allies] Caucus in particular. Dealing with pro-Israel evangelical Christians presents a considerable threat to Jews, claims Brasher, who specializes in the sociology of religion and divides her time between Jerusalem and Scotland's University of Aberdeen. "They believe that the Jews have a special relationship with God, but that, at the end of time, the Jews will no longer exist. Some-one who thinks you have no ultimate status is a problematic friend."

Moreover, she argues, "Since the Bible confirms Israel's right to the entire Land of Israel, evangelicals cannot theologically justify giv-ing back land." The trouble with that approach, she goes on, is that it oversimplifies Israel's challenges, amounting to overwhelming but utterly inflexible support for a very specific vision of Israel.

Rabbi David Rosen, international director of interreligious rela-tions at the American Jewish Committee, advocates what he calls an attitude of "respect and suspect." Stopping short of discouraging the Caucus, Rosen says, however, that the MKs must make clear that "though we are eager for Christian support," this should not be mis-understood by some of the participants as Israeli agreement to an End of Days vision.[23]

There are also a small number of non–religiously based ideological opponents of compromise. They believe in an expansive version of Zionism long rejected by mainstream Zionists. In his novel *The Counterlife*, Philip Roth created a character who defends this extremist position. He is an American dentist who makes aliyah (the immigration of Jews to Israel) to a Judaean settlement and becomes a disciple to a maximalist Zionist demagogue whose appeal lies in his substitution of certainty and fervor for prudence:

"The loser hates and is the virtuous one, and the winner wins and is wicked. Okay . . . I accept it. Let us be wicked winners for the next two thousand years, and when the two thousand years are over, when it is 3978, we will take a vote on which we prefer. The Jew will dem-ocratically decide whether he wants to bear the injustice of winning or whether he prefers living again with the honor of losing. And what-ever the majority wants, I too will agree, in 3978. But in the mean-time, *we do not give ground*!"[24]

Morton Klein, president of the Zionist Organization of America, holds similar views against territorial compromise. In *USA Today* he wrote, "The road map . . . imposes an un-American policy of ethnic discrimination by halting Jewish construction in the disputed Judea-Samaria territories while not limiting the much more widespread Arab construction in those areas."[25]

Finally, there are those who argue that Jews should have a right to live anywhere in the world, and especially in places—such as Hebron and the Etzion bloc[26]—in which Jews have lived for long periods of time and that are central to the Jewish history of the region.

There are also American Jews, and some Israelis, who are opposed to compromise—and especially to the establishment of a Palestinian state in the West Bank and Gaza—not on religious or ideological grounds, but rather on pragmatic and security grounds. They simply don't trust Palestinian promises of peace in exchange for land. They fear that an end to the occupation will mean an increase in terrorism and will weaken Israel's military capacity to prevent and control what they believe will be the inevitable violence that will follow the establishment of an independent Palestinian state. They point to the apparent unwillingness or inability of the Palestinian Authority to disarm the terrorist groups that persist in planning both rocket attacks and suicide bombings and that refuse to accept the two-state solution. As Morton Klein writes of the Gaza disengagement, "[S]uch a retreat would certainly exacerbate the terrorism problem, by making it much more difficult for Israel to combat Gaza-based terrorists."[27] The conservative *Boston Globe* columnist Jeff Jacoby elaborates this perspective:

Handing Gaza over to the gangsters of Hamas and the PLO will not leave them "stewing in their own juices" but celebrating their victory. As they take over the houses, farms, and schools of the people they demonized and terrorized for years, they will draw the obvious conclusion: Violence works and the Jews are on the run. . . . The Lebanon retreat inspired the Palestinian authority to launch a murderous terror war, the so-called "second intifadah." What fresh hell will the Gaza disengagement inspire?[28]

Some within these different groups that oppose the creation of a Palestinian state favor a continuation of the occupation. In March 2005, forty Jews from New York traveled to the Gaza settlement Gush

Katif to demonstrate against the government's disengagement plan,[29] prompting the *Jerusalem Post* to remark in a masthead editorial: "There is something awkward about Jews who have never in their lives paid taxes in Israel or worn an IDF uniform, not to mention seen a battlefield—let alone the way Ariel Sharon has—now coming here and accusing him of caving in to foreign pressure or, worse yet, betraying his nation."[30]

Others take the more extreme view of advocating the displacement of the Palestinian population. The Israeli minister of justice summarized—and criticized—these views in the following blunt language: "They believe there will come a point in the critical clash between us and the Palestinians when it would come time to transfer the Palestinians to Jordan; the second thing they hope for is the great American aliyah—a million more Jews coming to Israel. The third, and by far the most stupid, thing is that they believe God will help them."[31]

Fortunately, the numbers of Israelis who favor transfer are small, and their influence, both in Israel and in the United States, is negligible. The majority of Israelis favor the two-state solution, so long as terrorism can be effectively controlled.[32] In the United States as well, most Americans—Jews and non-Jews—support the U.S. policy of ending the occupation of Palestinian cities and establishing a peaceful Palestinian state.

Jews and non-Jews who do not live in Israel and who are not therefore in harm's way should not be more Israeli than the Israelis, especially when it comes to the security of the beleaguered nation. Let the Israeli people and their government make the difficult decisions regarding war, peace, and compromise.

On the other hand, there are religious groups that are trying to facilitate peace. They too invoke religious principles in support of their efforts. Rabbis for Human Rights cites the biblical tradition of caring for "the stranger in your midst" as a basis for their concern about Palestinian suffering. According to the Boston-born David J. Forman, founder of Rabbis for Human Rights:

> RHR offsets a portrayal of Judaism in Israel that is often characterized by a chauvinistic theology, in which a national ego is projected onto God, and any act is justified as a Divine right. When God is presumed to reside with one community above the other, then Yigal Amirs, Baruch Goldsteins and Jewish undergrounds are born. In this

world-view, anyone who opposes an extreme "particular" version of a "heavenly course" for the Jewish people in the Jewish state is a traitor. . . .

But more so, RHR is instructed by the biblical commandment: "When in a war against a city, if you have to besiege it a long time in order to capture it, you must not destroy its trees, wielding the ax against them." (Deuteronomy 20:19)[33]

But left-wing rabbis too sometimes go beyond their religious expertise and mis-cite theology in support of religious ideology. When Rabbi Michael Lerner demands that Israel "atone" for causing the Palestinian refugee problem and insists that the "Jewish people [must] acknowledge disproportionate responsibility for what happened to the Palestinian people,"[34] he displays abysmal historical ignorance. Even the historian Benny Morris, the foremost authority on the refugee problem and someone quite critical of Israel's role in it, acknowledges that "[t]he Arab leadership inside and outside Palestine probably helped precipitate the exodus."[35] Had the Arab leaders not declared a genocidal war against the new Jewish state, there would have been no refugee problem. Lerner should leave history to the historians, and limit himself to his expertise (whatever that might be). Yet he has pronounced on virtually every political, military, and economic issue facing Israel[36] and preached his religious or spiritual solutions to the Israeli government.

Israel is a vibrant democracy that is fully capable of making difficult choices. Its leaders and its citizens, who have experienced the costs of war and terrorism, should be the ones to decide whether to offer territorial and other compromises and whether the risks of making such compromises—and let no one doubt that there indeed are risks—are worth the potential benefits of an imperfect peace. Outsiders, many with the best of intentions, must stop being more Israeli than Israelis. The essence of a democracy is letting the citizens and their duly elected leaders decide the fate of their own nation. Being a democracy means having the power to make one's own mistakes and to correct them by democratic process. It also means that the power to make painful compromises in the hope of avoiding even more painful consequences must be left to its own citizens.

16 A Case Study in Hate and Intimidation

[T]he Jews do not merit a "second homeland" because they already have New York, with a huge Jewish population, Jewish-run media, a Jewish mayor, and domination of cultural and economic life.
—*Noam Chomsky, MIT professor of linguistics*[1]

I can't imagine why Israel's apologists would be offended by a comparison with the Gestapo.
— *Norman Finkelstein, assistant professor at DePaul University and author of* The Holocaust Industry[2]

I don't know there's enough exterior evidence to determine whether they [the claims that Israel perpetrated both 9/11 and the anthrax attacks] are true or not.
—*Alexander Cockburn, columnist for the* Nation *and editor of the Web newsletter* CounterPunch[3]

In this chapter, I will show how a small but influential group of anti-Israel, antipeace, and antitruth zealots has managed to intimidate many moderate voices for peace and the two-state solution on American university campuses. In exposing this new form of literary McCarthyism, I will necessarily have to focus on some of the attacks on me, because I have become a central focus of this intimidation since the publication of *The Case for Israel*. But the problem is much larger than any one person, and poses significant threats to the ongoing peace process.

I have often wondered why so few academics are willing to speak out in moderate support of Israel—or even of the two-state solution—on American university campuses. Some faculty members are prepared to play a behind-the-scenes role in counseling students who do speak out and some are willing to sign reactive petitions, such as the one against divestment. But on many campuses, perhaps even a majority, there is not a single professor who can be counted on to speak proactively about Israel, to write op-ed articles for the school newspaper, to present a pro-Israel or pro-two-state perspective on local talk radio or television shows, or in any other way to be identified publicly and positively with Israel.

I am not talking about support for all of Prime Minister Sharon's policies. I too am critical of some of these. I am talking about Israel's right to exist as a secular Jewish democracy, to defend itself against terrorism by proportional means, and to have its human rights record judged by a single standard. I am talking about Israel's right not to be demonized, delegitimated, singled out for unfair condemnation, and compared to the worst of regimes, especially the Nazis.[4]

This silence is particularly troubling in light of the raucousness of the anti-Israel rhetoric on so many university campuses, as described in chapter 14. The absence of a single pro-Israel voice among the faculty of a college or university—especially in contrast to the presence of so many anti-Israel voices—has a stifling effect on students and makes it seem as if there is no other side to the issues than that presented by the anti-Israel hard left. This threatens to produce a generation of graduates—future leaders—who take for granted that any show of support for Israel is immoral and politically incorrect. Indeed, it is these future leaders that the anti-Israel campus campaigns are specifically targeting.

This phenomenon contributes to an atmosphere that is not conducive to peace, because it encourages anti-Israel extremists to reject any compromise peace in the expectation that Israel will have little support among the next generation of leaders. It also encourages anti-Palestinian extremists in their belief that any compromise peace will only be a first step toward the eventual goal of Israel's enemies to destroy the Jewish state.

The reason for the faculty silence is not what is widely believed—namely, that few academics actually think that Israel or the two-state solution deserve their support. In my experience speaking on many campuses, there is unexpressed silent support for Israel—though certainly not for all of its policies—among many professors, and widespread support for the two-state solution. When I speak about these issues on a campus, I receive phone calls from faculty members thanking me for speaking out. When I respond by asking them why they don't speak out, I hear excuses galore: "I'm *not* an expert in the Middle East, so I really have no credentials for that issue." (I never hear that about other issues such as gay rights, abortion, or the Iraq war.) "I *am* an expert on the Middle East, so I can't take sides." (As if experts who are anti-Israel have any reluctance to take sides.) "I'm too busy with other projects."

Then there is the real reason, which I am now beginning to hear more often: "If I speak out in a way that is seen as in any way supportive of Israel, I will be attacked viciously by anti-Israel academics. My integrity and professionalism will be challenged. I will become the object of scorn and ridicule on the Internet. My academic career will be hurt." I have recently learned, from firsthand experience, that this is true and that the fear of becoming the target of unfair attacks by anti-Israel advocates is having a discernible impact on the willingness of academics to speak or write in support of Israel or the two-state solution.

The interesting news is that this is not haphazard or episodic. In fact, it is part of a well-orchestrated campaign to try to discredit pro-Israel advocacy on college campuses that has never previously been documented and exposed.

Since the publication of my book, *The Case for Israel*, I have become a prime target of this campaign of vilification. The Web is filled with personal attacks on me. The language is almost always the same. Pickets and protesters appear at my public speeches. False charges have been hurled against me in letters to the president, dean, and newspapers of Harvard. Boycotts of my classes have been proposed. My physical safety has been threatened.[5] All this despite—or perhaps because of—the fact that I have always presented a centrist, two-state approach to the Israeli-Palestinian conflict, which includes criticism of certain Israeli actions.[6] The attack on me is part of a broader campaign against moderate pro-Israel writers and professors that goes back many years and will likely continue unless it is exposed and confronted.

The attack team consists of Noam Chomsky, the MIT professor and noted linguist;[7] Norman Finkelstein, an obscure but prolific assistant professor of political science at DePaul University; and Alexander Cockburn, the extremist columnist for the *Nation* and editor of the radical political Web magazine *CounterPunch.*

The mode of attack is consistent. Chomsky selects the target and directs Finkelstein to probe the writings in minute detail and conclude that the writer didn't actually write the work, that it is plagiarized, that it is a hoax and a fraud. Cockburn publicizes these "findings," and then a cadre of fellow travelers bombard the Internet with so many attacks on the target that these attacks jump to the top of Google. Because no one has thus far exposed the pattern, each attack seems plausible on first impression. After all, some people do plagiarize. There are frauds and hoaxes, and some scholars deserve to have their integrity attacked. But when the pattern is examined and exposed, the entire enterprise becomes clear for what it is: a systematic attempt to chill moderate pro-Israel advocacy on university campuses by a form of literary McCarthyism.

Who Is Noam Chomsky?

Many people know who Noam Chomsky is. The jacket of one of his books describes him, without irony, as "arguably the most important intellectual alive."[8] He is well-known for his extreme hatred of the United States and Israel, having famously declared that "[i]f the Nuremberg laws were applied today, then every Post-War American president would have to be hanged."[9] But not many are aware of the even darker side of his record—including supporting, praising, and working with Holocaust deniers. Chomsky's most notorious bedfellow is Robert Faurisson, who called the Holocaust a "hoax," denied the existence of Hitler's gas chambers, claimed that the diary of Anne Frank was a "forgery," and described the Jewish claims for Holocaust reparations as a "fraud."[10] (These words have a tendency to recur in anti-Semitic and anti-Israel rhetoric.) Chomsky leaped to Faurisson's support. He did not limit himself to defending Faurisson's *right* to publish his false claims about the Holocaust, as a civil libertarian might.

Chomsky went out of his way to describe this Holocaust denier as a "a sort of relatively apolitical liberal,"[11] to praise him as a scholar who had done "extensive historical research," and to characterize his assertions about the Holocaust as historical "findings."[12] He also said that he did not see any "hint of anti-Semitic implications" in Faurisson's claim that the so-called Holocaust was a fraud perpetrated by the Jewish people. Chomsky, the linguist, assured his readers that "nobody believes there is an anti-Semitic connotation to the denial of the Holocaust . . . *whether one believes it took place or not*"[13] (thus implying that reasonable people could believe that it did *not* take place). Chomsky wrote an introduction to a Faurisson book, lending this Holocaust denier his academic imprimatur. Chomsky has also published his writings with a well-known neo-Nazi press.[14] As Paul L. Berman summarized Chomsky's record on these issues: "Chomsky's view of anti-Semitism is positively wild. His definition is so narrow, neither the *Protocols of the Elders of Zion* nor the no-Holocaust delusion fit into it. . . . I am afraid that his present remarks on anti-Semitism and Zionist lies disqualify him from ever being taken seriously on matters pertaining to Jews."[15]

Ever since his close association with Holocaust deniers compromised his credibility on "matters pertaining to Jews," Chomsky has tended to stay away from these issues—at least directly—leaving it to surrogates to continue his campaign of vilification against the Jewish community. His primary surrogate is Norman Finkelstein. In selecting as his intellectual hit man Finkelstein, Chomsky picked a real soul mate.

Chomsky and Finkelstein have remained, in Chomsky's words, "very close friends"[16] since they conspired back in 1984 to attack a writer named Joan Peters whom they regarded as pro-Israel. Chomsky has urged audiences "to come listen to" Finkelstein because he can speak about Israel "with more authority and insight . . . than anyone I can think of."[17] This about a man who repeatedly calls Israel a Nazi nation and who boasts of "publicly honoring" and showing "solidarity with Hezbollah."[18]

Chomsky has characterized Finkelstein as "a very fine scholar."[19] (Chomsky has also characterized the work of Ward Churchill—the Colorado professor who called the victims of the attack on the World Trade Center "little Eichmanns"[20]—as "excellent, penetrating and of high scholarly quality,"[21] and his achievements as "of inestimable value."[22]) In light of Chomsky's standards regarding scholarly quality, it should not be surprising that his own scholarship has been rigorously questioned. Professors Robert Levine and Paul Postal, both linguists at distinguished universities, have documented serious charges of plagiarism against him, accusing him of "the uncredited adoption of others' research ideas."[23] Others have documented denials by Chomsky of having made statements that appear on videotape. He has also been accused of "fabricat[ing] facts," concocting sources, mis-citing authorities, "lying," ignoring countersources, "intellectual corruption,"[24] "deliberate distortion,"[25] "intellectual misconduct,"[26] "playing fast and loose with the source material,"[27] and "massive falsification of facts, evidence, sources and statistics."[28] The historian Arthur Schlesinger, in summarizing the documented accusations against Chomsky, has labeled him an "intellectual crook."[29]

Who Is Norman Finkelstein?

Norman Finkelstein is a transient academic who describes himself as "in exile" at DePaul University because he has been—by his own account— "thrown out of every school in New York."[30] The former chairman of the political science department at one such college told me that Finkelstein was fired for "incompetence," "mental instability," and "abuse" of students with politics different from his own.

Finkelstein boasts, "Never has one of my articles been published in a scientific magazine,"[31] and for good reason. As Peter Novick, whose book *The Holocaust in American Life* Finkelstein characterized as "the initial stimulus for [his] book,"[32] wrote,

> As concerns particular assertions made by Finkelstein . . . the appropriate response is not (exhilarating) 'debate' but (tedious) examination of his footnotes. Such an examination reveals that many of those assertions are pure invention. . . . No facts alleged by Finkelstein should be assumed to be really facts, no quotation in his book should be assumed to be accurate, without taking the time to carefully compare his claims with the sources he cites.[33]

Novick called Finkelstein's book "trash"[34] and a "twenty-first century updating of the 'Protocols of the Elders of Zion.'"[35] When Finkelstein's own "stimulus" warns readers not to believe him, that warning must be taken seriously.

Nor should it be surprising in light of his methodology. When he was asked, "If you are a historian, why didn't you write a serious study about the subject? Why didn't you do research yourself? Interview people, etc.?" Finkelstein responded, "Why should I interview people?"[36]

Finkelstein has characterized Israeli counterterrorism actions a "holocaust" and said that he "can't imagine why Israel's apologists would be offended by a comparison with the Gestapo."[37] He has blamed September 11 on the United States ("[W]e [the U.S.] deserve the problem on our hands because some things Bin Laden says are true"),[38] and asserted that "Libya had nothing to do with [the blowing up of Pan Am 103]" (for which Libya has acknowledged responsibility).[39] He has said that most alleged Holocaust survivors—including Elie Wiesel—have fabricated their past and are bogus, and that those seeking reparations are cheats and greedy.

Marc Fisher, a columnist for the *Washington Post*, has observed that "Norman Finkelstein [is] a writer celebrated by neo-Nazi groups for his Holocaust revisionism and comparisons of Israel to Nazi Germany."[40] One actual Nazi (Ingrid Rimland, whose husband, the notorious Ernst Zündel, authored *The Hitler We Loved and Why*) referred to Finkelstein admiringly as the "Jewish David Irving"—a reference to the British Holocaust denier and Hitler admirer.[41] The comparison is apt because Finkelstein has reportedly praised Irving as a good historian[42] and as having "made an 'indispensable' contribution to our knowledge of World War II."[43] Martin Dietzsch, a German sociologist who is an expert on neo-Nazism, described him as a Jew who "supports anti-Semitism."[44] Like other anti-Semites, Finkelstein generalizes about "the Jews"; for example: "Just as Israelis, armed to the teeth by the United States, courageously put unruly Palestinians in their place, so American *Jews* courageously put unruly Blacks in their place."[45] Also like other anti-Semites, he blames the recurrence of anti-Semitism on the Jews: "[T]he worst enemies in the struggle against real anti-Semitism are the philo-Semites. . . . Alongside Israel ['American Jewish elites'] are the main fomenters of anti-Semitism in the world today. . . . They need to be stopped."[46] It should come as no surprise therefore that Finkelstein's books, which have no market in the United States, are widely read in Germany and distributed by neo-Nazi groups.[47]

Leon Wieseltier, literary editor of the *New Republic*, described Finkelstein as "poison, he's a disgusting self-hating Jew, he's something you find under a rock."[48] Gabriel Schoenfeld, senior editor of *Commentary* magazine, has labeled his views as "crackpot ideas, some of them mirrored almost verbatim in the propaganda put out by neo-Nazis around the world."[49] Prominent among these ideas is the old anti-Semitic canard of a "Jewish conspiracy" that includes Steven Spielberg, NBC, and Leon Uris. Finkelstein has condemned *Schindler's List* as an effort by American Jews to divert attention from America's Mideast policy: "Give me a better reason! . . . Who profits [from the movie]? Basically, there are two beneficiaries from the dogmas [of *Schindler's List*]: American Jews and the American administration."[50]

He believes that NBC decided to broadcast the series *Holocaust* in order to strengthen Israel's bargaining position with Egypt: "In 1978, NBC produced the series *Holocaust*. Do you believe, it was a coincidence, 1978? Just at this time, when peace negotiations between Israel and Egypt took place in Camp David?"[51]

And he accuses Leon Uris, the author of *Exodus*, of naming his central character "Ari" in order to promote Israel's "Nazi" ideology: "The name of the character is Ari Ben Canaan because Ari is the diminutive for Aryan. It is the whole admiration for this blond haired, blue eyed type."[52] (Ari is a traditional Hebrew name going back to the Bible.)

Normally, no one would take seriously the ridiculous claims Finkelstein makes, but he boasts that he "can get away with things which nobody else can"[53] because his parents were Holocaust survivors. As Alain Zucker, in his review of *The Holocaust Industry*, put it, "If Finkelstein wasn't Jewish, his book would have been dumped by the reviewers as a right extremist pamphlet."[54] Finkelstein accuses others of exploiting the memory of the Holocaust for personal purposes, yet it is clear that he himself ranks as one of that tragedy's most perverse exploiters. He quotes his mother as asking rhetorically, "If everyone who claims to be a survivor actually is one . . . who did Hitler kill?"[55] Finkelstein even doubted his own mother's denial that she was a kapo, asking whether her frequent statements that "the best didn't survive" constituted "an indirect admission of guilt?" The most he was willing to do was "assume" that his mother answered him "truthfully."[56] But he questioned even that assumption: "Still, if she didn't cross fundamental moral boundaries, I glimpsed from her manner of pushing and shoving in order to get to the head of a queue, which mortified me. . . . Really, how else would she have survived?" A ninety-year-old Holocaust survivor in Canada told me that "this Finkelstein man is, in some ways, worse than an outright Holocaust denier, because he acknowledges only the dead but not the living. It hurts so much to hear him say that we didn't actually suffer."

Who Is Alexander Cockburn?

The third member of this nasty triumvirate is Alexander Cockburn. Cockburn serves as the main megaphone for Chomsky's and Finkelstein's rants. He has used his column in the *Nation*, and his online radical hotspot *CounterPunch*, to publicize many of their most outrageous claims. His hatred for Israel knows no bounds. In 1984 he was suspended from the *Village Voice* for hiding a $10,000 "grant" he received from an anti-Israel organization.[57] When asked whether he believed the stories involving Israeli complicity in September 11 and in the anthrax attacks, his response was, "I don't know there's enough exterior evidence to determine whether they are true or not,"[58] thus legitimating these lies and those who spread them. The columnist Jon Margolis, after exposing several false charges made by Cockburn, asserted that "Cockburn has been abusing reality for decades" and that "as an accuser, Joe McCarthy was more responsible."[59]

Their Alliance—Their Mode—Their Attacks

The story of this unholy alliance among Chomsky, Finkelstein, and Cockburn began more than twenty years ago with the publication of a book entitled *From Time Immemorial*, by Joan Peters. The book, an unlikely best-seller, was largely a demographic study of the population of the area that eventually became Israel. Peters's conclusion was that the claim that the Palestinians who left or were expelled from Israel during the War of Independence (1947–1949) had lived in the area from time immemorial was exaggerated. She tried to prove—through land records, census figures, immigration data, eyewitness accounts, and other information—that many of these Palestinians were relatively recent transplants from the West Bank, Gaza, and other places. It was a controversial thesis, especially since the Ottoman records on which she partially relied were often incomplete. Indeed, I disagreed with some of her conclusions and said so in my book *The Case for Israel*.[60] But her major point—that not all of the refugees had lived for centuries in what became Israel—was supported by evidence and contributed an important new element to the debate.[61]

When Chomsky learned of Peters's book, he became outraged. He raised questions about whether Peters had actually written the book, writing that it was "*signed* by Joan Peters,"[62] but "probably it had been put together by some intelligence agency."[63] Chomsky telephoned Finkelstein, then a graduate student already notorious for the virulence of his anti-Zionism, and directed him to expose the book as "a fraud." According to Finkelstein's account, Chomsky told him that "if I go through the book more carefully, [I'd] probably discover that the whole thing is a fraud."[64] Any legitimate academic would have rejected this Alice-in-Wonderland approach: conclusion first and then a search for—or concocting of—evidence to support it. But here is how Finkelstein responded: "Well, you know, I'm a person of the left, and when you get a call from Professor Chomsky, his wish is your command."[65] And of course, Finkelstein granted Chomsky his wish: he "discovered"—surprise!—that Peters had perpetrated a "spectacular hoax," a "fraud from start to finish."[66] He also accused Peters of "plagiarism."[67]

Chomsky arranged for Finkelstein's critique of Peters's book to be published in an anti-Israel leftist magazine called *In These Times*.[68] Chomsky, who had not himself done the research, went even further than Finkelstein in attacking Peters's book. He said that the *entire book* "was completely faked" and that "the whole thing was a hoax."[69] (We will see that this pattern continues with regard to other books by pro-Israel academics as well.) With Finkelstein willing to devote his life to word-by-word scrutiny of every book contrary to Chomsky's political ideology, this was the start of a rather ugly collaboration.

The third member of the attack team, Alexander Cockburn, joined the orgy of name-calling calculated to destroy Peters's reputation. Cockburn characterized her conclusions as "fraudulent," "mad,"[70] and immoral. He called her book a "charnel house of disingenuous polemic"[71] and "nonsense which was duly exposed as fraudulent from start to finish."[72] He used his column in the *Nation* to publicize Finkelstein's charges of plagiarism—charges similar to the ones he has subsequently leveled against other pro-Israel writers.[73]

The Chomsky-Finkelstein-Cockburn mode of ad hominem attack proved successful against Peters because the words "hoax," "fraud," "fake," and "plagiarism" are so dramatic and unforgettable, as is the charge that Peters did not actually write the book, but merely signed a KGB-style forgery concocted by "some intelligence agency," presumably the Mossad or the CIA. The impression created by these charges is that the author (or the intelligence agency) actually made up all of her sources out of whole cloth, faked all the data, and forged all the documents. That is the meaning of "hoax" and "fake," as in the fake diary of Adolf Hitler or the forged *Protocols of the Elders of Zion*. It did not seem to matter that none of these charges was even close to the truth. All Finkelstein had managed to show was that in a relatively small number of instances, Peters may have misinterpreted some data, ignored counterdata, and exaggerated some findings—common problems in demographic research that often appear in anti-Israel books as well, including those of Chomsky.

Yet the anti-Israel press repeated the exaggerated charges against Peters as if they were gospel (and coming from Noam Chomsky, the high priest of the anti-Jewish hard left, they *were* gospel). Suddenly the name Joan Peters was associated in the minds of many with the words "hoax," "fake," "fraud," "plagiarism," and the claim that she was a front for the Mossad or the CIA. This hard-left version of literary McCarthyism had succeeded in damaging the academic reputation of one writer.[74] The Chomsky-Finkelstein-Cockburn tactic thus became the preferred mode of attack against other pro-Israel and pro-Jewish writers. The same words—"hoax," "fraud," "fake," and "plagiarism"—became the standard attack words, and other pro-Israel writers were falsely accused of the same literary crimes.

For example, Finkelstein has accused Elie Wiesel, whom he calls the "resident clown" of the Holocaust "circus"[75] and a "wimp,"[76] of being a liar who has made up stories of his past. Finkelstein finds it necessary to attack Wiesel's credibility because Wiesel's documentation of his experiences during the Holocaust is among the most important primary sources for historians of that tragic epoch in Jewish history. Just like Robert Faurisson, who falsely claims that the diary of Anne Frank is a "fraud" and a "hoax," Finkelstein claims—quite falsely—that Wiesel's account of his own life is false. To try to prove this defamation, Finkelstein focuses on a lighthearted anecdote in Wiesel's memoir that recounted how he read Immanuel Kant's *Critique of Pure Reason* in Yiddish and lost the interest of young women when he would mention the work in conversations. Finkelstein jumps on the story, insisting that

"*The Critique of Pure Reason* was never translated into Yiddish."[77] Finkelstein disregards the fact that a huge portion of Yiddish literature was destroyed or lost during and after the Holocaust. Moreover, former Oxford professor Dovid Katz, one of the world's most distinguished scholars of Yiddish literature, assures me that he has seen a Yiddish translation of the *Critique of Pure Reason* and that its substance was also included in a popular Yiddish philosophy compendium by Chaim Zhitlovsky. Moreover, even Finkelstein concedes that Kant's *Critique of Practical Reason*[78] was published in Yiddish by a Warsaw publishing house in 1929 and there is a copy in the Harvard library.

Other targets of Finkelstein are Edgar Bronfman, whom he called "the Jewish Ribbentrop";[79] Rabbi Israel Singer, who is according to Finkelstein "[Bronfman's] crooked sidekick . . . , a blackmailer, an extortionist . . . [who] belongs behind bars";[80] Abraham Foxman, whom Finkelstein called the "grand wizard"[81] of the ADL; and other Jewish leaders who support Israel and who work for reparations for Holocaust victims.[82]

Finkelstein's own claim to fame is a book called *The Holocaust Industry*, which was labeled an "irrational and insidious" "conspiracy theory" by the *New York Times* reviewer and historian Omer Bartov.[83] In this theory, Finkelstein accuses American Jewry of a conspiracy and of "shaking down" such helpless organizations as Swiss banks, German corporations, and European governments. As Finkelstein observed, "They [the Swiss banks] are so afraid of those hoodlums [the "Holocaust Industry"]. . . . They [the Jewish leaders] are so ruthless and reckless thugs."[84] The so-called "Holocaust Industry" is, in the world according to Finkelstein, a group of well-connected and powerful Jews using victim status to cover up for the sins of Israel and to line their own pockets with "Holocaust booty." In the *New York Times*, Bartov called Finkelstein's thesis "a novel variation on the anti-Semitic forgery, 'The Protocols of the Elders of Zion.'"[85]

To date, the Chomsky-Finkelstein-Cockburn attack team has targeted at least the following writers who support Israel and seek justice for Holocaust survivors: Stuart Eizenstat, Martin Gilbert, Burt Neuborne, Yehuda Bauer, Gerald Feldman, Richard Overy, and Abba Eban. They have called these distinguished Jews "hucksters," "hoaxters," "thieves," "extortionists," and worse. The pattern of attack is always similar.

After Wiesel, the other major targets of Finkelstein's bile are Daniel

Goldhagen and Burt Neuborne. Goldhagen, an eminent historian and best-selling author, was targeted by Finkelstein for his book *Hitler's Willing Executioners*, which Finkelstein accused of being another Holocaust Industry–sponsored example, a "hoax . . . with footnotes."[86] In reply, Goldhagen convincingly demonstrates that Finkelstein simply "fabricated" the charges against him.[87]

> This is a man who has made a career of attacking Israel's legitimacy. . . . Now, suddenly, he turns to Holocaust studies, which he discovers to be a Zionist conspiracy. . . . In addition to his documented inventions about my book, it is worth noting that Finkelstein has never before written anything on the Holocaust or German history and cannot read German . . . which means that he cannot read many of the sources on which he is passing his "expert" opinion.[88]

Burt Neuborne is one of the most distinguished civil liberties lawyers in the world today. Now a professor of law at New York University Law School, Neuborne previously served with distinction as the national legal director of the American Civil Liberties Union. In that capacity, he brought lawsuits against the government and in favor of the free speech rights of everyone ranging from the Palestine Liberation Organization to the Nazi party. In 1999, he was asked by a federal district court judge to serve as co-counsel for Holocaust survivors who were seeking compensation from the Swiss banks that had kept the money deposited by victims of the German atrocities. Neuborne brilliantly achieved a settlement for his clients, and everyone seemed satisfied with the results. Everyone except for Finkelstein (and, as we will soon see, Chomsky). Finkelstein began a vicious attack against Neuborne's integrity, accusing him of "tribal solidarity"[89] with the Jews, calling him a falsifier of documents,[90] a "blackmailer,"[91] a "shakedown" artist,[92] and "a liar,"[93] and publicly demanding his "disbarment."[94] In his replies, Neuborne demolished Finkelstein, pointing to made-up quotations,[95] faked facts,[96] and outright lies.[97] As usual, Finkelstein ignored the documented rebuttals to his false claims and repeated them in print.

Finkelstein even had his publisher take out an ad in the *Nation* calling Neuborne a liar. Neuborne responded by writing that "to be called a liar by Norman Finkelstein is like being called a traitor by Osama bin Laden. It means you must be doing something right."[98] Neuborne understood that Finkelstein's attack on him and Finkelstein's broader efforts at "minimizing the Holocaust" were motivated by an agenda that had little to do with the Holocaust itself and everything to do with the Israeli-Palestinian conflict. As he wrote: "When peace is achieved between a sovereign Palestinian state and a sovereign Israel, the political motives for minimizing the Holocaust will disappear."[99] Finally, Neuborne wrote the following: "I have no illusions that you will alter your chapter to bring it closer to the truth. You appear to be so obsessed with waging your private political war against militant Zionism and the Jewish establishment that you simply cannot see anything except corruption and bad faith. . . . But your stridency and rage prevents your work from playing any constructive role. Rather, you just become fodder for *someone else's* political obsessions"[100] (emphasis added).

When I asked Burt Neuborne to whom he was referring when he wrote about "someone else's political obsessions," he replied, "Chomsky, of course. He's behind this."[101]

One more incident will illustrate this pattern. Professor Werner Cohn sent me an e-mail stating that when he wrote a book exposing Chomsky's flirtation with Holocaust deniers, one of Chomsky's acolytes accused Cohn of not having written his own book. The CIA and the Mossad have apparently been kept quite busy "writing" books of which Chomsky disapproves.

Their Attacks against Me

Having attacked Joan Peters, Elie Wiesel, Daniel Goldhagen, Burt Neuborne, Werner Cohn, and so many other Jewish supporters of Israel and Holocaust reparations, it was only natural that the anti-Israel triumvirate would target me after *The Case for Israel* became a bestseller and, according to Finkelstein, "got great reviews everywhere."[102] One of my critics, who has expressed indebtedness to Finkelstein for providing him source material, reported in an overstatement characteristic of the triumvirate and their followers, that "no book in recent memory has received such unvarying praise from both the American intellectual establishment and the American and world press," and that it had become quite "influential among policy makers."[103] It was necessary therefore to subject my book to "the treatment" accorded other influential pro-Israel writings. The carefully coordinated response to my book employed exactly the same words they had used so successfully against Peters (and others).

I have the resources to counter their attack and disprove their false charges, but younger, less-established academics could have their careers hurt or even destroyed by such false accusations. Finkelstein boasts of having destroyed at least two promising academic careers and has made it plain that he will go after others who write in support of Israel or Holocaust reparations.

The attack against me began with my appearance on a radio show called *Democracy Now!* (recorded on September 24, 2003) on which I was supposed to debate Chomsky. Finkelstein showed up instead, having arranged with the host to "expose" my book, and having coordinated the attack with Chomsky and Cockburn, who stood ready to publicize it in the *Nation* and other left-wing media. They first claimed—as they had with Peters—that I did not "write this book," that I did not even "read it," and that I "had no idea what was in the book."* The implication was that some Israeli intelligence agency wrote it and had me sign it—exactly as they claimed was the situation with Peters's and Cohn's books. The problem for them is that I don't type or use a computer, so every word of the text was hand-written by me in my own handwriting—and I still have the original, handwritten manuscript.[104]

Well, if I did actually write it in my own hand, I must have copied it or plagiarized it. That was the next charge. And guess who I plagiarized it from? Joan Peters, according to Finkelstein, Chomsky, and Cockburn. The problem with their charge—in addition to its complete falsity—is that Peters's book was entirely demographic and historical, whereas more than 90 percent of my book deals with contemporary events that took place years *after* the publication of Peters's book in 1984. The other, even more serious problem for them is that they could not come up with a *single* sentence, phrase, or idea in my book that came from another source and was used without quotation marks,

---

*Recently Finkelstein claimed that I don't write any of my books: "[I]t's sort of like a Hallmark line for Nazis. . . . [T]hey churn them out so fast that he has now reached a point where he doesn't even read them." (Norman Finkelstein "Ambushes" Alan Dershowitz [Part II]: an original transcript from *theExperiment*, December 6, 2003, accessible at www .theexperiment.org/articles.php?news_id=1991.)

attribution, and citation. I explicitly cited Peters's book numerous times while disclaiming reliance on its conclusions because I disagreed with some of them. That, of course, means there was no plagiarism.

Moreover, Finkelstein has publicly stated that he does not take the issue of plagiarism seriously, virtually acknowledging that he uses it only as a tactic against his ideological enemies: "I'm a leftist and I don't get too excited about plagiarism, I have to admit it."[105] Despite Finkelstein's lack of excitement about plagiarism, and his obvious realization that I had not engaged in it, he knew from his previous experience that the false charge of plagiarism, if leveled, would be more likely to garner media attention than simple criticism of my conclusions.

That is why the charge of plagiarism has become a central element of their standard attack plan. Finkelstein's claim of plagiarism against me is laughable. His charge is that I originally came across several quotations that I use in my book—for example, one from Mark Twain—in Peters's book. Although he acknowledged that I put the Twain quote in quotation marks and cited it to Twain, he says I should have cited it to Peters. In any event, I didn't even find the Twain quote (and others that Finkelstein points to) in Peters's book. I have been speaking about the Israel-Palestine conflict for decades—well before Peters published her book—and was using many of these quotes in my debates and speeches, as I can conclusively prove.[106] Chomsky knew this because I used quotations from Mark Twain, the *Encyclopaedia Britannica*, and the Peel Commission in debates with *him*. It is true that I first came upon some obscure diplomatic letters in Peters's book, but I then checked them against the originals in the Harvard library and cited them to their original sources. When I could not find the original sources, I cited them to Peters. *This* became the charge of plagiarism— that I cited some quotations to their *original* sources rather than all of them to the *secondary* source in which I first came across them. That is not plagiarism. It is what the style books mandate and scholars do— except in the mind of the Chomsky-Finkelstein-Cockburn attack team, and only when pro-Israel writers do it, not when they themselves do it!

In order to level his spurious charge of plagiarism, Finkelstein had to make up a false quotation, which he called the "smoking gun":[107] "[I]n the [galley] proofs, it . . . says: *Copy from* Joan Peters.[108] It does. . . . There was no question about it." He thus alleges that I instructed a research assistant to "copy"[109] from another author without citations. But he simply makes up the word "copy." The note says precisely the opposite: "*cite* sources on pp. 160, 485, 486, footnotes 141–145" (emphasis added). The instruction is to be certain that the material is properly *cited*. This is not proof of plagiarism; it is proof of scholarship.

That is why James O. Freedman, the former president of Dartmouth, the University of Iowa, and the American Academy of Arts and Sciences, concluded after reviewing the Finkelstein charge:

> I do not understand [Finkelstein's] charge of plagiarism against Alan Dershowitz. There is no claim that Dershowitz used the words of others without attribution. When he uses the words of others, he quotes them properly and generally cites them to the original sources (Mark Twain, Palestine Royal Commission, etc.) [Finkelstein's] complaint is that instead he should have cited them to the *secondary* source, in which Dershowitz may have come upon them. But as *The Chicago Manual of Style* emphasizes:
>
>> With all reuse of others' materials, it is important to identify the original as the source. This not only bolsters the claims of fair use, it also helps avoid any accusation of plagiarism.
>
> This is precisely what Dershowitz did. Moreover, many of the sources quoted both by Dershowitz and Peters are commonly quoted in discussions of this period of Palestinian history. Nor can it be said that Dershowitz used Peters' ideas without attribution. He cites Peters seven times[110] in the early chapter of his book, while making clear that he does not necessarily accept her conclusions. This is simply not plagiarism, under any reasonable definition of that word.

Professor Charles Fried, the former solicitor general of the United States and the Beneficial Professor of Law at Harvard, called the Finkelstein accusation "stupid, unfair and ridiculous . . . from biased accusers,"[111] and concluded that my use of citations was absolutely proper and usual among academicians. The distinguished chief librarian at Harvard Law School was asked for an opinion on the matter and concluded that citing "the first source, not the repeater" is "certainly correct" and that my use of citations was absolutely proper.[112]

Finkelstein was furious that Harvard cleared me of his entirely false and politically motivated charges of plagiarism. In December 2004, he sent an e-mail to the dean of Harvard Law School in which he complained about the decision that had "completely exonerated" me of all charges. He then had the gall to cite his own lie about the galley proof of my book that he said "conclusively demonstrated that Dershowitz instructed his research assistants to copy the quotations and citations in his book from Joan Peters's hoax, *From Time Immemorial.*" He also claimed that he could prove that I "almost certainly didn't write the book, and perhaps didn't even read it prior to publication." Dean Kagan ignored Finkelstein's missive, treating it as the nut mail it is. Indeed, in June 2005 Dean Kagan awarded me a "writing prize . . . to honor exceptional scholarship, for your publication this year of *Rights from Wrongs.*"

Finkelstein, of course, knows that his politically motivated accusations against me are complete fabrications, but he also knows that false charges once made tend to stick, even if they have been authoritatively disproved. The media regards plagiarism as such an explosive charge that even absolute innocence is no defense. After the charge against me was dismissed as wholly without merit,[113] it continued to be recycled in some newspapers and magazines. In this case, the false charge has grown in size. In the well-coordinated Internet attack on me, Finkelstein's tiny accusation about the citation form for a handful of quotations—totally false as it is—has ballooned into a charge that I plagiarized "all" or "large parts" of my book from Peters. For example, here is what Chomsky has said (after characterizing me as "a passionate opponent of civil liberties"[114]): "*large parts* of the book were simply plagiarized from a well-known hoax" (emphasis added). This charge was then transmogrified into the usual accusation that my *entire* book was a "hoax," a "fraud," a "fake," and a "lie." It sounds familiar, doesn't it? The only new element in this tired tactic is the creative use of the Internet. When I was Googled in June 2005, the third entry under my name was Cockburn's headline "Alan Dershowitz, Plagiarist?" Finkelstein's headline "The Dershowitz Hoax" was not far below. There were hundreds of Google results on Alan Dershowitz and plagiarism and even several for "Dershowitz admits plagiarism,"[115] though I have always denied that false charge and was completely exonerated by Harvard. When the phrase "Dershowitz didn't write *The Case for Israel*" is plugged in, dozens more results appear. These false allegations remain on the Internet, even though Finkelstein was forced by his publisher to drop them from the text of his book.

In addition to the charges that I didn't write *The Case for Israel* and that if I did I must have plagiarized it, Finkelstein also claimed that "every substantive sentence in his [Dershowitz's] book is fraudulent."[116] In order to prove *this* absurd charge, Finkelstein himself resorts to what his "stimulus" Peter Novick previously accused him of doing: he simply makes up quotations and facts. A couple of examples will illustrate this pattern. Finkelstein claims that in *The Case for Israel* I "never once—I mean literally, not once—mention[ed] any mainstream human rights organization. Never a mention of Amnesty's findings, never a mention of Human Rights Watch's findings, never a mention of B'Tselem's findings . . . none."[117] But a simple check of the index reveals that I repeatedly discuss—and criticize—the findings of these very organizations. He then purports to quote a judicial opinion in support of his claim that I distorted the facts of "a famous case in 1995 of a Palestinian who was shaken to death while in detention."

> And *I'm quoting now* from the High Court of Justice Judgment; "All agree that Harizat died from the shaking." If you go to Dershowitz's book, he discusses the case and says, *quote*, "an independent inquiry found that *he didn't die from the shaking*, but from a previous illness."[118]

There is simply no statement in the High Court judgment that says, "All agree that Harizat died *from* the shaking," nor in my book that "he didn't die from shaking."[119] He simply makes up both quotes, as he has others.[120]

Another made-up quotation by Finkelstein is his claim that in my book *Chutzpah* I analogized "ethnic cleansings" to "urban renewal."[121] I say nothing of the kind in *Chutzpah*. I never even mention "ethnic cleansing."[122] He also claims that I actually wrote "at the very beginning" of *The Case for Israel* that I only "became actively involved in supporting Israel *after June* 1967." I urge anyone to look at what I actually say, to see how deceptive Finkelstein is. I was among the leaders of the faculty campaign at Harvard in support of Israel during the months, weeks, and days leading up to the Six-Day War.[123]

Finkelstein has even alleged that the autobiographical account of my life in *Chutzpah*—growing up as an Orthodox Jew in Brooklyn in the 1940s and 1950s—does not "have much to do [with] what has actually happened in [my] life."[124] Well, I guess he caught me there: I'm actually a thirty-year-old Norwegian-American woman raised in Minnesota during the 1980s. (I'm sure Finkelstein will quote this "admission" from me in his next speech! It will certainly surprise my ninety-one-year-old mother, who still thinks I am her son who grew up in Brooklyn.)

In the face of Finkelstein's long and well-documented record of making up fake quotations and false facts—a record exposed several years ago by the very scholar who inspired him to write his own major book—one would expect that no reputable publisher would go near him. After all, journalists have been fired for much less and have never been published again.[125] But Finkelstein's career and reputation on the anti-Israel hard left has not suffered from these revelations. If anything, it has soared on Planet Chomsky. The best proof of this phenomenon occurred in April 2005, when a group of students prepared a series of David Letterman–type top ten lists of Finkelstein's greatest literary sins that documented his made-up quotations and false facts. Finkelstein's reaction was to post the lists on his own Web site, acknowledging that they were accurate except for a few typographical errors.[126] Had he caught one of his enemies making up even a single quote—which, of course, he has not—he would demand that the sinner be fired and never again published. But just as he does not take plagiarism seriously when committed by his compatriots on the anti-Israel hard left, but only when alleged against his ideological enemies, so too with making up false quotations.

Finkelstein can get anything he writes published, regardless of its demonstrable falsehoods, because Noam Chomsky has enormous influence on the hard-left press. When no one would publish Finkelstein's falsehoods about Joan Peters, Chomsky boasted that "I finally managed to place a piece of it in *In These Times.*"[127] More recently, when one publishing house refused to publish Finkelstein's most recent book that claimed, among other falsehoods, that I plagiarized and didn't write *The Case for Israel,* Chomsky persuaded another, more sympathetic press to publish the book. Chomsky's criteria for praise, condemnation, and publishability seem to have more to do with ideology than accuracy, as evidenced by his praise of not only Finkelstein, but also Ward Churchill, another hard-left academic who has also been accused of making things up.[128]

The same is true with regard to the third member of the triumvirate, Alexander Cockburn. Because he has his own Web site and would welcome the publicity of a defamation lawsuit, he can publish anything he chooses, regardless of its accuracy. Even his column in the *Nation* is subjected to less vetting than the rest of the magazine. When I told the publisher of the *Nation* that his magazine had published false information by Cockburn, he shrugged and said, "Don't judge the rest of the magazine by what we allow Cockburn to say."

Therein lies the reason why young academics who support Israel and the two-state solution are so intimidated and frightened by this anti-Israel triumvirate. They realize that no matter how false and easily disprovable the charges against them may be, those charges will still be widely circulated. The marketplace of ideas, a marketplace in which falsehoods are supposed to sink by their own weight, simply does not operate on the anti-Israel hard left. Instead, a kind of Gresham's law seems to govern, by which the bad currency of made-up quotations drives the good currency of truth out of circulation. For example, the publisher of the University of California Press, which is publishing a book by Finkelstein, has said that Finkelstein has "an incredible amount of documentation."[129] That is literally true: his documentation is "incredible."

Despite his long and well-documented record of demonstrable lies and made-up quotations, Finkelstein remains a popular speaker at anti-Israel events on university campuses around the world. He is not quite as popular as Chomsky and Cockburn, but he is paid handsomely by student groups anxious to promote his anti-Zionist rants. The members of the McCarthyite triumvirate are invited to campuses far more frequently than centrist, moderate pro-Israel and pro-two-state-solution speakers. But now that the well-coordinated pattern of literary McCarthyism dating back more than twenty years has been exposed, perhaps the picture will change—at least among objective, well-intentioned, and open-minded audiences. The boy who cried "wolf" was eventually ignored. The anti-Israel extremists who cry "fraud," "hoax," and "plagiarism" whenever a pro-Israel book becomes successful must also now be ignored because they have been proved to be fabricators of truth. They are also enemies of peace, and relegating these naysayers to the dustbin of history would eliminate a significant barrier to a peaceful compromise between Israel and the Palestinians.

Postscript: As this book was going to press, a serious charge of real plagiarism was leveled at one of the triumvirate's favorite anti-Israel professors—Rashid Khalidi, the Edward Said Professor of Arab Studies at Columbia University and director of its Middle East Institute. The details of this charge are set out in the note.[130] Although this charge is far more serious than any leveled by the triumvirate against pro-Israel writers, you can be sure that Finkelstein will not examine it, Chomsky will not complain about it, and Cockburn will not publicize it. Nor will they demand sanctions against their ideological soul mate, as they have against me and other pro-Israel writers. The same double standard that is directed against Israel by these selective condemners is also directed against pro-Israel and pro-peace academics.

17 Will Anti-Semitism Decrease as Israel Moves toward Peace with the Palestinians?

May 2003 (in the midst of the violence)

The vote: Britain's largest professors' union defeats a proposed academic boycott by a two-to-one margin.

April 2005 (after Israel announces its intention to withdraw from the Gaza Strip and parts of the West Bank and a cease-fire is reached)

The vote: The executive board of the union approves the boycott by a vote of 96 to 92.[1] It was rescinded several weeks later following an international outcry.

Spring 2002

Nearly six hundred Harvard and MIT students and faculty sign a petition endorsing divestment from Israel; nearly six thousand signed the counterpetition.[2] The original petition fails.

April 2005

Divestment proposals are suddenly revived as students hold a panel discussion supporting the Presbyterian divestment[3] and a rally in favor of divesting.

How can the following phenomenon be explained: just as Israel is moving most dramatically toward peace with the Palestinians—ending the occupation of the Gaza Strip, agreeing to dismantle some of its West Bank settlements, stopping house demolitions and targeted killings, meeting with leaders of the Palestinian Authority—there seems to be an increase in worldwide anti-Semitism and efforts to boycott and divest from Israel?

Many of those who most stridently attack the Jewish state deny that they are in any way motivated by anti-Jewish or anti-Semitic feelings. It is, of course, impossible to take an X-ray of human motivations, but there are relatively objective ways of discerning such a phenomenon. A "natural" experiment is occurring right now. If attacks on the Jewish state were motivated entirely by disagreements over its policies, then it should follow that as these policies "improve" (as defined by those who level the attacks) the nature, degree, and frequency of the attacks should diminish. On the other hand, if the alleged disagreement over policies were merely a cover for more intractable hatred of the Jewish state (or Jews or other Jewish institutions) then the attacks would not diminish with improvement in Israel's policies. That is the natural experiment: it has a null hypothesis, measurable factors, and objective criteria.

The two variables are Israel's policies and anti-Jewish attitudes. No reasonable person could disagree with the following conclusion: since 2003, Israel has announced that it will dismantle all Jewish settlements in the Gaza Strip and compel the evacuation of all Jewish settlers; that it will end the use of house demolitions and targeted killings against terrorist commanders, leaders, and operatives (except if it is the only way to prevent an imminent terrorist attack); that it has begun the process of handing over Jericho and Tulkarm to the Palestinian Authority;[4] and that it has released hundreds of Palestinian prisoners.[5]

Whether one believes Israel is doing "enough," it is impossible to dispute that its decisions and actions constitute an improvement—as judged from a pro-Palestinian perspective—over prior decisions and actions. Palestinian leaders, as well as Palestinians on the ground, agree that there has been an improvement (while, understandably, demanding more).[6]

Yet there is no evidence of any decrease in the most hateful expressions of anti-Jewish or anti-Semitic attitudes during this period of improvement in policies. If anything, anti-Semitism seems to be on the rise. According to the Anti-Defamation League's annual audit of anti-Semitic incidents released in April 2005, "hate attacks" have hit the "highest level in nine years."[7] And this is in the United States. In other parts of the world it is far worse.[8] Take England, for example. Since Israel announced its disengagement plans, London's Mayor Ken Livingstone likened a Jewish journalist to "a Nazi concentration camp guard," and Israeli self-defense to "terror aimed at ethnic cleansing," while at the same time "rolling out the red carpet for Sheik Qaradawi, whose fatwas sanction female Palestinian suicide terrorist attacks."[9] "Oona King, Labor MP for Bethnal Green, was pelted with onions and eggs by Muslim constituents . . . when she participated in a memorial to Jewish victims of WWII's last German V2 missile attack on London."[10] The actions by the Association of University Teachers (AUT), described in chapter 14, also illustrate this phenomenon at work. Two years after its first failed boycott resolution, the AUT passed the blacklist, just as Israel was taking its greatest risks and making its broadest concessions to Palestinians since Camp David in 2000. The fact that it ultimately rescinded the boycott—at least for the moment—says more about its attitude toward academic freedom than it does about its attitude toward Israel.

Why this renewal of interest in sanctions against Israel?

From the Palestinian perspective, the political and social climate is objectively improved over what it was two years ago. In the first half of 2005, Prime Minister Sharon and Palestinian president Abbas have signed a cease-fire agreement, Israel released hundreds of Palestinian prisoners, and Israel is about to withdraw from all of the Gaza Strip and four West Bank settlements. The second intifada has effectively ended, and Palestinians are preparing to police their own streets after the Israelis disengage. By any reasonable standard, things are better for Palestinians today than they were in 2003.[11] The Palestinians themselves acknowledge this,[12] but that is not good enough for those who voted for sanctions in 2005. As the *Jerusalem Post* wondered, "Why is it that just as the Palestinians are about to receive the greatest unilateral concession ever from Israel they urge a boycott? It is hardly the manifestation of goodwill that would encourage Israelis to support yet greater existential risks."[13] The London *Guardian* concurred, pointing out a troubling double standard: "Singling out Israel raises other questions. AUT members are not proposing, after all, to boycott universities in North Korea, Zimbabwe or Sudan, where the government has been accused of perpetrating genocide against its own people."[14]

This renewed effort to impose sanctions against Israel makes clear that when Israel does precisely what its detractors demand that it do, even then—especially then!—extreme left-wing academics will only despise Israel more for putting the lie to the professors' hate-filled views. By targeting Israeli Jews, Britain's Professors Against Peace— that's what those who voted for a boycott really should be called—have displayed bigotry against Jews, done violence to academic freedom and antidiscrimination laws, and are fast closing a window of opportunity for reconciliation in the Middle East.

The same can be said of divestment efforts, which failed during the height of the conflict, but seem to be gaining strength, as evidenced by the Presbyterian divestment proposal and its support from *Tikkun*'s publisher, Michael Lerner, just as Israel is moving toward peace. Harvard, along with every other major university, refused to divest from Israel back in 2002, but the divestment proponents were back at Harvard following Israel's decision to withdraw from the Gaza Strip and part of the West Bank. Harvard's Society of Arab Students (SAS) organized and cosponsored a panel discussion on divestment, sponsored by the Presbyterian Church (USA). And just as the British AUT originally refused to let boycott opponents speak out in opposition against the resolution,[15] so too did the divestment advocates at Harvard stifle all rebuttals. When a student in attendance remarked on the one-sidedness of the panel, the SAS Political Action Committee chair told the audience, "It's not meant as a debate." Following the talk, the panel moderator asked the audience to avoid expressing "value judgments" during the question-and-answer period.[16]

Even Palestinian moderates seem closer to the Israelis than to the outsiders who hate Israel so much that Israel's progress toward peace cannot even be acknowledged. On January 24, 2005, President Abbas confirmed that "there has been significant progress in the talks. Our differences have diminished, and therefore we are bound to reach an agreement very soon."[17] On the ground as well, the Palestinian-appointed mayor of Qalqilyah acknowledged that "things are definitely improving"[18] for Palestinians. But for advocates of boycotts, divestment, and continuing hate speech against Israel, it is entirely irrelevant how the Palestinians themselves feel about the progress toward peace.[19]

This natural experiment lends support to what many have long suspected: namely, that much of the most extreme forms of Israel-bashing is motivated not by reasonable disagreements over policies, but rather by intractable hatreds. A natural control experiment corroborates this conclusion. That experiment is taking place in Israel itself, where criticism of particular Israeli policies is an ever-present phenomenon, even among Israel's five million Jewish citizens. But Jews (with some striking exceptions)[20] tend not to be motivated by anti-Semitism. Their criticism of Israel's policies tends to be genuinely motivated by disagreement over policies. And the difference shows. In Israel, there is a direct correlation between stridently anti-Israel rhetoric and Israeli policies. When Israeli policies toward Palestinians "improve," there is a diminution in the rhetoric by those on the left who see improvement (to be sure, there is also an increase in the rhetoric among some on the right who disagree that there has been an improvement).[21]

There are those who argue—whether they believe this argument is another matter—that anti-Semitism is "caused" by Israel's policies, as well as by Jewish leaders who support these policies. The most strident proponent of this "blame the victim" explanation of anti-Semitism is a Jew who has himself been described as an "anti-Semite." In an article in *Tikkun* magazine, Norman Finkelstein has opined that Israel and "American Jewish elites" are "the main fomenters of anti-Semitism in the world today."[22]

This too is a testable proposition, and it fails any reasonable test. If much of the most strident hatred of Israel is in fact more a function of anti-Semitism than of disagreement with specific Israeli policies, what can be done to "normalize" Israel? Obviously, to the extent that anti-Semitism can by reduced, it would follow that anti-Semitically motivated Israel-bashing would diminish as well. And there are steps that can be taken to address this worldwide problem, through education and the reduction of hate speech and statements by leaders. But these have all been tried, with varying degrees of success, but without eliminating anti-Semitism. A different tack might be tried: zero tolerance for anti-Semitism and its various permutations.

Today, a double standard of tolerance exists toward the expression of views that are in fact anti-Semitic but that wear the disguise of anti-Zionism or singular condemnations of Israeli policies. Every halfway intelligent anti-Semite who cares about his or her reputation has learned how to hide that bigotry under a more acceptable label. A case in point is Patrick Buchanan. In the 1980s, Buchanan spoke in explicitly anti-Jewish terms. In a column criticizing Jewish concerns about the Polish decision to maintain a Catholic convent at Auschwitz, he invoked

"Catholic rage" against the Jews. Instead of urging his readers to understand the pain that some Jewish survivors of Auschwitz must feel at Polish efforts to de-Judaize Hitler's final solution, Buchanan declared that "to orthodox Catholics, the demand that we be more 'sensitive' to Jewish concerns is becoming a joke." Then, in a tone reminiscent of an incitement to a nineteenth-century religious pogrom, he prophesied that "the slumbering giant of Catholicism may be about to awaken." Lest there be any doubt about the target of this giant's wrath, Buchanan pointed to "those who so evidently despise our Church"—namely "the Jews."[23] It was classic anti-Semitism with little effort at disguise.

In the past decade, Buchanan has been more careful and indirect in his vitriol. As the *Nation* reported, he continues to instigate distrust of American Jews by insinuating that their loyalties are split between the United States and Israel: "Recently the specter of 'dual loyalties,' long a trigger of anti-Semitic bigotry, was raised when Patrick Buchanan, the ultra-right commentator and former presidential candidate, cast aspersions on those who 'harbor a passionate attachment to a nation not our own.'"[24]

Buchanan has also lashed out against the "neoconservatives," which, for some, has become a euphemism for Jewish conservatives who support Israel. According to *Foreign Policy*:

> With varying degrees of delicacy, everyone from fringe U.S. presidential candidates Lyndon LaRouche and Patrick Buchanan to European news outlets such as the BBC and *Le Monde* have used neocon as a synonym for Jew, focusing on Richard Perle, Paul Wolfowitz, Eliot Cohen, and others with obvious Jewish names. Trying to resurrect the old dual-loyalties canard, they cite links between some neocons and the Likud Party to argue that neocons wanted to invade Iraq because they were doing Israel's bidding.[25]

Sometimes Pat Buchanan still slips and uses the J-word. Again, from the *Nation*: "Pat Buchanan blamed the US invasion of Iraq on a 'cabal' of Jewish intellectuals willing to 'conscript American blood to make the world safe for Israel.'"[26]

As Gloria Borger of *U.S. News and World Report* summed up Buchanan's take on the Jewish precipitation of the two Gulf wars:

Predictably, none other than Pat Buchanan (he who coined the "amen corner" moniker for those in support of the first Gulf War) was happy to join the fray. This time, it was a polemic in his magazine declaring that a small cabal of neoconservatives with ties to the administration are willing "to conscript American blood to make the world safe for Israel." The names he names—Wolfowitz, Perle, Kristol, Podhoretz—are all Jewish. Thank goodness Buchanan assures us their Jewishness is not the issue. No, they just happen to be Jews who have single-handedly persuaded this administration to wage a war with Iraq "not in America's interests" after "colluding with Israel to ignite those wars." So they are traitors.[27]

This was not the first time Buchanan used surnames in a failed effort disguise his anti-Semitism. During the first Gulf war, in one column, he went out of his way to list only Jews who supported the war—A. M. Rosenthal, Charles Krauthammer, Richard Perle, and Henry Kissinger—though most of the support, both from within and without the administration, came from non-Jews. Then in another column four days later, he went out of his way to list only non-Jewish names when describing the "American" kids who are likely to die in the war—"kids with names like McAllister, Murphy, Gonzales and Leroy Brown," though Jewish kids have been killed in every American war.[28] It was this juxtaposition of names, among others, that led William F. Buckley Jr. to conclude that Buchanan's statements "amounted to anti-Semitism."[29]

The word "neoconservative" has now become a code word for "Jew" to such an extent that even I was accused of being "the intellectual neo-conservative who is a double super-patriot of the US and Israel."[30] This bigoted charge by Brendan O'Leary elevates stereotype over fact. Yes, I am a Jew; yes, I am an American; and yes, I support Israel, but I am certainly not a super-patriot of any kind. I opposed the American invasion of Iraq. I opposed the reelection of President George Bush. I am in fact a liberal Democrat who has written critically of neoconservatives. The bigotry has gotten so bad that one writer even accused me of being a neocon, like Paul Wolfowitz, because our names both end with the same suffix!

Another case, though somewhat less disguised, is that of Amiri Baraka. As I argued in chapter 14, Baraka and those who defend his anti-Semitic falsehoods while attacking his critics by invoking anti-Semitic stereotypes, tend to get a free pass on many American campuses. If the shoe were on the other foot—if a Jew were to invoke comparable anti-black or anti-Arab stereotypes—he or she would be justly condemned, or worse.

Consider, for example, the recent decision by DePaul University to suspend and then terminate a pro-Israel professor for conduct that is common, and often much worse, among anti-Israel academics, but that is not punished. Adjunct Professor Thomas Klocek challenged members of two student groups—Students for Justice in Palestine, and United Muslims Moving Ahead—at an activities fair. The *DePaulia*, the university's student newspaper, quoted the president of Students for Justice in Palestine:

> He began to engage the people behind the [United Muslims Moving Ahead] booth in conversation. . . . He began by saying he was a professor at DePaul and was speaking about how he had gone to a Catholic university in Jerusalem. He then continued to talk about how Christians have more of a right to Palestine than Muslims or Jews. . . . He quoted [a *Chicago Tribune*] passage as saying "not all Muslims are terrorists but all terrorists are Muslims."[31]

According to Klocek, "One of the SJP members said that the Israeli treatment of 'Palestinians' is as bad as the way Hitler treated the Jews. I took vast umbrage with this scurrilous statement. . . . At no time did I threaten any of the students physically or verbally, but the volume of the talking turned loud on both sides."[32] For this—vigorously challenging university students to defend a viewpoint with which he disagreed—Klocek was suspended. A week after the *DePaulia* reported Klocek's exchange with the students, a dean from the school wrote to the newspaper:

> A university is a sacrosanct place, a place where persons gather for the sole purpose of learning and seeking truth and coming to understand the human condition. . . . The university must serve as a forum at which individuals are able to express contrary ideas, debate opposing positions, challenge assumptions, press areas of the unknown, and consider unimagined possibilities. Vital to such a forum is the climate of openness.

On Sept. 15 . . . these assumptions were violated. The students' perspective was dishonored and their freedom demeaned. Individuals were deeply insulted.

Our college acted immediately by removing the instructor from the classroom. . . . He has no further responsibilities with the university at this time.

In my meeting with the students on Sept. 23, I apologized to them for the insult and disrespect they had endured, acknowledged the seriousness of the offense, and informed them that this teacher had been removed from class. I repeat that apology now. I sincerely regret the assault on their dignity, their beliefs, their individual selves, and I continue to be saddened by the fact that they have experienced such pain.[33]

Firing a professor because his arguments made pro-Palestinian supporters feel bad about themselves hardly seems to further the university's "sole purpose of learning and seeking truth and coming to understand the human condition." And this from a university that happily continues to employ an anti-Semite and anti-Zionist who has no respect for the truth—Norman Finkelstein. Talk about a double standard! Nor has there been any outcry about the firing of Professor Klocek from those who defend the academic freedom-of-speech rights of anti-Israel academics and who are rallying around Professor Ward Churchill. For many of these people, it is not academic freedom that is being neutrally defended, but rather the freedom only to criticize Israel and the United States.

DePaul's treatment of Klocek stands in stark contrast to Columbia University's treatment of Joseph Massad. Massad, like Klocek, did not have tenure. Massad, like Klocek, purportedly challenged students (though the allegation against Massad was far more serious in that he demanded students leave his class if they disavowed "Israeli atrocities"). But while Massad supports anti-Israel efforts, Klocek opposed them. Massad kept his job, while Klocek did not. Massad has an army of supporters, while Klocek stands nearly alone.

This double standard is unacceptable, but all too typical of universities throughout the world. The easy acceptance of anti-Semitic speech on campuses, even campuses with "speech codes" and other mechanisms for enforcing political correctness, is a symptom of a much larger problem: namely, a not-so-subtle assumption that attacking Jews, the

Jewish state, and Jewish supporters of the two-state solution is different from criticizing other ethnic groups, because Israel is a political issue and political speech must remain untrammeled. I agree that political speech must remain robust and free, but discussions of Arab terrorism, affirmative action, gay rights, and women's equality are also political issues. Universities must practice what I call "ism equity." The rules of discourse must be the same for all "isms," including Zionism and Judaism. Had a Jewish assistant professor threatened to throw an Arab student out of his class for refusing to acknowledge publicly that "Arabs are terrorists" or that "Arab governments support terrorism," he would be fired, as would any professor who made a student recite similar "acknowledgments" against any ethnic, racial, or other protected group. But Jews and the Jewish state are treated differently and a more permissive standard is applied to them on many campuses.

So long as this double standard is tolerated, anti-Semitism and hate speech directed against Israel and its supporters will continue to increase, regardless of what steps Israel takes toward peace. The natural experiment that is currently under way proves beyond any doubt that much of this hate speech and these hateful actions are neither the result of, nor an attempt to influence, Israeli policies with regard to peace. They are simply, to quote one of the most virulent haters (Susan Blackwell), designed to strike a blow at the very existence of what she and her fellow haters regard as the "illegitimate state" of Israel. Since illegitimacy cannot be cured by policy changes, the only action Israel could take to end the hate would be to commit politicide. That will not happen. Nor would it even work, as evidenced by the fact that anti-Semitism persists even in countries where there are no longer any Jews.[34]

One of the great moral issues of the twenty-first century is whether Israel's efforts at making peace and defending its citizens from terrorism will become the latest (and lamest) excuse for a renewal of the oldest of bigotries: the singling out of Jews and Jewish institutions for demonization and discrimination. If you, the readers, want to help promote peace between Israelis and Palestinians, there is something concrete you can do: refuse to become complicit in this bigotry. Marginalize and confront those who persist in their hate speech even while Israel and the Palestinians move toward peace. Do not stand idly by the blood libels of your neighbors.

CONCLUSION
The Contributions Peace Can Make

The Israeli people and the Palestinian people are among the most innovative, creative, and energetic in the world. Unfortunately for them, as well as for the world at large, these talents have been diverted over the past century to ongoing strife. The peace dividend that could accompany the end of this tragic conflict is virtually limitless.

Because of the ever-present threats to Israel, both external and internal, that nation has developed one of the most high-tech military establishments in the world. From sophisticated robotics to state-of-the-art military software and hardware, Israel has devoted enormous resources—intellectual as well as financial—to technologies designed to prevent terrorism and assure military superiority against external enemies. Existential necessity has surely been the mother of military invention. Some of Israel's most innovative scientists have gotten their start in the military and have then turned the knowledge they honed in the army into nonmilitary technologies that have benefited world health, the environment, agriculture, computers, and other causes and businesses.

Imagine how much more these Israeli scientists and technologists could do for humanity if they did not have to place such a high priority on the defense of their country.

Israel has national health insurance, which guarantees health care to all of its citizens, regardless of race or religion. Access to such care has helped Israeli Arabs to enjoy both a longer life expectancy and a lower infant mortality rate than their Arab neighbors. Though life expectancy is somewhat lower for Israeli Arabs than for Israeli Jews—seventy-seven years for women and seventy-four for men rather than eighty and seventy-six respectively—it is still well above that of Syria, which is only in the upper sixties for both. In truth, Israeli health care has likely saved more Palestinian lives than all the care available in many of the neighboring countries combined.

The Israeli economy also creates health benefits beyond its borders. Israel has become a world leader in biotechnology, with Israeli companies leading the way in elements of cancer and autoimmune disease research. There are now more than 160 biotech companies in Israel,[1] with hundreds of millions of private dollars invested, providing thousands of jobs and hundreds of health-improving products—80 percent of which are solely for export. With close ties to Israel's flourishing research universities and educational system, as well as support from the government, Israeli biotech has become industry-leading, providing advances in research on Parkinson's, Alzheimer's, multiple sclerosis, and other diseases that are the cause of great suffering. Now, tragically, it has become the world's leader in the medical treatment of injuries caused by terrorism. Israeli companies and Israeli government research dollars are saving lives both in Israel and abroad, and the same simply cannot be said of any other country in the region despite their much greater share of natural resources. An Israel at peace could contribute more than it does today to lifesaving medical technologies. Even today, despite its engagement in constant conflict, Israeli medical innovations probably save more lives per capita (from a nation whose population is smaller than that of New York City) than do those of any other nation in the world.

In 1996, I met with then King Hussein of Jordan. The Oslo process was still alive and peace seemed possible, if not likely. The king talked excitedly about the prospects for joint medical teams—Israeli, Palestinian, and Jordanian—to bring the best of Israeli medicine to the Arab world. The point often ignored is that Israel has become, through hard work, ingenuity, and, most of all, dedication to freedom and the rule of law, a flourishing and diverse democracy with a bustling economy, a vibrant and critical media, a creative artistic culture, and a commitment to equality based on gender, sexual orientation, and race. Other countries in the region, which have greater natural resources and comparable amounts of foreign aid, have failed to translate these assets into benefits to their people and others. Moreover, the relatively strong Israeli economy materially contributes to the well-being of *all* Israelis, regardless of their religion, ethnicity, or race—and the gap between Jewish and non-Jewish Israelis will surely close even more if peace is achieved.

Israel is an educational mecca. Universities and specialized schools of every kind have sprouted up everywhere. Even the Israeli occupation brought with it Palestinian universities that were prohibited during the Egyptian and Jordan occupation of those same areas. Peace can bring with it the prospect of Israeli educational innovations throughout the Middle East.

The Palestinian people thirst for education, for health care, and for a better life. They envy their Arab brothers who live in Israel, despite lingering problems of inequality between Jewish and Arab Israelis. Some of these inequalities are a function, at least in part, of the conflict. For example, many benefits flow from military service, and most Arabs (along with most ultra-Orthodox Jews) do not serve in the army. A real peace could end, or at least reduce, this inequality. Everybody, except those extremists for whom no compromise can be a real peace, will benefit from an end to the hostilities. That is why to be pro-peace and pro–the two-state solution is to be pro-Palestinian *and* pro-Israel.

In *The Case for Israel* I wrote that "I support Israel precisely *because* I am a civil libertarian and a liberal," not despite those values. Similarly, I am pro-peace because I am pro-Israel and pro-Palestinian.

During a speech delivered at the University of Toronto in March 2005, I declared that I was both pro-Israel and pro-Palestine, since I favored the two-state solution, the end of the occupation, and the dismantling of Israeli settlements in areas that will become part of the Palestinian state. There were boos and heckles from anti-Israel extremists who believe that everyone must choose sides in a zero-sum game and that to be pro-Israel necessarily means that one is anti-Palestinian. That is simply not the case. I have always been pro-Palestinian. Since 1967, I have urged Israel to trade captured land for peace, as provided by Security Council Resolution 242, which I helped (in a very small way) to draft. I opposed the building of Israeli settlements since the early 1970s and have been critical of the Israeli occupation of Palestinian population centers. Many Israelis and many American supporters of Israel share these "pro-Palestinian" views. It has not been we who have opposed the establishment of a democratic, peaceful Palestinian state in exchange for peace and the recognition of Israel. That has been the rejectionist Arab states, the rejectionist Palestinian leaders, and those outsiders who are more Palestinian than the Palestinians. It has not been we who have stolen money earmarked for Palestinian health care, education, and infrastructure. That was Yasser Arafat and other corrupt Palestinian politicians who looted the Palestinian treasury to line their own pockets. It was not we who wired Palestinian men, women, and children to blow themselves up with dynamite strapped to their chests. That was Hamas, Islamic Jihad, the Al-Aqsa Martyrs Brigades, and other Islamic extremists who have incited and legitimated suicide bombing. It was not we who turned down the Clinton-Barak offer of Palestinian statehood in 2000 and 2001. That was the late Yasser Arafat. It was not we who have preached hatred to our children, kept "refugees" and their descendants in horrible camps, and misled them into believing that soon they will march triumphantly "back" to Haifa and Jerusalem. That too was the Palestinian leadership and their supporters.

The primary difference between pro-Israel and anti-Israel advocates is that most of the former are also pro-Palestinian, whereas many of the latter are more interested in the destruction of Israel than in the creation of a democratic Palestinian state living in peace with a democratic Israel. It is telling that a new book by a virulently anti-Israel academic named Michael Neumann is entitled *The Case against Israel*, rather than *The Case for Palestine*.

The important change that now seems to be occurring within some elements of the Palestinian Authority, though not yet among many European and American supporters of Palestinians, is that these Palestinians do not see support for reasonable Palestinian aspirations as inconsistent with support for reasonable Israeli aspirations. This is a positive development.

The road to peace will be long, difficult, tedious, and full of pitfalls and stumbling blocks. But peace is not impossible, as Noam Chomsky pessimistically asserts. It is only impossible for those who refuse to compromise.

In this book I have purposely tried to avoid getting bogged down in the logistics of my own "ideal" peace agreement. My project here has not been to micromanage a peace accord. There are two reasons for this. First, it is not my place to identify the exact timetable, territory, and compensation bargains best suited to a permanent agreement.[2] Israelis and Palestinians alone have the right to set the exact negotiation parameters; the particulars belong to the participants. Second, the basic outline is already apparent. Peace will involve partition, supplemented with mutual respect by Israelis and Palestinians for each other's lives and each other's ways of life. It will also require the normalization of Israel—the end to demonization, delegitimation, and discrimination—by the international community, far-left academics, and bigoted religious leaders.

In the past I have written that *The Case for Israel* is not an argument that cuts along a left-right divide. The same holds true for *The Case for Peace*. Whether the American administration is Democratic or Republican, whether the Israeli coalition forms around Labor or Likud, history has shown that peace-loving liberals and conservatives alike will expend limitless resources and take brave risks for a just peace. Peace is an argument made by men and women of goodwill and tolerance, some tough-minded, some conciliatory.

In the end, the case for peace is really a case for self-determination and security. It is a case for democracy and human rights and a robust rule of law. It is also a case for continuity—one that will allow two distinct ethnicities with rich histories and cultures to command their own affairs and destinies. Peace is both a radical and a traditional solution.

The case for peace is a hope for two homelands, side by side and prospering, with mutual respect for democratic governance and an enduring season of *shalom* and *salaam*.

NOTES

Introduction: The Case for Peace

1. Lorenz Jäger, "Schlägerschatten. Folter, noch einmal: Wolffsohn, Dershowitz und Israel," *Frankfurter Allgemeine Zeitung*, June 18, 2004, p. 35 (translated from the German).
2. "Justice for Palestine? Noam Chomsky interviewed by Stephen R. Shalom and Justin Podur," March 30, 2004, www.chomsky.info/interviews/20040330.htm.
3. Chomsky lecture, Harvard University, November 25, 2002.
4. Noam Chomsky, *Keine Chance für den Frieden. Warum mit Israel und den USA kein Palästinenserstaat zu Machen Ist* [No chance for peace: why it is impossible to establish a Palestinian state with Israel and the U.S.] (Hamburg: Europa Verlag, 2005).
5. "Abbas Wins a Popular Mandate; the Palestinian Presidential Vote," *Economist.com*, January 14, 2005.
6. James Bennet, "The Interregnum," *New York Times*, March 13, 2005.

Introduction to Part I

1. Imam Achmad Cassiem, "Zionist Israel: Hypocrisy Has No Limits," Radio 786, May 23, 2002, accessible at www.radio786.co.za/news/analysis/articles.asp?id=3&pv=1.

CHAPTER 1
The End Result: Two States with Secure and Recognized Borders

1. Bill Clinton, quoted in "Clinton Defends Decision Not to Strike at Bin Ladin Compound," *PR Newswire*, February 5, 2002.
2. Dennis Ross, *The Missing Peace* (New York: Farrar, Straus and Giroux, 2004), p. 779.
3. Marwan Jilani, quoted in Matthew Gutman, "Geneva Pact Seeks Limelight," *Jerusalem Post*, January 7, 2004, p. 3.
4. See, for example, Mark Silva, "Bush Tells Sharon to Stick to Peace Plan," *Chicago Tribune*, April 12, 2005.
5. Ibrahim Barzak, "Hamas Supporters Vow to End Cease-Fire If Jewish Extremists March on Mosque Compound," *Associated Press*, April 8, 2005.
6. See Alan Dershowitz, *Why Terrorism Works* (New Haven, CT: Yale University Press, 2002), chapter 2.
7. UN Security Council, Resolution 242, November 22, 1967. Emphasis added.
8. See Michael Oren, *Six Days of War* (Oxford, UK: Oxford University Press, 2002), pp. 325–26.
9. Both the French and Arabic versions of the resolution include the definite article, but "the official English-language version" deliberately omitted the word "the." Michael Oren, *Six Days of War*, p. 326.
10. S/PV.1377, November 15, 1967, Security Council Official Records, http://domino.un.org/unispal.nsf/0/faa6138b684a6e8605256724004d8394?OpenDocument.
11. Arthur Goldberg, speech to AIPAC policy conference, May 8, 1973, quoted in Mitchell G. Bard, *Myths and Facts: A Guide to the Arab-Israeli Conflict* (Chevy Chase, MD: American Israeli Cooperative Enterprise, 2002), p. 67.
12. "Corrections," *New York Times*, January 23, 2001.
13. Dennis Ross, *The Missing Peace*, pp. 202–203.
14. Geneva Accords, art. 4.1.i.
15. Steven Erlanger, "Israel, on Its Own, Is Shaping the Borders of the West Bank," *New York Times*, April 19, 2005, p. 10.
16. Ibid.
17. See map in Alan Dershowitz, *The Case for Israel* (Hoboken, NJ: Wiley, 2003), p. 49.

18. Palestine Royal Commission Report (Peel Report) (London: His Majesty's Stationery Office, 1937), pp. 59, 141.
19. Ibid., p. 376.
20. Abba Eban, *Abba Eban: An Autobiography* (New York: Random House, 1977), p. 446.
21. "By signing the Camp David agreement in 1979, Egypt in effect renounced any claim to Gaza, leaving it without any Arab state protector." Thomas L. Friedman, "Mubarak and Hussein Discuss Gaza," *New York Times*, May 23, 1986.
22. Howard M. Sachar, *A History of Israel from the Rise of Zionism to Our Time*, 2d ed. (New York: Knopf, 1996), p. 864.
23. Benny Morris, "The Rejection," *New Republic*, April 21–28, 2003.
24. Alan Dershowitz, *The Case for Israel* (Hoboken, NJ: Wiley, 2003), p. 8.
25. For a description of the Alon Plan, see ibid., pp. 98–99.
26. Ruth R. Wisse, "At Home in Jerusalem," *Commentary*, April 2003; Etgar Lefkovits, "Gilo Residents Await Funds for Bulletproof Windows," *Jerusalem Post*, December 15, 2000. Israel has already officially annexed Gilo through the Jerusalem Law of 1980. Joshua Hammer, "Code Blue in Jerusalem," *Newsweek*, July 1, 2002.
27. Steven Erlanger, "Israel on Its Own, Is Shaping the Borders of the West Bank," *New York Times*, April 19, 2005, p. 10.
28. Ibid.
29. In a 2000 poll conducted by the Arab-Israeli weekly *Kul Al-Arab*, 83 percent of Palestinian residents in Um Al-Fahm opposed the transfer of their city into a Palestinian state. They wanted to remain within the Israeli democracy. Joseph Algazy, "Um Al-Fahm Prefers Israel," *Ha'aretz*, August 1, 2000. For the full text see http://memri.org/bin/articles.cgi?Page=countries&Area=israel&ID=SP11700; see also Yossi Klein Halevi, "Umm El Fahm Dispatch: Benign Neglect," *New Republic*, February 23, 2004.
30. Yossi Klein Halevi, "The Pattern of Palestinian Rejectionism," *Jerusalem Post*, July 9, 2004.
31. As Michael B. Oren and Yossi Klein Halevi reported in their article "Fantasy" in the *New Republic*, December 15, 2003:
    Geneva undermines these objectives by rewarding terrorism, compromising democratic norms, and strengthening dictatorial rule. Consider the trajectory of concessions offered by the Israeli left. At the Camp David talks in 2000, the Barak government proffered 92 percent of the West Bank. When the Palestinians rejected that offer and responded with terrorism, Ehud Barak proceeded to up the offer to 96 percent. When that, too, was rejected and terrorism intensified, a part of the Israeli left proceeded to negotiate what became the Geneva Accord, which is willing to forfeit all of the territories, the Temple Mount, the ability of Israel to defend itself, and Israel's inviolate opposition to the Palestinians' right of return. The trajectory was not lost on Mamdouh Nowfal, Arafat's military adviser, who told Jordan's *Al Rai*, "What was proposed at Taba was better than what was proposed at Camp David, but what was proposed at Geneva is twice the progress."
32. Steven Erlanger, "For Arabs Uneasy Calm, Little Hope for Lasting Peace," *New York Times*, February 13, 2005, p. 10.
33. Ibid.
34. Ibid.
35. Anne Bayefsky, "Never Again?" *National Review*, January 27, 2005.
36. James S. Tisch, "Human Rights, UN-Style," *Jerusalem Post*, April 14, 2005.
37. The current situation is better reflected by the joke about the American minister who goes to the Biblical Zoo in Jerusalem and is astounded to see in one enclosure a wolf and a lamb. "I must tell you how wonderful this is," he exclaims to the director. "Here we are in this violent land. Yet I see, as the biblical prophecy has it, a wolf and a lamb lying down together. How do you do it?" The director shrugs. "Easy. Every morning we toss in another lamb."
38. Amos Oz, *Israel, Palestine, and Peace* (New York: Vintage, 1994), p. 113.

CHAPTER 2

Is the One-State Solution a Barrier to Peace?

1. Tony Judt, "Israel: The Alternative," *New York Review of Books*, October 23, 2003.
2. Leon Wieseltier, "Israel, Palestine, and the Return of the Bi-National Fantasy. What Is Not to Be Done," *New Republic*, October 27, 2003, p. 20.
3. Amos Oz, *Israel, Palestine, and Peace* (New York: Vintage, 1994), p. 17.
4. "One thinks at once of Yugoslavia, where in the course of a successful social revolution, the old conflict-provoking ethnic ties (Serb, Croat, and so forth) give some evidence of being less 'irrational' and less binding, with more individuals thereby willing to think of themselves quite simply as individuals operating within a broad Yugoslav context." Noam Chomsky, *Middle East Illusions* (Lanham, MD: Rowman & Littlefield, 2003), p. 62 (quoting George Zaninovich, *Development of Socialist Yugoslavia* [Baltimore: Johns Hopkins University Press, 1968], p. 105).
5. Michael Tarazi, "Two Peoples, One State," *New York Times*, October 4, 2004.
6. Tony Judt, "Israel: The Alternative," *New York Review of Books*, October 23, 2003.
7. For a description of Prince Bandar's criticism of Arafat, see Alan Dershowitz, *The Case for Israel* (Hoboken, NJ: Wiley, 2003), pp. 118–120.
8. Dennis Ross, *The Missing Peace* (New York: Farrar, Straus and Giroux, 2004), p. 758.
9. Tony Judt, "Israel: The Alternative," *New York Review of Books*, October 23, 2003.
10. Leon Wieseltier, "Israel, Palestine, and the Return of the Bi-National Fantasy. What Is Not to Be Done," *New Republic*, October 27, 2003.
11. Israelis overwhelmingly support the endurance of Israel as a Jewish state. According to a 2003 poll conducted by the Tami Steinmetz Center for Peace Research of Tel Aviv University, only 6 percent of Israelis support a one-state solution, while 78 percent favor a two-state solution. Palestinians, likewise, aspire to self-determination free of demographic competition with Jews. They too are largely opposed to the one-state solution. Of those polled, 75.5 percent prefer the two-state solution, with only 7 percent advocating a binational combination. Ephraim Yaar and Tamar Hermann, "The Peace Index/Israeli Jews Fret Over Possibility of a Binational State," *Ha'aretz*, May 11, 2003.
12. The Ramallah-based Palestinian Center for Policy and Survey Research found that "a majority of Palestinians view the structure of the democratic regime in Israel as a model that they would like to institute in a future Palestinian state." Khaled Abu Toameh, "Palestinians Want Democracy 'Like Israel,'" *Jerusalem Post*, June 8, 2004.
13. See Daniel Pipes, "The Hell of Israel Is Better Than the Paradise of Arafat," *Middle East Quarterly*, spring 2005. See also Joseph Algazy, "Um Al-Fahm Prefers Israel," *Ha'aretz*, August 1, 2000.
14. Edward Rothstein, "Seeking an Alternative to a Jewish State," *New York Times*, November 22, 2003.
15. See Dershowitz, *The Case for Israel*, pp. 42–43 (recounting the Hebron massacre of 1929) and pp. 88–89 (describing in detail Jewish treatment in Arab nations following Israeli independence, culminating in the creation of 850,000 Jewish refugees); Michael Oren, *Six Days of War: June 1967 and the Making of the Modern Middle East* (Oxford, UK: Oxford University Press, 2002), pp. 3–4 (the 1936–1939 Arab pogrom against Jews in Palestine, Baghdad, Cairo, Tunis, and Casablanca), pp. 306–7 (cataloging the expulsion and pogroms of Jews in Arab countries following the Six-Day War).
16. Benny Morris, "Politics by Other Means," *New Republic*, March 22, 2004.
17. Ibid.
18. David Frum, "The Alternative," *National Review Online*, www.nationalreview.com/frum/diary101403.asp.
19. Michael Walzer, "An Alternative Future: An Exchange," *New York Review of Books*, December 4, 2003.

CHAPTER 3

Is a Noncontiguous Palestinian State a Barrier to Peace?

1. Edward Said, "We Know Who 'We' Are," *London Review of Books*, October 17, 2002.
2. Noam Chomsky, "The Solution Is the Problem: The US Presents Itself as the Peace-Broker in the Middle East. The Reality Is Different," *Guardian* (London), May 11, 2002.
3. Deborah Sontag, "And Yet So Far: A Special Report; Quest for Mideast Peace: How and Why It Failed," *New York Times*, July 26, 2001.
4. Dennis B. Ross, "Yasir Arafat; Think Again," *Foreign Policy*, July 1, 2002.
5. "Discussion with Former U.S. Envoy to Middle East Dennis Ross; A Discussion with Former Senator Gary Hart—Part 1," *Charlie Rose Show* transcripts, August 17, 2004.
6. Justin Lonergan, "Connecting the West Bank and Gaza Strip: Questions of 'Safe Passage,'" Macro Center at Roger Williams University Web page, http://macrocenter.rwu.edu/2004/briefingpapers/paper4.htm.
7. Miguel Moratinos, "Moratinos Documents," published in *Ha'aretz*, February 14, 2002.
8. Steven Erlanger, "Israel, on Its Own, Is Shaping the Borders of the West Bank," *New York Times*, April 19, 2005, p. 10.
9. Other such nations include Brunei, Malaysia, Oman, Uzbekistan, Russia, and Turkey.
10. Bret Stephens, "The Inevitability Myth," *Jerusalem Post*, August 27, 2004.
11. Palestine Royal Commission Report (Peel Report) (London: His Majesty's Stationery Office, 1937), p. 385.
12. Bret Stephens, "Toilets in the Sand," *Jerusalem Post*, September 3, 2004, p. 24.
13. Bret Stephens, "The Inevitability Myth."
14. Ibid.
15. James Bennet, "The Day after Peace: Designing Palestine," *New York Times*, May 15, 2005.

CHAPTER 4

Can Peace Be Achieved without Compromising Rights?

1. Hamas Charter, 1988, accessible at www.palestinecenter.org/cpap/documents/charter.html.
2. Amos Oz, *Israel, Palestine, and Peace* (London: Vintage, 1994), p. 120.
3. Thomas L. Friedman, *From Beirut to Jerusalem* (New York: Doubleday, 1995), p. 555.
4. Quoted in Leslie Susser, "Days of Rage," *Jerusalem Report*, March 21, 2005.
5. Ina Friedman, "'No One Is Obligated to Accept a Rabbinical Opinion,'" *Jerusalem Report*, July 28, 2003.
6. See Mary Ann Glendon, *Rights Talk: The Impoverishment of Political Discourse* (New York: Free Press, 1991).
7. Amos Oz, *Israel, Palestine and Peace*, p. 102.
8. *Beirut Telegraph*, August 6, 1948, quoted in Joan Peters, *From Time Immemorial: The Origins of the Arab-Jewish Conflict over Palestine* (New York, Harper & Row, 1984), p. 13.
9. Dewey Anderson, et al., "Arab Refugee Problem and How It Can Be Solved," proposals submitted to the United Nations General Assembly, December 1951, p. 77, citing *Al-Misri*, October 11, 1949, quoted in Peters, p. 22.
10. *Al Nahar* (Beirut), May 15, 1975, quoted in Peters, p. 30.
11. Dan Fisher, "Death, Rebirth of a Kibbutz Recalled; Joy and Sorrow: Israelis Mark 40th Anniversary," *Los Angeles Times*, April 21, 1988.
12. *Al Nahar* (Beirut), May 15, 1975, quoted in Peters, pp. 29–30.
13. William Safire, "On Language," *New York Times Magazine*, April 17, 2005.

CHAPTER 5

Is the Division of Jerusalem a Barrier to Peace?

1. Etgar Lefkovitz, "Sharansky Denies Bush Plan Includes Call to Divide Jerusalem," *Jerusalem Post*, October 17, 2001.

2. Churchill to diplomat Evelyn Shuckburgh, 1955, *Descent to Suez: Diaries 1951–1956* (London: Weidenfeld and Nicolson, 1986), quoted in Jewish Virtual Library, www.jewishvirtuallibrary.org/jsource/Quote/jeruq.html.

3. "Palestinian Negotiator on the Jerusalem Issue," *Al-Hayat* (London), September 26, 1999, MEMRI Special Dispatch Series—No. 47.

4. "East Jerusalem and the Holy Places at the Camp David Summit," *Kul Al-Arab*, August 18, 2000, MEMRI Special Dispatch Series—No. 121.

5. "Abu Mazen Discusses Jerusalem and the Refugees," *Al-Hayat* (London-Beirut), November 23, 2000, MEMRI Special Dispatch Series—No. 157.

6. According to *Ha'aretz* in 2001, "The population of Jerusalem is 657,900; 444,900 Jews (68 percent) and 201,300 Arabs (31.1 percent)." "The Facts on Jerusalem in 2001," *Ha'aretz*, May 21, 2001. The next year, *USA Today* reported, "City statistics show about 200,000 Palestinians and 200,000 Jews live in East Jerusalem. The population of East and West Jerusalem combined is about 600,000, two-thirds Jewish." Vivienne Walt, "Homes Built in the Way of Division in Jerusalem," *USA Today*, June 12, 2002. Two years later, in the *Jerusalem Post*: "At the end of 2003, 67 percent of Jerusalem's 693,000 residents were Jewish, and the remaining 33% were Arab, according to the Statistical Yearbook of Jerusalem put out by the Jerusalem Institute for Israel Studies." Etgar Lefkovitz, "Capital's Jewish Population Slides," *Jerusalem Post*, September 3, 2004.

7. Dennis Ross confirmed Clinton's strong views on this matter:

    Since we would be discussing the options on the Haram, I anticipated that Arafat might well again declare that the Temple—the most sacred place in Jewish tradition—did not exist in Jerusalem but was in Nablus. I did not want to turn this issue into Arafat the Muslim debating me the Jew. I wanted Gamal [Helal, special adviser and translator], a Christian of Coptic origin who was originally from Egypt, to tell Arafat that this was an outrageous attempt to delegitimize the Israeli connection to Jerusalem. Gamal was happy to take on this role. . . .

    What ensued surprised even me. Gamal started very politely, suggesting to Arafat that whatever his personal views, the one core premise of any process must be that one side did not question the religious faith of the other side. But Arafat would not back down, telling Gamal that he knew nothing of religion, whereas he (the Chairman) was an expert on all religions, especially on Judaism, and the Temple did not exist in Jerusalem. They began to argue, and Gamal said if the Jews believe the Temple existed in Jerusalem, then for our purposes it existed in Jerusalem.

    Finally, after nearly ten minutes of increasing invective, I intervened and said, "Mr. Chairman, regardless of what you think, the President of the United States *knows* that the Temple existed in Jerusalem. If he hears you denying its existence there, he will never again take you seriously. My advice to you is never raise this view again in his presence."

    Arafat may not have been willing to engage on any of the four options on the Haram, but he stopped his argument with Gamal and never again raised his myth on the Temple in either the President's presence or mine. (Of course, that did not prevent him from raising it with countless others.)

    Dennis Ross, *The Missing Peace* (New York: Farrar, Straus and Giroux, 2004), p. 718.

8. Jeff Jacoby, "Slice Up Jerusalem? Unthinkable!" *Boston Globe*, January 4, 2001. See also the following editorial from the *Weekly Standard*:

    Among the many myths propagated by the Arabs are that there is such a thing as a "Palestinian nation" (it's a concept that is not more than 40 years old); that the Israelis (Jews) are "occupiers" (if they were, who would be the sovereign that they displaced?); that Jerusalem is Islam's "third holiest city" (it's never once mentioned in the Koran, but hundreds of times in the Jewish Bible); the transformation of the age-old provinces of Judea/Samaria into the "West Bank"; the concept of "settlements" (with its connotation of illegality); and much more.

    "You Deserve a Factual Look at . . . the So-Called 'Peace Process'; Does It Lead Down the Road to Another Holocaust?" *Weekly Standard*, March 1, 1999.

9. Harold B. Shugar, "Aksa Mosque No Basis for Muslim Holy City Claim," *Albany Times Union*, March 8, 2001.

10. Dennis Ross, *The Missing Peace*, p. 655.
11. Ibid., p. 686.
12. Based on an article by Ben Caspit in *Ma'ariv*, July 27, 2000. The list is found at the online Jewish Virtual Library, www.jewishvirtuallibrary.org/jsource/Peace/jerdivide.html.
13. Dennis Ross, *The Missing Peace*, p. 694.
14. Ibid., p. 803.
15. Ibid., p. 723.
16. Ibid., p. 803.
17. From Elsa Walsh, "The Prince: How the Saudi Ambassador Became Washington's Indispensable Operator," *New Yorker*, March 24, 2003:

    On January 2, 2001, Bandar picked up Arafat at Andrews Air Force Base and reviewed the plan with him. "Did he think he could get a better deal?" Bandar asked. "Did he prefer Sharon to Barak?" he continued, referring to the upcoming election in Israel. "Of course not," Arafat replied. Barak's negotiators were doves, Bandar went on, and said, "Since 1948, every time we've had something on the table we say no. Then we say yes. When we say yes, it's not on the table anymore. Then we have to deal with something less. Isn't it about time we say yes?" Bandar added, "We've always said to the Americans, 'Our red line is Jerusalem. You get us a deal that's O.K. on Jerusalem and we're going, too.'"

    Arafat said that he understood, but still Bandar issued something of an ultimatum: "Let me tell you one more time. You have only two choices. Either you take this deal or we go to war. If you take this deal, we will all throw our weight behind you. If you don't take this deal, do you think anybody will go to war for you?" Arafat was silent. Bandar continued, "Let's start with the big country, Egypt. You think Egypt will go to war with you?" Arafat had had his problems with Egypt, too. No, he said. "I'll prove it to you, just to confirm," Bandar went on. Bandar called the Egyptian Ambassador. Bandar reported that the Egyptian Ambassador, who was to join them shortly, was willing to support the peace process. "Is Jordan going to go to war? Syria go to war? So, Mr. Arafat, what are you losing?" . . .

    Bandar believed that the White House had hurt its cause by not pressing an ultimatum. Arafat, though, was committing a crime against the Palestinians—in fact, against the entire region. If it weren't so serious, Bandar thought, it would be a comedy. He returned to Arafat's room and sat down, trying to remember: "Make your words soft and sweet." Bandar began, "Mr. President, I want to be sure now. You're telling me you struck a deal?" When Arafat said it was so, Bandar, still hiding his fury, offered his congratulations. His wife and children were waiting for him in Aspen, he said, and he wanted to go. Bandar could see the life draining out of Arafat. He started to leave, then turned around. "I hope you remember, sir, what I told you. If we lose this opportunity, it is not going to be a tragedy. This is going to be a crime." When Bandar looked at Arafat's staff, their faces showed incredulity.

18. Under a decision by the Supreme Court of Israel, an area of the wall is supposed to be set aside for prayer by men and women together, which is today prohibited at the prayer section of the wall.

CHAPTER 6
Are the Informal Geneva Accords a Basis for or a Barrier to Peace?

1. "Noted & Quoted; Soundbites," *New York Times*, January 12, 2004.
2. Ravi Nessman, "'Geneva Accord' Touted at Ceremony," *New York Sun*, December 2, 2003.
3. Ibid.
4. Ibid.
5. Bill Clinton, "Citizens Show Peace Is Possible," *USA Today*, December 4, 2003.
6. Marc Levine, "A Problematic Peace Plan," accessible at www.israelforum.com/board/archive/index.php/t-4344.html.
7. Prime Minister Ariel Sharon's Address at the Opening of the Knesset Winter

Session, accessible at www.embassyofisrael.org/articles/2003/October/2003102000
.htm.

8. Most troubling to many was the accord's failure to commit the Palestinian negotiators to abandon a full right of return:

> So, while Israel is to tangibly repudiate its claim to Greater Israel by removing settlements, the Palestinians under Geneva aren't even obliged to verbally renounce their claim to Greater Palestine. "The assertion that the Accord cancels the right of return . . . is inaccurate," Palestinian signatory Jamal Zaqout recently wrote, "It was spread by Israeli figures trying to make the document more palatable to Israelis." Zaqout is correct: The Accord cites both the Saudi peace plan for the Middle East and U.N. resolution 194, both of which say that refugees should return to Israel. So, while the Accord does recognize "the right of the Jewish people to statehood" (without saying that Israel is the fulfillment of that right), that concession is effectively nullified by the implicit endorsement of the right of return, which would make Jewish statehood untenable.

Michael B. Oren and Yossi Klein Halevi, "Fantasy," *New Republic*, December 15, 2003.

9. Bret Stephens, "Talk about Force," *Jerusalem Post*, September 24, 2004, p. 19.
10. As Michael Oren and Yossi Klein Halevi put it:

> Geneva undermines these objectives by rewarding terrorism, compromising democratic norms, and strengthening dictatorial rule. Consider the trajectory of concessions offered by the Israeli left. At the Camp David talks in 2000, the Barak government proffered 92 percent of the West Bank. When the Palestinians rejected that offer and responded with terrorism, Ehud Barak proceeded to up the offer to 96 percent. When that, too, was rejected and terrorism intensified, a part of the Israeli left proceeded to negotiate what became the Geneva Accord, which is willing to forfeit all of the territories, the Temple Mount, the ability of Israel to defend itself, and Israel's inviolate opposition to the Palestinians' right of return. The trajectory was not lost on Mamdouh Nowfal, Arafat's military adviser, who told Jordan's Al Rai, "What was proposed at Taba was better than what was proposed at Camp David, but what was proposed at Geneva is twice the progress."

Michael B. Oren and Yossi Klein Halevi, "Fantasy," *New Republic*, December 15, 2003.

11. Thomas L. Friedman, "Suicidal Lies," *New York Times*, March 31, 2002, p. 9.
12. The columnist Bret Stephens is less solicitous toward private peace agreements. He wrote:

> Procedurally, Geneva was a flagrant attempt by private citizens to usurp the elected Israeli government's exclusive right to conduct the country's foreign policy. In the United States, there's a law against that: It's called the Logan Act, and it's been on the books since 1798. No such law exists in Israel, so Beilin did nothing technically wrong. Then again, if Israel were so eager for his medicine, it probably would have found a space for him in the Knesset.

Bret Stephens, "Talk About Farce," *Jerusalem Post*, September 24, 2004.

Commentary magazine took a similar stance: "This is extraordinary. It is as if an American citizen, say, for instance, Al Gore or Pat Buchanan, were to negotiate with an Iraqi confidant of Saddam Hussein about the American-Iraqi relationship." "You Deserve a Factual Look at . . . the 'Geneva Accord': Is It the Way to Lasting Peace in the Middle East or to Disaster?" *Commentary*, February 1, 2004.

13. See the epigraphs beginning chapter 3.

CHAPTER 7
Can Israel Make Peace and Prevent Terrorism at the Same Time?

1. Clyde Haberman, "Eye on the Ball for Israel; Peace and Terror: Search for Balance," *New York Times*, April 1, 1993.
2. Michael Freund, "When Sharon Meets Bush," *Jerusalem Post*, October 16, 2002.
3. Ed Koch, "Keep American Troops out of Israel," *Jewish World Review*, June 18, 2003.
4. Cam Simpson, "Rice Praises Restraint after Blast in Israel; Calmness Following Suicide Attack Friday Called Positive Sign," *Chicago Tribune*, March 1, 2005.

5. Benny Morris, *Righteous Victims: A History of the Zionist-Arab Conflict, 1881–1999* (New York: Knopf, 1999), p. 636.
6. Ibid.
7. Ibid.
8. Quoted in Alan Dershowitz, *Why Terrorism Works* (New Haven, CT: Yale University Press, 2002), p. 79. "A few days after the failure of the Camp David summit in July 2000, the Palestinian Authority's monthly magazine, *Al-Shuhada* (*The Martyrs*), published the following letter on July 25: 'From the negotiating delegation at Camp David, led by the commander and symbol, Abu Ammar (Yasser Arafat) to the brave Palestinian people, be prepared. The Battle for Jerusalem has begun.'" Khaled Abu Toamech, "How the War Began," *Jerusalem Post*, September 20, 2002.
9. Ibrahim Barzak, "Hamas Backers Threaten to End Truce," *Boston Globe*, April 9, 2005, p. A4.
10. Megan K. Stack, "Israel Widens Fight, Bombs Camp in Syria; An Airstrike against a Suspected Terrorist Compound Signals a Willingness to Retaliate across Borders and Sparks Mideast Outrage," *Los Angeles Times*, October 6, 2003.
11. Egyptian president Mubarak remarked, "We condemn what happened today concerning the aggression against a brotherly state under the pretext that some organizations exist there." German chancellor Gerhard Schröder said regional peace efforts "become more complicated when . . . the sovereignty of a country is violated. This is why the action in Syria is not acceptable." Finally, "U.S. Ambassador John Negroponte said he and other U.S. officials have repeatedly made clear to Syria that its support of terrorist groups is 'unacceptable and intolerable.'" "Syria Asks U.N. to Condemn Israel," *CNN.com*, October 6, 2003.
12. Greg Myre, "Arab Slain by Israeli Troops; Abbas Calls It Truce Violation," *New York Times*, April 15, 2005.
13. Steven Erlanger, "Israel Vows Tough Stance with Restraint, in Gaza," *New York Times*, May 20, 2005.
14. Thomas L. Friedman, "Expanding Club NATO," *New York Times*, October 23, 2003.
15. Thomas L. Friedman, "How About Sending NATO Somewhere Important?" *New York Times*, September 3, 2001.
16. Thomas L. Friedman, "Go Slow-Mo, NATO," *New York Times*, December 11, 2002.
17. Martin Indyk, "A Trusteeship for Palestine?" *Foreign Affairs*, May–June 2003.
18. Ibid.
19. Ibid.
20. Indyk addressed this concern by noting, "The notion that Israel cannot accept foreign forces defending its citizens is belied by the fact that in 1991 and again in 2003 Israel welcomed American Patriot antimissile teams to help defend it from an Iraqi attack." This is hardly satisfactory. It is unlikely to persuade Israeli moderates, many of whom believe that Israel's restraint in 1991 was taken as a sign of its weakness.
21. Quoted in Jonathan S. Tobin, "Quagmire: Keep Out," *Jerusalem Post*, September 4, 2003.
22. Bill Sammon, "U.S. Troops' Role in Mideast Dismissed; Bush Urges Sides to Unite to Fight Terror," *Washington Post*, June 17, 2003.
23. Dana Milbank, "Bush Still Hopeful on Mideast Peace; President Blames Hamas for Violence," *Washington Post*, June 16, 2003.
24. Bill Sammon, "U.S. Troops' Role in Mideast Dismissed; Bush Urges Sides to Unite to Fight Terror," *Washington Post*, June 17, 2003.
25. The full text of the Geneva Accords may be found at www.haaretz.com/hasen/pages/ShArt.jhtml?itemNo=351461.

CHAPTER 8

Are Israeli Counterterrorism Measures the Cause
of Suicide Bombings and a Barrier to Peace?

1. Reporter Hilary Brown, "Israel's Policy of Targeted Assassinations Favored in Israel, Condemned Abroad," ABC News *Nightline*, August 2, 2001.

2. Gil Hoffman and Janine Zacharia (Melissa Radler contributing), "Sharon to Powell: Targeted Killings Will Continue," *Jerusalem Post*, August 2, 2001.
3. Joshua Muravchik, "EU v. Hamas," *National Review*, April 27, 2004.
4. Alan Dershowitz, "Killing Terrorist Chieftains Is Legal," *Jerusalem Post*, April 23, 2004.
5. Gil Hoffman and Janine Zacharia (Melissa Radler contributing), "Sharon to Powell: Targeted Killings Will Continue," *Jerusalem Post*, August 2, 2001.
6. Patrick W. Higgins, "Netanyahu: 'I Want to Talk about a Real Peace,'" *University Wire*, April 23, 2002.
7. Gil Hoffman and Janine Zacharia (Melissa Radler contributing), "Sharon to Powell: Targeted Killings Will Continue," *Jerusalem Post*, August 2, 2001.
8. Neil MacFarquhar, "Saudis Support a Jihad in Iraq, Not Back Home," *New York Times*, April 23, 2004.
9. Ibid.
10. Adam Karatnycky, "Murder and Martyrdom," *Wall Street Journal*, April 19, 2002.
11. David Remnick, "Rage and Reason: Will Anyone Listen to the P.L.O.'s Voice of Restraint?" *New Yorker*, May 6, 2002.
12. Patrick E. Tyler and Don van Natta Jr., "Militants in Europe Openly Call for Jihad and the Rule of Islam," *New York Times*, April 26, 2004.
13. Charles A. Radin, "Courier, 11, Seen as Pawn in Mideast Terror: Boy Was Unaware He Carried a Bomb," *Boston Globe*, March 17, 2004.
14. Ibid.
15. Jonathan Wells, Jack Meyers, Maggie Mulvihill, and Kevin Wisniewski, "Radical Islam; Outspoken Cleric, Jailed Activist Tied to New Hub Mosque," *Boston Herald*, October 28, 2003.
16. "Embassy of Israel Briefing: Palestinian Exploitation of Children," United Jewish Communities: The Federation of North America, January 21, 2003, www.ujc.org/content_display.html?ArticleID=69109.
17. Alan M. Dershowitz, *The Case for Israel* (Hoboken, NJ: Wiley, 2003), p. 184, discussing Israel's Supreme Court decision.
18. Greg Myre, "Putin Visits Israel and Tries to Allay Its Security Worries," *New York Times*, April 29, 2005.
19. Basic Law: The Knesset (Amendment No. 9), www.knesset.gov.il/laws/special/eng/basic2_eng.htm.
20. As Raphael Cohen Almagor points out in his article "Disqualification of Political Parties in Israel: 1988–1996," "Meir Kahane justifies his position by advancing the idea that the Torah commands the Jews to separate themselves from the non-Jews. It is important to recognize that it is this type of religious argument that needs to be marginalized for the peace process to move forward." Raphael Cohen Almagor, "Disqualification of Political Parties in Israel: 1988–1996," www.law.emory.edu/EILR/volumes/spg97/ALMAGOR.html. Almagor cites Sections 144 (A–E) of Penal Law, Amendment No. 20 (1986).
21. Ibid.
22. Ibid.
23. Bureau of Democracy, Human Rights, and Labor, "Israel and the occupied territories: Country Reports on Human Rights Practices—2003," February 25, 2004, accessible at the U.S. Department of State Web site, www.state.gov/g/drl/rls/hrrpt/2003/27929.htm#occterr.
24. Eight European Union countries currently outlaw Holocaust denial: Germany, Austria, Poland, the Netherlands, Belgium, Spain, and Switzerland. John Sack, "Inside the Bunker; In-Depth Look at Those Who Deny the Holocaust," *Esquire*, February 1, 2001.
25. "Palestinian Paper Publishes Latest PNA Draft Constitution, Proposed Alternatives," *BBC Monitoring International Reports*, February 1, 2003.
26. "Voices of Hatred," *Canada Post*, May 17, 2005.
27. "Palestinians Remove Hate Text from Web Site," Reuters, May 19, 2005.

CHAPTER 9

What If a Palestinian State Became a Launching Pad for Terrorism?

1. Uri Dan, "Yasser Feels Ariel's Angry Boot Again," *New York Post*, August 12, 2001.
2. *Al-Arabi* (Egypt), June 24, 2001, translated in "Faysal Al-Husseini in His Last Interview: The Oslo Accords Were a Trojan Horse; The Strategic Goal Is the Liberation of Palestine from the [Jordan] River to the [Mediterranean] Sea," MEMRI Special Dispatch Series—No. 236.
3. Caroline Glick, "The Problem Is with the People," *Jerusalem Post*, June 18, 2002.
4. The Palestinian Center for Policy and Survey Research found the following in a survey conducted March 10–12, 2005:

   - Support for bombing (or suicide) attacks inside Israel drops from 77% last September to 29% in this poll. But support for arrest of the perpetrators of suicide attacks does not exceed 40%.

   - 84% support return to negotiations and 59% prefer a permanent, rather than interim agreement. 59% believe that it is possible to reach a compromise agreement with the Israeli leadership.

   - 59% support the Road Map and 35% oppose it.

   - 79% support the participation of Hamas in the negotiations with Israel while 79% prefer to see more active American involvement in the search for a peace agreement.

     A majority believes that the Oslo peace process failed because Israel was not forthcoming and continued to build Israeli settlements. Similarly, a majority blames Israel for the failure of the Camp David Summit believing the Israeli offer was insufficient.
   PSR Survey Research Unit: Public Opinion Poll #15, March 10–12, 2005, accessible at www.pcpsr.org/survey/polls/2005/p15a.html.
5. Thomas L. Friedman, "Reeling but Ready," *New York Times*, April 28, 2002.

CHAPTER 10

Will Civil Wars Be Necessary to Bring About Peace?

1. Victor Davis Hanson, "As Democracy Spreads, the Noose Tightens," *Chicago Tribune*, March 25, 2005.
2. "Arafat," *New Republic*, November 22, 2004.
3. "Palestinian President Urges Factions to Adhere to Non-Violence," *BBC Worldwide Monitoring*, March 17, 2005.
4. "Abbas Sends in His Men; The New Palestinian Leader Takes Action," *Economist.com*, January 21, 2005.
5. Greg Myre, "Putin Visits Israel and Tries to Allay Its Security Worries," *New York Times*, Friday, April 29, 2005.
6. "Quote Unquote," *Jerusalem Report*, April 18, 2005.
7. Richard W. Stevenson, "Bush Supports Plan by Sharon for a Withdrawal from Gaza," *New York Times*, April 12, 2005.
8. Lee Keath, "Hamas, Islamic Jihad to Halt Attacks on Israel but Reject Long-Term Truce," *Associated Press*, March 17, 2005.
9. Uri Dan, "Dancing with Abbas," *Jerusalem Post*, March 23, 2005.

CHAPTER 11

Is the Security Fence a Barrier to Peace?

1. Rosemary Church, *Q&A with Jim Clancy*, CNN, July 16, 2003.
2. Jay DePapper, anchor, "Senator Chuck Schumer, Democrat of New York, Discusses Foreign Policy as Well as State and National Politics," *News Forum*, WNBC-TV, November 14, 2004.
3. Yossi Klein Halevi, "Reaching beyond the Security Fence," *New Republic*, August 6, 2004.
4. "Politicizing Terrorism," *Nation*, July 10, 2004.

5. Aharon Barak, Supreme Court of Israel, *Beit Sourik Village Council v. 1. The Government of Israel, 2. Commander of the IDF Forces in the West Bank*, accessible at www.jewishvirtuallibrary.org/jsource/Peace/fencesct.html.

6. "Our Very Own Berlin Wall," *Daily Telegraph* (London), February 24, 2004.

7. "Although only about five per cent of the barrier is concrete wall, opponents have dubbed it the 'apartheid wall' and drawn comparisons with racist segregation in South Africa and with the Berlin Wall." Toby Harnden, "Sharon to Boycott UN Court Hearing on Security Barrier," *Daily Telegraph* (London), February 13, 2004. "While the barrier is monotonously called a wall by Palestinian advocates, almost all of it will be a chain-link fence—much like the one the UN has recently announced its intention to build to protect its Manhattan headquarters. Exceptions are 30-foot-high concrete sections, totaling about fifteen of the barrier's 400 miles (or less than 4 percent), being built to block three areas where Palestinian snipers have shot at cars traveling on the trans-Israel highway." Andrew C. McCarthy, "The End of the Right of Self-Defense? Israel, the World Court, and the War on Terror," *Commentary*, November 1, 2004. See also Joshua Brilliant, "Palestinians Agree on Truce," UPI, February 8, 2005; Ben Thein, "Is Israel's Security Barrier Unique?" *Middle East Quarterly*, Fall 2004; Martin Sieff, "Sharon, Abbas, Angels of Peace?," UPI, February 9, 2005; Andrew Levin, "Another NPR Winter of Distortion," *Jerusalem Post*, March 25, 2005.

8. As the Yom Kippur War came to a close, the U.S. secretary of state, along with the Soviet Union, proposed a cease-fire resolution that would become UN Security Council Resolution 338 (October 22, 1973). Part 2 of Resolution 338 "calls upon all parties concerned to start immediately after the cease-fire the implementation of Security Council Resolution 242 (1967) in all of its parts."

9. "Exchange of Letters between PM Sharon and President Bush," Israel Ministry of Foreign Affairs, April 14, 2004, www.mfa.gov.il/MFA/Peace+Process/Reference+Documents/Exchange+of+letters+Sharon-Bush+14-Apr-2004.htm.

10. Andrew C. McCarthy, "The End of the Right of Self-Defense? Israel, the World Court, and the War on Terror," *Commentary*, November 1, 2004.

11. Eric A. Posner, "All Justice, Too, Is Local," *New York Times*, December 30, 2004, p. 23.

12. See Jonathan L. Snow, "Backgrounder: Security Fences around the World," the Foundation for the Defense of Democracies, February 23, 2004, accessible at www.defenddemocracy.org/publications/publications_show.htm?doc_id=211945. The Foundation for the Defense of Democracies is a nonpartisan and nonprofit think tank dedicated to fighting terrorism. Their backgrounder points out that countries other than Israel have often built security fences—sometimes in disputed territories—to prevent the free movement of terrorists and smugglers. For example, India has built a fence on disputed territory to block terrorists from Pakistan, Saudi Arabia is using a fence to try to stem the flow of terrorists and smugglers from Yemen, and Islamic terrorists from Kyrgysztan prompted Uzbekistan to secure its borders with a fence. The list does not end there; the United States, Botswana, Spain, Ireland, and Cyprus all have security fences. In 1991, even the United Nations installed a security barrier to protect Kuwait from Iraq.

CHAPTER 12

Is a Militarized Palestine a Barrier to Peace?

1. "Israel's Peres Hails Palestinian Official's Backing of Demilitarised State," Agence France-Presse, January 13, 2002.

2. May 25, 2003, Jewish Virtual Library, accessible at www.jewishvirtuallibrary.org/jsources/Peace/road1.html.

3. Michael Lerner, "An International Conference for the Mideast," *Tikkun*, July/August 1987, quoted in Louis Rene Beres, "Tikkun's Early Hope: A Demilitarized Palestine," accessible at www.freeman.org/m_online/oct00/beres1.htm.

4. Dennis Ross, *The Missing Peace* (New York: Farrar, Straus and Giroux, 2004), pp. 702, 720.

5. In my view the 1947–1949 War of Independence was entirely justified as a defensive war; the 1956 invasion of Egypt was questionable; the 1967 and 1973 wars were justified; the 1981 attack on the Iraqi nuclear reactor was justified; the 1992 invasion of

Lebanon, at least the scope of it, was questionable; and the continuing war against terrorism has been justified. See my forthcoming book *Preemption: A Knife That Cuts Both Ways* for a detailed analysis of these issues.

CHAPTER 13

Is the Iranian Nuclear Threat a Barrier to Peace?

1. "Kharrazi Criticizes 'Double Standard' on Iran's Nuclear Activities," *BBC Worldwide Monitoring*, July 16, 2004.

2. *Kayhan* (Iran), August 19, 2004; *Akhbar Al-Khaleej* (Bahrain), August 19, 2004, from Ayelet Savyon, "Iran's Nuclear Policy Crisis," MEMRI Special Dispatch Series—No. 189.

3. Noam Chomsky, "Iran's Threat," July 26, 2004, accessible at http://blog.zmag.org/ttt/archives/000911.html.

4. Gerald M. Steinberg, "No It's Not a Double Standard; Israel's Nuclear Program," *International Herald Tribune*," October 1, 2004.

5. Nasser Karimi, "Iran Rejects US Overtures on Nuclear Program," *Jerusalem Post*, March 13, 2005.

6. Francis Harris, "America Would Back Israel Attack on Iran," *Daily Telegraph* (London), February 18, 2005.

7. Suzanne Fields, "Confronting the New Anti-Semitism," *Washington Times*, July 25, 2004.

8. "Rafsanjani Says Muslims Should Use Weapons Against Israel," *Iran Press Services*, accessible at www.iran-press-service.com/articles_2001/dec_2001/rafsanjani_nuke_threats_141201.htm.

9. Steven Stalinsky, "Iranian Talk of an Attack on America," *New York Sun*, August 18, 2004; *Al-Sharq Al-Awsat* (London), May 28, 2004, MEMRI Special Dispatch Series—No. 723.

10. In fact, the State Department recently called on Israel "to forswear nuclear weapons." Amir Oren, "U.S. Says Israel Must Give Up Nukes," *Ha'aretz*, March 4, 2005.

11. Israel Shahak, *Open Secrets: Israeli Nuclear and Foreign Policy* (Chicago: Pluto Press, 1997), pp. 44–45.

12. Steven R. Weisman, "Sharon, Ending U.S. Visit, Says Israel Has No Plan to Hit Iran," *New York Times*, April 14, 2005, p. 14.

13. "Before Meeting with King, Peres Claims Israel's Nuclear Arsenal Was Built for Peace," *Jordan Times*, July 14, 1998, quoted in Warren D. Farr, LTC, U.S. Army, "The Third Temple's Holy of Holies: Israel's Nuclear Weapons," September 1999, www.au.af.mil/au/awc/awcgate/cpc-pubs/farr.htm.

14. It did bomb the outskirts of Beirut, targeting terrorist bases.

15. Warren D. Farr, LTC, U.S. Army, "The Third Temple's Holy of Holies: Israel's Nuclear Weapons," September 1999, www.au.af.mil/au/awc/awcgate/cpc-pubs/farr.htm.

16. Barbara Amiel, "Islamists Overplay Their Hand but London Salons Don't See It. It Has Been Fashionable to Blame Israel for Causing Terrorism. But Barbara Amiel Predicts a Reassessment Following US Success in Afghanistan." *Daily Telegraph* (London), December 17, 2001. Amiel also recounted an incident in which the host of a private lunch "made a remark to the effect that she couldn't stand Jews and everything happening to them was their own fault." When faced with a shocked silence, the hostess snapped, "Oh come on . . . you all feel like that." Ibid.

17. Norman Finkelstein, "The Occupation's Spillover Effect," *Tikkun*, March/April 2005, p. 14.

18. Larry Rather, "Little Common Ground at Arab–South American Summit Talks," *New York Times*, May 11, 2005, p. A3.

19. Theodor Herzl, *The Jewish State: An Attempt at a Modern Solution of the Jewish Question* (New York: American Zionist Emergency Council, 1946), p. 157.

20. Michael B. Oren, *Six Days of War: June 1967 and the Making of the Modern Middle East* (Oxford, UK: Oxford University Press, 2002), p. 315.

21. Gerald M. Steinberg, "Boycotting the Jews," *Wall Street Journal, European Edition*, April 30, 2005.

Introduction to Part II

1. See, for example, Guy D. Garcia, reported by Christine Gorman (New York) and Jon D. Hull (Jerusalem), "Middle East; Where Hatred Begets Hatred; Even in Death, Meir Kahane Makes Israel an Angrier Place," *Time*, November 19, 1990.

CHAPTER 14

More Palestinian Than the Palestinians

1. Edward Said, "Second Thoughts on Arafat's Deal; Yasir Arafat's Peace Accord with Israel," *Harper's*, January 1994.

2. Robert Fisk, "Arafat Prepares for More Capitulation," *Independent* (London), August 24, 2000.

3. Dinitia Smith, "A Stone's Throw Is a Freudian Slip," *New York Times*, March 10, 2001, accessible at www.nytimes.com/2001/03/10/arts/10PROF.html?ex =11169936000&en=6706e1a6953bb174&ei=5070.

4. From editor's comment to Daniel Barenboim, "Ein Freund; Zum Tode von Edward Said," *Frankfurter Allgemeine Zeitung*, June 18, 2004, p. 35 (translated from the German).

5. Lorenz Jäger, "Schlägerschatten. Folter, noch einmal: Wolffsohn, Dershowitz und Israel," *Frankfurter Allgemeine Zeitung*, June 18, 2004, p. 35 (translated from the German).

6. Justin Reid Weiner, "'My Beautiful Old House' and Other Fabrications by Edward Said; Palestinian Arab Rights Advocate Has Fabricated His Earlier Life," *Commentary*, September 1, 1999.

7. Janny Scott, "Israeli Says Palestinian Thinker Has Falsified His Early Life," *New York Times*, August 26, 1999. But see Christopher Hitchens, "*Commentary*'s Scurrilous Attack on Edward Said," *Salon.com*, September 7, 1999.

8. In fact, Said's own birth certificate lists his home residence as Cairo—he was born in Jerusalem on a family visit to his aunt and uncle's home—leaving blank the line asking for a permanent mandatory address. Jeff Jacoby, "Professor Said's Untrue Stories," *Boston Globe*, August 30, 1999. Said even told a West Bank university audience in 1992 that Martin Buber had lived in his family's Jerusalem home, and that Buber apparently "didn't mind living in an Arab house whose inhabitants had been displaced." The truth is, Buber rented a room in the home from Said's aunt, who evicted Buber in 1942, five years before Said's "entire family" supposedly became refugees. Justin Reid Weiner, "'My Beautiful Old House' and Other Fabrications by Edward Said; Palestinian Arab Rights Advocate Has Fabricated His Earlier Life," *Commentary*, September 1, 1999.

9. Chairman Hamid Debashi, excerpted from Debashi's article in *Al-Ahram*, an Egyptian newspaper, September 23, 2004, accessible at www.columbiaunbecoming.com/script.htm.

10. Professor Joseph Massad, lecture at Oxford University, March 2002, accessible at www.columbiaunbecoming.com/script.htm; Jonathan Calt Harris, "Tenured Extremism," *New York Sun*, May 4, 2004.

11. *Columbia Unbecoming*, quoting a student, accessible at www.columbiaunbecoming.com/script.htm.

12. Jonathan Calt Harris, "Tenured Extremism," *New York Sun*, May 4, 2004.

13. Professor Massad Al-Ahram, January 30, 2003, accessible at www.columbiaunbecoming.com/script.htm.

14. Samantha Shapiro, "How the ADL Counts Anti-Semites," *Slate*, July 9, 2002; Douglas Feiden, "Vile Words of Hate That Shame Top University: Daily News Special Report on Anti-Semitism at New York's Most Prestigious Seat of Learning," *New York Daily News*, November 21, 2004.

15. Karen Alexander, "West Bank; San Francisco Dispatch," *New Republic*, June 24, 2002.

16. Alisa Solomon, "Tipping toward Hate," *Village Voice*, May 21, 2002; Dahlia Lithwick, "Free Speech 101," *Slate*, September 19, 2002.

17. Ibid. (Solomon).

18. Karen Alexander, "West Bank; San Francisco Dispatch," *New Republic*, June 24, 2002.

19. Chris Gaither, "Berkeley Course on Mideast Raises Concerns," *New York Times*, May 16, 2002.

20. For a catalog of past reported anti-Semitic incidents at SFSU involving students and professors, see Aleza Goldsmith, "Bigotry by the Bay," *Jerusalem Post*, June 7, 2002.

21. Dahlia Lithwick, "Free Speech 101," *Slate*, September 19, 2002.

22. "Barak's Speech in Canada Canceled," *Jerusalem Post*, October 6, 2004.

23. Lou Marano, "Jewish Group Fights Suspension in Montreal," December 8, 2002; Andrew Sullivan, "The Weekly Dish," UPI, *Washington Times*, December 6, 2002.

24. David Sax, "No Harmony at Concordia," *Jerusalem Post*, January 31, 2003.

25. James Kirchick, "Applauding Falsehoods at a University," *Yale Daily News*, February 26, 2003.

26. David Kocieniewski, "Politics and Poetry Are Volatile Mix in New Jersey," *New York Times*, June 28, 2003.

27. Pamela George, "In Defense of Inviting Amiri Baraka," *Yale Daily News*, February 25, 2003.

28. Sahm Adrangi, "Not Just Another Conspiracy Theory: Manipulating Anger," *Yale Daily News*, February 26, 2003.

29. See, for example, the ADL's Web site cataloging acts of anti-Arab and anti-Muslim bigotry across the United States following September 11, along with the ADL's aggressive responses to these incidents. "Terrorism Strikes America: ADL Responds to Violence and Harassment against Arab Americans and Muslim Americans," Anti-Defamation League Web site, accessible at www.adl.org/terrorism_america/adl_responds.asp.

30. "ADL Condemns Falwell's Anti-Muslim Remarks; Urges Him to Apologize," *U.S. Newswire*, October 4, 2002; Anwar Iqbal, "Falwell Asked to Apologize," United Press International, October 6, 2002.

31. Glen Owen, "Oxford Professor Suspended for Rejecting Israeli," *Times* (London), October 28, 2003.

32. Charlotte Edwardes, "Fury as Academics Are Sacked for Being Israeli; American Scholar Leads Condemnation of 'Repellant' British Action," *Sunday Telegraph* (London), July 7, 2002.

33. Ibid.

34. "In Brief: Professor in the Clear," *Guardian* (London), January 31, 2003.

35. Will Woodward, "Lecturers Reject Call to Boycott Israel: Union Votes for Maintaining Links to Support Progressive Academics," *Guardian* (London), May 10, 2003.

36. The AUT targeted one of the universities, Haifa, based on Professor Ilan Pappe's allegation that Haifa had discriminated against him due to his pro-Palestinian views. In fact, Pappe, a tenured professor at Haifa, "has never been subject to a disciplinary committee." Talya Halkin, "UK Weighs New Boycott of Israeli Academics," *Jerusalem Post*, April 7, 2005. Even after Pappe precipitated a national boycott against his own school, Haifa University undertook no retributive disciplinary action against him. Talya Halkin, "Haifa U Won't Fire Pappe for Backing Ban," *Jerusalem Post*, April 26, 2005.

37. Yaakov Lappin and Talya Halkin, "Israel Fumes at UK Academics' Boycott," *Jerusalem Post*, April 22, 2005.

38. Matthew Taylor, Polly Curtis, and Conal Urquart, "Lecturer Defends Israeli Boycott Plan on Eve of Vote," *Guardian* (London), April 22, 2005.

39. "Don't Boycott Us, Plead Israeli Academics," *Guardian Unlimited*, April 18, 2005.

40. Sarah Harris, "Row as Dons Boycott Israeli Universities," *Daily Mail* (London), April 23, 2005.

41. Polly Curtis and Matthew Taylor, "Lecturers Vote to Boycott Israeli Universities," *Guardian* (London), April 23, 2005.

42. Efraim Karsh, "College Coarse," *New Republic Online*, www.tnr.com.

43. Polly Curtis and Matthew Taylor, "Lecturers Vote to Boycott Israeli Universities," *Guardian* (London), April 23, 2005.

44. Yaakov Lappin, "UK Teachers' Boycott of Israel May Be Overturned," *Jerusalem Post*, April 29, 2005.

45. Matthew Taylor, Polly Curtis, and Conal Urquart, "Lecturer Defends Israeli Boycott Plan on Eve of Vote," *Guardian* (London), April 22, 2005, p. 3.
46. According to an article in *Political Science and Politics*, "Professors generally felt that their academic freedom was safeguarded, although responses ranged from 92% in Israel to 16% in Russia." Thomas W. Smith, "Teaching Politics Abroad, the Internationalization of a Profession," *Political Science and Politics*, March 1, 2000.
47. Freedom House, Freedom in the World 2004, accessible at www.freedomhouse .org/research/freeworld/2004/countryratings/israel.htm.
48. Jenni Frazer, "Fertile Mind," interview with Dame Ruth Deech, *Jewish Chronicle*, April 22, 2005, p. 27.
49. Barbara Amiel, "Islamists Overplay Their Hand but London Salons Don't See It. It Has Been Fashionable to Blame Israel for Causing Terrorism. But Barbara Amiel Predicts a Reassessment Following US Success in Afghanistan," *Daily Telegraph* (London), December 17, 2001.
50. Ibid.
51. Robin Shepherd, "In Europe, an Unhealthy Fixation on Israel," *Washington Post*, January 30, 2005.
52. Amos Oz, *A Tale of Love and Darkness*, trans. Nicholas de Lange (Orlando, FL: Harcourt, Inc., 2003), p. 60.
53. Manfred Gerstenfeld, "Calling Jews, Nazis," *Jerusalem Post*, April 18, 2004.
54. Leon Wieseltier, "After Peace; The First Palestinian-Israeli War," *New Republic*, April 15, 2002.
55. Donald MacIntyre, "Coalition Deal Faces Delay over Peres Role," *Independent* (London), December 20, 2004.
56. Omayma Abdel-Latif, "That Weasel Word," *Al-Ahram Weekly On-Line*, April 4–10, 2002.
57. Tom McGurk, "Israeli Holocaust in Palestine," *Sunday Business Post*, April 14, 2002.
58. Ian Buruma, "How to Talk About Israel," *New York Times Magazine*, August 31, 2003, p. 28.
59. Robin Shepherd, "In Europe, an Unhealthy Fixation on Israel," *Washington Post*, January 30, 2005.
60. Lawrence Hart, "The Apartheid Slur," *Canadian Jewish News*, December 9, 2004.
61. "An Apartheid State?" *Jerusalem Post*, November 11, 2002.
62. Gerald M. Steinberg, "NGOs Make War on Israel; Nongovernmental Organizations," *Middle East Quarterly*, June 22, 2004.
63. Julia Duin, "Palestinian Lectures Anger Georgetown Jewish Students," *Washington Times*, May 1, 1998.
64. Jay Nordlinger, "Rude Awakenings: Some Effects of the Middle East Wars on U.S. Campuses," *National Review*, July 15, 2002.
65. Benjamin Pogrund, "Is Israel the New Apartheid?" www.jewschool.com/israpartheid.htm.
66. Anne Bayefsky, "Fatal Failure," *National Review*, November 30, 2004.
67. Richard Cohen, "Boycotting Common Sense," *Washington Post*, May 24, 2005.
68. "An Apartheid State?" *Jerusalem Post*, November 11, 2002.
69. Omer Bartov, "He Meant What He Said," *New Republic*, February 2, 2004.
70. The survey, taken in November 2003 across fifteen European Union states, found that 59 percent of respondents consider Israel the greatest "threat to world peace." The United States came in second, ahead of Iran and North Korea. Berb Keinon, "EU poll: Israel Greatest Threat to World Peace," *Jerusalem Post*, November 1, 2003.
71. Natan Sharansky, "Seeing Anti-Semitism in 3D," *Jerusalem Post*, February 24, 2004.
72. Irwin Cotler writes of "indices that may serve to illustrate this new anti-Jewishness," which he calls "discrimination against Jews as people" rather than "discrimination against Jews as individuals." These include:

   • "[E]xistential or genocidal anti-Semitism. I am referring here to the public call for the destruction of Israel and the Jewish people."
   • "[T]he discrimination against, or denial of, the legitimacy, if not the existence, of the State of Israel . . . an assault upon whatever is the core of Jewish self-definition

at any moment in time—be it the Jewish religion at the time of classical anti-Semitism, or the State of Israel as the 'civil religion' of the Jewish people under this new anti-Jewishness."

- "[T]he 'demonizing' of Israel—the attribution to Israel of all the evils of the world—the portrayal of Israel as the enemy of all that is good and the repository of all that is evil."

- "[T]he melange of attitudes, sentiments, innuendo and the like—in academe, in parliaments, among the literati, public intellectuals, and the human rights movement—the discourse of the 'chattering classes' and enlightened elites."

Irwin Cotler, "Identifying the New Anti-Semitism," Aish.com, February 29, 2004, accessible at www.aish.com/jewishissues/jewishsociety/Identifying_the_New _Anti-Semitism.asp.

73. Natan Sharansky has defined the boundary between legitimate criticism of Israel and anti-Semitism with his "3-D test." According to the test, criticism is not genuine but hateful when it employs demonizing language ("trying to paint modern-day Israel as the embodiment of evil"), double standards ("[D]o similar policies by other governments engender the same criticism?"), or delegitimation ("[T]he denial of Israel's right to exist is always anti-Semitic. If other people have a right to live securely in their homelands, then the Jewish people have a right to live securely in their homeland."). Sharansky, "Seeing Anti-Semitism in 3D," *Jerusalem Post*, February 24, 2004.

74. President Lawrence H. Summers said in his address at morning prayers:

Of course academic communities should be and always will be places that allow any viewpoint to be expressed. And certainly there is much to be debated about the Middle East and much in Israel's foreign and defense policy that can be and should be vigorously challenged.

But where anti-Semitism and views that are profoundly anti-Israeli have traditionally been the primary preserve of poorly educated right-wing populists, profoundly anti-Israel views are increasingly finding support in progressive intellectual communities.

Serious and thoughtful people are advocating and taking actions that are anti-Semitic in their effect if not their intent.

For example:

- There have been synagogue burnings, physical assaults on Jews, or the painting of swastikas on Jewish memorials in every country in Europe. Observers in many countries have pointed to the worst outbreak of attacks against the Jews since the Second World War.
- Candidates who denied the significance of the Holocaust reached the runoff stage of elections for the nation's highest office in France and Denmark. State-sponsored television stations in many nations of the world spew anti-Zionist propaganda.
- The United Nations-sponsored World Conference on Racism—while failing to mention human rights abuses in China, Rwanda, or anyplace in the Arab world—spoke of Israel's policies prior to recent struggles under the Barak government as constituting ethnic cleansing and crimes against humanity. The NGO declaration at the same conference was even more virulent.

. . .

- And some here at Harvard and some at universities across the country have called for the University to single out Israel among all nations as the lone country where it is inappropriate for any part of the university's endowment to be invested. I hasten to say the University has categorically rejected this suggestion.

Lawrence Summers, address at morning prayers, September 17, 2002, accessible at www.president.harvard.edu/speeches/2002/morningprayers.html.

75. "Criticizing Israel is not anti-Semitic, and saying so is vile. But singling out Israel for opprobrium and international sanction—out of all proportion to any other party in the Middle East—is anti-Semitic, and not saying so is dishonest." Thomas L. Friedman, "Campus Hypocrisy," *New York Times*, October 16, 2002.

76. Concurring opinion, *Jacobellis v. Ohio*, 378 U.S. 184 (1964), at 197.

77. See discussion of *La Stampa* cartoon, *supra* pp. 131–132. See also Josef Joffe, *Nations We Love to Hate: Israel, America and the New Anti-Semitism* (Jerusalem: Vidal Sassoon International Center for the Study of Antisemitism, 2005).

78. For example, Finkelstein comments, "I can't imagine why Israel's apologists would be offended by a comparison with the Gestapo." Norman Finkelstein and John Dirlik, "Canadian Jewish Organizations Charged with Stifling Campus Debate," *Washington Report on Middle East Affairs*, April/May 1992, p. 43. When challenged to defend his frequent comparison between Jews and Nazis, Finkelstein has responded, "Nazis never like to hear they're being Nazis." Simon Rosenblum and Len Rudner, "In a nasty neighbourhood, Israel needs to be tough," *Record*, June 16, 2003.

79. A survey, taken in November 2003 across fifteen European Union states, found that 59 percent of the respondents said that they consider Israel the greatest "threat to world peace." The United States came in second, ahead of Iran and North Korea. Berb Keinon, "EU Poll: Israel Greatest Threat to World Peace," *Jerusalem Post*, November 1, 2003. Professor Irwin Cotler notes that there is a

> variant of political anti-Semitism. I am referring here to the "demonizing" of Israel—the attribution to Israel of all the evils of the world—the portrayal of Israel as the enemy of all that is good and the repository of all that is evil. This is the contemporary analogue to the medieval indictment of the Jew as the "poisoner of the wells." In other words, in a world in which human rights has emerged as the new secular religion of our time, the portrayal of Israel as the metaphor for a human rights violator is an indictment of Israel as the "new anti-Christ"—as the "poisoner of the international wells" encompassing all the "teaching of contempt" for the "Jew among the Nations," this new anti-Semitism implies.

Irwin Cotler, "Identifying the New Anti-Semitism," *Jewish People Policy Planning Institute*, November 2002, accessible at www.aish.com/jewishissues/jewishsociety/ Identifying_the_New_Anti-Semitism.asp.

80. See discussion of Durban, *infra* pp. 144–146 and Susan Sachs's exposé of anti-Semitism in the Arab world, *infra* p. 148.

81. See discussion of the call for divestment by the Presbyterian Church, *infra* pp. 154–156, and Michael Lerner's support for unfair divestment from Israel, *infra* p. 156.

82. See discussion of the British professor Mona Baker, who fired Israeli academics based on their nationality and the refusal by Oxford professor Andrew Wilkie to accept a Ph.D. student because he was Israeli, *supra* pp. 129–130.

83. Again Finkelstein:

> [I]t's too simple to (and convenient) to label the notion of Jewish power anti-Semitic. Jews now rank as the wealthiest ethnic group in the United States; with this economic power has accrued substantial political power. Their leaders have wielded this power, often crudely, to mold U.S. policy regarding Israel. These leaders have also utilized this power in other realms. Under the guise of seeking "Holocaust reparations," American Jewish organizations and individuals at all levels of government and in all sectors of American society entered into a conspiracy. . . . And who can seriously believe that the pro-Jewish bias of the corporate media has nothing to do with the influential Jewish presence at all levels of it? . . . Alongside Israel, [Jewish American elites] are the main fomenters of anti-Semitism in the world today.

Norman Finkelstein, "The Occupation's Spillover Effect," *Tikkun*, March/April 2005, p. 14.

84. See discussion of Tony Judt's comment that "Israel is not good for the Jews," *supra* pp. 30–31.

85. Professor Cotler observes:

> When it comes to European anti-Semitism, we are witnessing an explosion of European anti-Semitism without parallel or precedent since World War II, whose atmospherics are reminiscent of the 1930s. Some examples, to which I can personally attest to, following my visits to European capitals these past two years, include assaults upon and desecration of synagogues, cemeteries and Jewish institutions; attacks upon

identifiable Jews; convergence of the extreme left and the extreme right in public demonstrations calling for "death to the Jews"; atrocity propaganda against Israel and Jews (e.g., Israel injects the AIDS virus into Palestinians); the ugly canard of double loyalty; the demonization of Israel through the escalating ascription of Nazi metaphors; indifference or silence in the face of horrific acts of terror against Israel and the threatening of sanctions against Israel for exercising its right of self-defense against these acts of terror. In the words of Joel Kotek of the University of Brussels: "One's position on the Arab-Israeli conflict has become a test of loyalty. Should he become a supporter of Israel, he becomes a supporter of a Nazi state."

Irwin Cotler, "Identifying the New Anti-Semitism," Aish.com, February 29, 2004, accessible at www.aish.com/jewishissues/jewishsociety/Identifying_the_New _Anti-Semitism.asp.

86. See the *Foreign Policy* article that pointed out how some have labeled Jews neo-conservates, *infra* p. 194.

87. Gore Vidal, for example, has accused Norman Podhoretz—and by strong implications all American Jews—of dual loyalty: "[H]e was not planning to become an 'assimilated American,' . . . but rather, his first loyalty would always be to Israel. Yet he and Midge [Podhoretz's wife] will stay among us." He called Podhoretz and his wife members of the "Israeli Fifth Column Division." He then said to Podhoretz's wife, "I don't like your country, which is Israel." Gore Vidal, "The Empire Lovers Strike Back," *New Republic*, March 22, 1986, pp. 30, 32.

On the eve of the Iraq war the *Guardian*'s senior political commentator, Hugo Young, made the same point:

Only in Washington does one get a true sense of the obsession of these Pentagon civilians. Conversationally, it is common talk that some of them, not including Rums-feld, are as much Israeli as American nationalists. Behind nervous confiding hands come sardonic whispers of an American outpost of Likud. Most striking of all, how-ever, is how unmentionable this is in the American liberal press. The aura of a dirty little secret surrounds the possibility—the perfectly intelligible and even reasonable possibility—that the emotional thrust of the anti-Saddam campaign, from the most hawkish hawks, contemplates the security of one country, Israel, which he really threatens, more than that of another, the US itself, which his weapons of mass destruction have no chance of reaching.

Hugo Young, "Blair Has Not Been a Poodle, but Poodleism Still Beckons: Hugo Young in Washington: America's Hawks Are Obsessive in Their Pursuit of War," *Guardian* (London), November 14, 2002, p. 26.

88. As Professor Cotler notes:

As for cultural anti-Semitism, I am referring here to the melange of attitudes, sen-timents, innuendo and the like—in academe, in parliaments, among the literati, pub-lic intellectuals, and the human rights movement—the discourse of the "chattering classes" and enlightened elites—as found expression in the remarks of the French Ambassador to the U.K. to the effect of, why should the world risk another world war because of "that shitty little country Israel"; or as British journalist Petronella Wyatt put it, "Anti-Semitism, and its open expression, has become respectable at London dinner tables once more—not just in Germany or Catholic Central Europe."

Irwin Cotler, "Identifying the New Anti-Semitism," Aish.com, February 29, 2004, accessible at www.aish.com/jewishissues/jewishsociety/Identifying_the_New _Anti-Semitism.asp.

89. See the remark by Professor De Genova from the MEALAC at Columbia University, *supra* p. 124; see also discussion of Holocaust denial and revisionism in the Arab world, *infra* pp. 150–152. See generally Finkelstein's writings on this issue.

90. Again Professor Cotler:

I am referring here to the singling out of Israel for differential, if not discriminatory, treatment amongst the family of nations; with Israel emerging, as it were, as "the col-lective Jew among the Nations." Some examples include the World Conference Against Racism in Durban, which turned into a conference of racism against Israel, where Israel was the only state singled out for indictment; the UN Commission on Human Rights, where Israel is the only country singled out for a country-specific condemnation even before the annual session begins, where 30 percent of all resolutions condemn Israel alone, while the major human rights violators enjoy exculpatory immunity; the Conference of the Contracting Parties to the Geneva Conventions, where Israel became the first country in 52 years to be the object of a country-specific indictment, while the perpetrators of horrific killing fields—be it Cambodia, Sudan, etc.—have never been the object of a contracting party's enquiry; the systemic and systematic discrimination against Israel in the major decision-making bodies of the United Nations and its specialized agencies; the exclusion of Magen David Adom, Israel's humanitarian aid agency, from the International Federation of Red Cross and Red Crescent Societies; the conversion of refugee camps under UNRWA's management into bases and sanctuaries of incitement and terror, in breach of fundamental principles of international humanitarian and refugee law.

Irwin Cotler, "Identifying the New Anti-Semitism," Aish.com, February 29, 2004, accessible at www.aish.com/jewishissues/jewishsociety/Identifying_the_New _Anti-Semitism.asp. ·

91. As Finkelstein observed: "Alongside Israel, [Jewish American Elites] are the main fomenters of anti-Semitism in the world today." Norman Finkelstein, "The Occupation's Spillover Effect," *Tikkun*, March/April 2005, p. 14. Rabbi Michael Lerner stated: "Please don't say, 'Well, the Jewish state is causing . . . anti-Semitism.'" Earlier on in the article, he says, "I have argued that some of the policies of the State of Israel have actually intensified pre-existing anti-Semitism and have generated anger at the Jewish people from many who had no previous history of anti-Semitism." Michael Lerner, "Divestment and More: A Strategy Exploration," *Tikkun*, March/April 2005, pp. 42, 38.

92. For example, Susannah Heschel, associate professor of Jewish Studies at Dartmouth College, made this demonstrably false claim: "We often hear that criticism of Israel is equivalent to anti-Semitism." Susannah Heschel, "Ad Condemning Anti-Semitism on Campuses Misses the Point," *JTA Jewish Global News*, October 14, 2002, accessible at www.jta.org/page_view_story.asp?intartcleid=11944&intcategoryid=5.

As I wrote in *The Case for Israel*: "I . . . challenge anyone who claims that mere criticism of Israel is 'often' labeled anti-Semitism to document that serious charge by providing actual quotations, in context, with the source of the statements identified. I am not talking about the occasional kook who writes an anonymous postcard or e-mail. I am talking about mainstream supporters of Israel who, it is claimed, have 'often' equated criticism of Israel with anti-Semitism." Alan Dershowitz, *The Case for Israel* (Hoboken, NJ: Wiley, 2003), p. 209.

Susannah Heschel and the others who spread this canard have not responded to this challenge.

93. See discussion of Chomsky's remark that "nobody believes there is an anti-Semitic connotation to the denial of the Holocaust . . . whether one believes it took place or not." *Infra* p. 171.

94. See discussion of AUT boycott in England, *supra* pp. 130–133.

95. See *infra*, p. 153.

96. Irwin Cotler, "Durban's Troubling Legacy One Year Later: Twisting the Cause of International Human Rights against the Jewish People," Jerusalem Center for Public Affairs Web site, Vol. 2, No. 5, August 20, 2002, www.jcpa.org/brief/brief2-5.htm.

97. Anne Bayefsky, "U.N. vs. Israel," *National Review Online*, April 20, 2004.

98. Irwin Cotler, "Durban's Troubling Legacy One Year Later: Twisting the Cause of International Human Rights against the Jewish People," Jerusalem Center for Public Affairs Web site, Vol. 2, No. 5, August 20, 2002, www.jcpa.org/brief/ brief2-5.htm.

99. "Show of Farce," *New Republic*, September 10, 2001.

100. Michael J. Jordan, "Inside the Durban Debacle," *Salon.com*, September 7, 2001.

101. Arch Puddington, "The Wages of Durban; United Nations World Conference against Racism, 2001," *Commentary*, November 1, 2001.

102. Michael Kelly, ". . . Or a Good Time to Take a Hike?" *Washington Post*, September 5, 2001.

103. Arch Puddington, "The Wages of Durban; United Nations World Conference against Racism, 2001," *Commentary*, November 1, 2001.

104. Barbara Amiel, "A Pathetic Discussion of Racism," *Chicago Sun-Times*, September 11, 2001.

105. Arch Puddington, "The Wages of Durban; United Nations World Conference against Racism, 2001," *Commentary*, November 1, 2001.

106. Michael J. Jordan, "Inside the Durban Debacle," *Salon.com*, September 7, 2001.

107. Ibid.

108. Ibid.

109. Michael Kelly, ". . . Or a Good Time to Take a Hike?" *Washington Post*, September 5, 2001.

110. Elizabeth Neuffer, "Elie Wiesel Assails UN Chief, Says Annan Speech at Racism Meeting Set a Divisive Tone," *Boston Globe*, September 5, 2001.

111. Ibid.

112. Irwin Cotler, "Durban's Troubling Legacy One Year Later: Twisting the Cause of International Human Rights against the Jewish People," Jerusalem Center for Public Affairs Web site, Vol. 2, No. 5, August 20, 2002, www.jcpa.org/brief/brief2-5.htm.

113. John L. Allen Jr., "A Whiff of Anti-Semitism in Rome's Assessment of Sex Abuse Crisis; a Boost for Tettamanzi; Lawyers Target Holy See," *National Catholic Reporter*, July 19, 2002, accessible at www.nationalcatholicreporter.org/word/word0719.htm; James Carroll, "One Cardinal's Old Impulse to Blame Jews," *Boston Globe*, August 12, 2003, p. A13.

114. For a series of 59 political cartoons, collected from Arab newspapers, depicting Jews and Israelis as Nazis, see www.memri.org/bin/cartoons.cgi?cat2. For a collection of 142 anti-Semitic cartoons from Arab papers, see www.memri.org/bin/cartoons .cgi?cat3. For a collection of 154 cartoons suggesting that Israel or Jews control the United States, see www.memri.org/bin/cartoons.cgi?cat1.

115. Susan Sachs, "Anti-Semitism Is Deepening among Muslims; Hateful Images of Jews Are Embedded in Islamic Popular Culture," *New York Times*, April 27, 2002.

116. Ibid.

117. Umayma Ahmad al-Jalahma, "The Jewish Holiday of Purim," *Al-Riyadh* (Saudi Arabia), March 2002. For a translation of the text, see http://memri.org/ bin/articles.cgi?Page=archives&Area=sd&ID=SP35402 (MEMRI Special Dispatch Series—No. 354).

118. Ibid.

119. Ibid.

120. Ibid.

121. Hussam Wahba, *Al-Gomhuriya* (Egypt), August 10, 2004. For a translation of the text, see http://memri.org/bin/articles.cgi?Page=subjects&Area=anti semitism&ID=SP76304 (MEMRI Special Dispatch Series—No. 763).

122. Ibid.

123. Galal Duweidar, *Al-Akhbar* (Egypt), November 3, 2002. For a translation of the text, see http://memri.org/bin/articles.cgi?Page=subjects&Area=antisemitism&ID=IA10902 (MEMRI Special Dispatch Series—No. 109).

124. "No to Ideological Terrorism," *Al-Akhbar* (Egypt), November 12, 2002. For a translation of the text, see http://memri.org/bin/articles.cgi?Page=subjects&Area =antisemitism&ID=IA11302 (MEMRI Special Dispatch Series—No. 113).

125. Ab Al-'Aziz Al-Sweid, *Al-Riyadh* (Saudi Arabia), November 5, 2002. For a translation of the text, see http://memri.org/bin/articles.cgi?Page=subjects&Area =antisemitism&ID=IA11302 (MEMRI Special Dispatch Series—No. 113).

126. Seif 'Ali Al-Jarwan, "Jewish Control of the World Media," *Al-Hayat Al-Jadida* (Palestine), July 2, 1998. For a translation of the text, see http://memri. org/bin/articles.cgi?Page=subjects&Area=antisemitism&ID=SP0198 (MEMRI Special Dispatch Series—No. 1). Curiously, in the same column Al-Jarwan accused

Rupert Murdoch of being Jewish (he's not) and of owning "three magazines that specialize in spreading prostitution."

127. Rif'at Sayyed Ahmad, "The Lie about the Burning of the Jews," *Al-Liwaa Al-Islami* (Egypt), June 24, 2004. For a translation of the text, see http://memri.org/bin/articles.cgi?Page=subjects&Area=antisemitism&ID=SP75604 (MEMRI Special Dispatch Series—No. 756).

128. Fatma Abdallah Mahmoud, "Accursed Forever and Ever," *Al-Akhbar* (Egypt), April 29, 2002. For a translation of the text, see http://memri.org/bin/articles.cgi?Page=subjects&Area=antisemitism&ID=SP37502 (MEMRI Special Dispatch Series—No. 375).

129. Ahmad Ragab, "Half a Word," *Al-Akhbar* (Egypt), April 18, 2001. For a translation of the text, see http://memri.org/bin/articles.cgi?Page=subjects&Area=antisemitism&ID=SP20801 (MEMRI Special Dispatch Series—No. 208).

130. 'Abd Al-'Aziz Al-Rantisi, "Which Is Worse—Zionism or Nazism?" *Al-Risala*, August 23, 2003. For a translation of the text, see http://memri.org/bin/articles.cgi?Page=subjects&Area=antisemitism&ID=SP55803 (MEMRI Special Dispatch Series—No. 558).

131. Ahmad al-Muslih, *Al-Dustour* (Jordan), September 13, 2001. For a translation of the text, see http://memri.org/bin/articles.cgi?Page=subjects&Area=jihad&ID=SP27001 (MEMRI Special Dispatch Series—No. 270).

132. Rakan al-Majali, *Al-Dustour* (Jordan), September 13, 2001. For a translation of the text, see http://memri.org/bin/articles.cgi?Page=subjects&Area=jihad&ID=SP27001 (MEMRI Special Dispatch Series—No. 270).

133. Sheikh Muhammad Al-Gamei'a, interviewed for the Web site www.alilatalqadr.com. For a translation of the text, see http://memri.org/bin/articles.cgi?Page=subjects&Area=jihad&ID=SP28801 (MEMRI Special Dispatch Series—No. 288).

134. Joseph Nasr, "Egyptian Magazine: Israel-US Caused Tsunamis," *Jerusalem Post*, January 7, 2005.

135. Quoted in ADL Press Release, "Presbyterian Church Leaders Meet with Terrorists in Lebanon; ADL Says 'Irresponsible' Decision Furthers Interfaith Rift," October 20, 2004, accessible at www.adl.org/PresRele/ChJew_31/4578_31.htm.

136. Michael Lerner, "Divestment and More: A Strategy Exploration," *Tikkun*, March/April 2005, p. 42.

137. Ibid.

138. Ibid.

139. Ibid.

CHAPTER 15

More Israeli Than the Israelis

1. Max Blumenthal, "Born-Agains for Sharon," *Salon.com*, November 1, 2004.

2. Jessica Graham, "11 Jews Here Arrested in Anti-Barak Protest," *New York Post*, May 22, 2000.

3. Uriel Heilman, "US Jewish Right to Step Up Anti-Pullout Campaigning," *Jerusalem Post*, April 15, 2005.

4. Sam Allis, "'Frontline' Takes an Unsettling Look at Extremist Israeli Settlers," *Boston Globe*, April 5, 2005.

5. Leora Eren Frucht, "The Flame That Died," *Jerusalem Post*, November 10, 2000.

6. Jeffrey Goldberg, "Among the Settlers; Will They Destroy Israel?," *New Yorker*, May 31, 2004.

7. Ibid.

8. Ibid.

9. "Rabbi's Note on Killing Those Who Give Up Land Stirs Up 'Storm' in Israel," *BBC Worldwide Monitoring*, July 1, 2004.

10. Deuteronomy 30:19.

11. Larry Derfner, "Answering to a Higher Authority," *Jerusalem Post*, October 22, 2004.

12. Sanhedrin 4:1 (22a).

13. Theodor Herzl, *The Jewish State: An Attempt at a Modern Solution of the Jewish Question* (New York: American Zionist Emergency Council, 1946), p. 146.
14. Robert O. Smith, "Between Restoration and Liberation: Theopolitical Contributions and Response to U.S. Foreign Policy in Israel/Palestine," *Journal of Church and State*, September 22, 2004.
15. Max Blumenthal, "Born-Agains for Sharon," *Salon.com*, November 1, 2004 (emphasis added).
16. Melissa Radler, "True Friendship," *Jerusalem Post*, August 22, 2003.
17. Ralph Reed, "Israel and the US: An Enduring Friendship, An Essential Alliance," speech delivered to the Anti-Defamation League National Leadership Conference, April 29, 2003, www.adl.org/Israel/israel_us.asp.
18. Peter Beinart, "Bad Move," *New Republic*, May 20, 2002.
19. Calev Ben-David, "Some of Our Best Friends Are . . . ?" *Jerusalem Post*, June 4, 2003.
20. Sheldon Kirshner, "Journalist Advises Israel to 'Transfer' Palestinians," *Canadian Jewish News*, December 9, 2004.
21. Don Melvin and George Edmonson, "'Values' Agenda a Concern; Evangelicals' Views on Worldwide Matters Jangle Some Nerves," *Atlanta Journal-Constitution*, December 5, 2004.
22. Megan K. Stack, "DeLay Tells Israeli Hawks Not to Fear; GOP House Leader Pledges Support on Holy Land Tour," *Chicago Tribune*, July 31, 2003.
23. Zev Nagel, "With Friends Like These . . . ," *Jerusalem Report*, September 6, 2004.
Most evangelicals insist that their support for Israel is not contingent on the End of Days prophecy. As the *Chicago Sun-Times* reported:
> Many Jews have long feared what they presume to be evangelical Christians' main reason for supporting Israel—their hope that it would usher in Jesus' second coming and the conversion of the Jews to Christianity. But a new poll that seeks to understand evangelicals' motivation for standing with Israel finds a very different agenda.
> The poll, commissioned by the Stand for Israel project of the International Fellowship of Christians and Jews, found that, among evangelicals who expressed support for Israel well over half attributed their support to non-theological factors. Israel's democratic system of government, the value it places on freedom, the country's status as a long-standing ally of the United States in the war against terror, and the fact that Jews have been persecuted for centuries and need a homeland were the most commonly cited factors.
> Even when pressed to cite the top theological reason for supporting Israel, 54 percent of evangelicals cited Hebrew Bible passages that God promised the land to the Jewish people and that those who bless the Jews will themselves be blessed. A minority of 30 percent cited New Testament passages related to the prophesied second coming.

Rabbi Yechiel Eckstein, "Christians, Jews on the Same Page," *Chicago Sun-Times*, October 30, 2002.
24. Philip Roth, *The Counterlife* (New York: Random House, 1986), p. 122.
25. Morton A. Klein, "'Road Map Threatens Peace,' Today's Debate: Israeli-Palestinian Conflict," *USA Today*, May 1, 2003.
26. The Etzion bloc is a group of settlements south of Jerusalem with a current population of approximately 20,000. Gush Etzion was the first West Bank settlement following the Six-Day War.
27. Morton A. Klein, "Israel Isn't in Charge of Gaza," *Sun-Sentinel* (Fort Lauderdale, FL), May 26, 2004.
28. Jeff Jacoby, "Retreat from Gaza Is a Victory for Terrorists," *Boston Globe*, March 31, 2005.
29. Tovah Lazaroff, "US Jews Head to Gaza in Solidarity," *Jerusalem Post*, March 14, 2005.
30. "The Diaspora's Task," *Jerusalem Post*, March 15, 2005.
31. Jeffrey Goldberg, "Among the Settlers; Will They Destroy Israel?" *New Yorker*, May 31, 2004.

32. At the height of the second intifada, in early 2002, a poll taken by *Yediot Aharonot* showed that 73 percent of Israelis supported the statement that Israel should reengage in peace talks for a Palestinian state provided terrorism was halted. But in a more frequently cited poll, by the Jaffee Center, 46 percent of respondents supported some form of transfer of Palestinians. Glenn Frankel, "Israelis' Hope for the Future Yields to Fear of the Past; Military Action Nonetheless Forges New Unity," *Washington Post*, April 7, 2002.

33. David J. Forman, "Rabbis for Human Rights," *Jerusalem Post*, January 10, 2002.

34. Michael Lerner, "Divestment and More: A Strategy Exploration," *Tikkun*, March/April 2005, p. 41.

35. Benny Morris, *The Birth of the Palestinian Refugee Problem, 1947–1949* (Cambridge University Press, 1988), p. 289.

36. See, for example, the following: "Using the excuse of responding to acts of terror by some Palestinians, Sharon recently set out to destroy the institutions of Palestinian society and has done so with murderous brutality, with little regard for human rights and with great harm to many civilians." Michael Lerner, "Jews for Justice," *Nation*, May 20, 2002.

CHAPTER 16
A Case Study in Hate and Intimidation

1. Noam Chomsky, *Lies of Our Time*, January 1, 1990, quoted in Werner Cohn, "Chomsky and Holocaust Denial," in Peter Collier and David Horowitz, eds., *The Anti-Chomsky Reader* (San Francisco: Encounter Books, 2004), p. 117.

2 John Dirlik, "Canadian Jewish Organizations Charged with Stifling Campus Debate," *Washington Report on Middle East Affairs*, April/May 1992, p. 43.

3. Franklin Foer, "Relativity Theory; Alexander Cockburn's Dubious Theories," *New Republic*, April 22, 2002, p. 12.

4. For an excellent discussion of the differences between legitimate criticism of Israeli policies and illegitimate singling out of Israel for unique condemnation, see the talk given by President Lawrence Summers of Harvard in 2002, quoted in Alan M. Dershowitz, *The Case for Israel* (Hoboken, NJ: Wiley, 2003), pp. 201–202.

5. Alan Dershowitz, *Bigotry outside Faneuil Hall*, accessible at www.beliefnet.com/story/141/story_14167_1.html.

6. As one reviewer of *The Case for Israel* wrote, "In his view the two-state solution is not only desirable but also inevitable. He does not believe that the cessation of all Palestinian terrorism should be a prerequisite for the creation of a Palestinian state; that, as he wisely observes, would be to give the terrorists a veto over progress towards peace—a veto which they would exercise with violence." Ian McIntyre, "On the Road Map to Nowhere," *Times* (London), October 11, 2003.

7. After President Summers made his moderate talk in which he encouraged reasonable criticism of Israel, Chomsky attacked him as among the "extremists who want to maximize U.S.-Israeli atrocities and crimes." See Dershowitz, *The Case for Israel*, p. 202.

8. Noam Chomsky, *What Uncle Sam Really Wants* (Tucson, AZ: Odonian Press, 1993).

9. Quoted in "Who Runs America? Forty Minutes with Noam Chomsky," *Boston Phoenix*, April 1–8, 1999, www.bostonphoenix.com/archive/features/99/04/01/NOAM_CHOMSKY.html.

10. For examples of Faurisson's stances, see Robert Faurisson, "The Leaders of the Arab States Should Quit Their Silence on the Imposture of the 'Holocaust,'" Institute for Historical Review Beirut Conference, March 22, 2001, accessible at www.ihr.org/conference/beirutconf/010331faurisson.html; and Robert Faurisson, "The Diary of Anne Frank: Is It Genuine?" *Journal of Historical Review* 19, no. 6 (November/December 2000), accessible at www.ihr.org/jhr/v19/v19n6p-2_Faurisson.html.

11. "Faurisson est une sorte de liberal relativement apolitique." Robert Faurisson, *Mémoire en defense contre ceux qui m'accusent de falsifier l'Histoire. La question des chambres à gaz. Précédé d'un avis de Noam Chomsky* [Memory in defense against those who accuse me of falsifying history. The question of the gas chambers. Precede by an opinion of

Noam Chomsky.] (Paris: A Vieille Taupe, 1980), pp. xiv–xv; Pierre Vidal-Naquet, *Assassins of Memory: Essays on the Denial of the Holocaust* (New York: Columbia University Press, 1993), p. 67.

12. Werner Cohn, "Chomsky and Holocaust Denial," in Peter Collier and David Horowitz, eds., *The Anti-Chomsky Reader*, p. 124.

13. Scot Lehigh, "Men of Letters," *Boston Phoenix*, June 16–22, 1989, p. 30 (emphasis added).

14. Chomsky published the French version of his *Political Economy of Human Rights* (written with Edward Herman) with La Vieille Taupe, the publisher of the Holocaust denier Robert Faurisson, although he could have published it with a commercial firm. He also wrote the preface for Faurisson's book *Mémoire en defense*. Werner Cohn, "Chomsky and Holocaust Denial," in Peter Collier and David Horowitz, eds., *The Anti-Chomsky Reader*, pp. 124–133.

15. Paul L. Berman, reply to "Chomsky: Freedom of Expression? Absolutely," *Village Voice*, July 1–7, 1981, p. 13.

16. Peter R. Mitchell and John Schoeffel, eds., *Understanding Power: The Indispensable Chomsky* (New York: New Press, 2002).

17. Noam Chomsky, March 21, 2004, listed at Norman Finkelstein's May 15, 2004, speech in Vancouver, Canada, accessible at www.normanfinkelstein.com/content.php?pg=9.

18. Norman Finkelstein, "A Reply to Michael Young," accessible at www.normanfinkelstein.com/article.php?pg=4Aar=15.

19. Noam Chomsky, e-mail to Gary Greenberg, February 27, 2004.

20. Ward Churchill, "'Some People Push Back': On the Justice of Roosting Chickens," 2001, accessible at www.kersplebedeb.com/mystuff/s11/churchill.html.

21. Dave Curtin and Howard Pankratz, "CU Prof's Writings Doubted," *Denver Post*, February 10, 2005, p. A1.

22. Ward Churchill, *Acts of Rebellion: The Ward Churchill Reader* (New York: Routledge, 2003), back cover.

23. They have also accused Chomsky of "a deep disregard and contempt for the truth," "outright invention, unanchored by demonstrable fact," "intentional deception," "adopting other linguists' research proposals without credit," and a chronic "profound and massively arrogant contempt for truth." Robert D. Levine and Paul M. Postal, "A Corrupted Linguistics," in Peter Collier and David Horowitz, eds., *The Anti-Chomsky Reader*, pp. 204–205, 213.

24. Robert D. Levine and Paul M. Postal, "A Corrupted Linguistics," in Peter Collier and David Horowitz, eds., *The Anti-Chomsky Reader*, p. 205.

25. Ibid., p. 217.

26. Ibid., p. 205.

27. Stephen J. Morris, "Whitewashing Dictatorship in Communist Vietnam and Cambodia," in Peter Collier and David Horowitz, eds., *The Anti-Chomsky Reader*, p. 13.

28. Paul Bogdanor, "Chomsky's War Against Israel," in Peter Collier and David Horowitz, eds., *The Anti-Chomsky Reader*, p. 87.

29. Ibid., p. 98.

30. "'I Won't Lie Down and Take the Insults,'" *Irish Times*, July 1, 2003, p. 13.

31. Ibid.

32. Norman Finkelstein, *The Holocaust Industry: Reflections on the Exploitation of Jewish Suffering* (New York: VERSO, 2000), p. 4.

33. Peter Novick, "Offene Fenster und Tueren. Ueber Norman Finkelsteins Kreuzzug" [Open Windows and Doors. About Norman Finkelstein's Crusade.], in Petra Steinberger, ed., *Die Finkelstein-Debatte* [The Finkelstein Debate] (München: Piper Verlag, 2001), p. 159 (translated from the German). Even David Cesarani, a left-wing scholar, points out Finkelstein's "questionable use of sources," "[s]elective quotation," and "other misuse of evidence." David Cesarani, "Finkelstein's Final Solution," *Times Higher Education Supplement*, August 4, 2000.

34. *Tagesspiegel*, February 6, 2001 (translated from the German).

35. Peter Novick, "Offene Fenster und Tueren. Ueber Norman Finkelsteins Kreuzzug," in

Petra Steinberger, ed., *Die Finkelstein-Debatte* (München: Piper Verlag, 2001), p. 159 (translated from the German).

36. Victor Frlke, "Shoah Business," *Salon.com*, August 30, 2000, accessible at http://dir.salon.com/books/int/2000/08/30/finkelstein/index.html.

37. John Dirlik, "Canadian Jewish Organizations Charged with Stifling Campus Debate," *Washington Report on Middle East Affairs*, April/May 1992, p. 43.

38. Don Atapattu, "How to Lose Friends and Alienate People: A Conversation with Professor Norman Finkelstein," *CounterPunch*, December 13, 2001, accessible at www.counterpunch.org/finkelstein1.html.

39. Interview with Norman Finkelstein, "The Holocaust Industry," March 10, 2004, Part 1 of DVD, accessible at www.snowshoefilms.com.

40. Marc Fisher, "Campus Should Cultivate Its Seeds of Debate," *Washington Post*, December 3, 2002.

41. Martin Dietzsch and Alfred Schobert, eds., *Ein "jüdischer David Irving"? Norman G. Finkelstein im Diskurs der Rechten—Erinnerungsabwehr und Antizionismus* [The "Jewish David Irving"? Norman G. Finkelstein in the Discourse of the Right—Defense against Remembrance and Antizionism] (Duisburg, Germany: DISS, 2001), p. 11. Another admirer of Finkelstein called him "the Jewish Ward Churchill." Portland Independent Media Center, http://portland.indymedia.org/en/2005/03/312868.shtml.

42. Anne Applebaum, "The Battle for the Holocaust Legacy," *Sunday Telegraph*, July 16, 2000, accessible at www.anneapplebaum.com/other/2000/07_16_tel_holocaust.html.

43. Finkelstein, *The Holocaust Industry*, p. 71.

44. Martin Dietzsch and Alfred Schobert, eds., *Ein "jüdischer David Irving"?* p. 6.

45. Finkelstein, *The Holocaust Industry*, p. 38 (emphasis added).

46. "The Occupation's Spillover Effect," *Tikkun*, March/April 2005, p. 14.

47. Martin Dietzsch and Alfred Schobert, eds., *Ein "jüdischer David Irving"?* pp. 9–26.

48. Accessible at www.normanfinkelstein.com/article.php?pg=3&ar=41.

49. Gabriel Schoenfeld's response to critics, "Holocaust Reparations," *Commentary*, January 2001, p. 20.

50. Bas Blokker, "'Joden zijn immuun voor elke vorm van kritiek'" [Jews are immune against any sort of criticism], *NRC Handelsblad*, August 5, 2000, quoted in Leon de Winter, "Der Groll des Sohnes" (The Son's Anger), in Petra Steinberger, ed., *Die Finkelstein-Debatte* (München: Piper Verlag, 2001) (translated from the German).

51. Ibid.

52. Interview with Norman Finkelstein, "The Holocaust Industry," March 10, 2004, Part 1 of DVD, accessible at www.snowshoefilms.com.

53. Ibid.

54. Quoted in Hans Stutz, "Ein Buch, erschienen wie gerufen" [A book, published just at the right time], *Jüdische Rundschau*, March 8, 2001 (translated from the German).

55. Finkelstein, *The Holocaust Industry*, p. 81. According to the Claims Conference, which describes itself as "The Conference on Jewish Material Claims Against Germany," it is not possible to pinpoint the exact number of Jewish Holocaust survivors who sought benefits after the war because only the numbers of applications are recorded. But according to estimates by the Claims Conference in Frankfurt, only 1.5 million people submitted applications for benefits. These include non-Jews who were persecuted. Another difficulty with attempting to ascertain an exact number of Jewish survivors is that many Jews never lodged a claim, because either they wouldn't accept money from the German government or they didn't know of the BEG (*Bundesentschaedigungsgesetz* is a term referring to the federal law for the payment of compensation between 1953 and 1965). Many survivors couldn't lodge a claim because they lived in Eastern Europe and were excluded from the BEG.

There were also thousands of people who spent the war in hiding places or served as Nazi slaves outside of labor camps. As the Fritz Bauer Institute points out, "If you look at Finkelstein's 3rd Chapter, *The Double Shakedown*, carefully, it becomes evident that Finkelstein hasn't understood his sources and literature, or that he even consciously misread them." Fritz Bauer Institute, *Newsletter No. 21, Fall 2001* (translated from the German), accessible at www.fritz-bauer-institut.de/rezensionen/nl21/hoppe.htm.

56. Norman G. Finkelstein, "Haunted House" excerpt from a political memoir in progress, www.normanfinkelstein.com.

57. "Village Voice Suspends Alexander Cockburn Over $10,000 Grant," *Wall Street Journal*, January 18, 1984, p. 12.

58. Franklin Foer, "Relativity Theory; Alexander Cockburn's Dubious Theories," *New Republic*, April 22, 2002, p. 12.

59. Jon Margolis, "A Treatise on Columnist Alexander Cockburn," *High Country News*, May 11, 1998.

60. For instance, on page 24 I write, "Palestine was certainly not a land empty of all people. It is impossible to reconstruct the demographics of the area with any degree of precision, since census data for that time period are not reliable."

61. One reviewer wrote: "*From Time Immemorial* is the often repetitive, sometimes overwhelming result, part historic primer, part polemic, part revelation, and a remarkable document in itself," wrote one reviewer. Timothy Foote, "Which Land Is Their Land?" *Washington Post*, June 24, 1984, p. 11. Another wrote, "Peters is partly driven to this interpretation of recent history by her exhaustive examination of past centuries and by an interesting—and original—attempt to compare Arab and Jewish population figures throughout the 19th century." Anthony Verrier, "Disputed Territory," *Financial Times*, March 2, 1985, p. 16.

62. Peter R. Mitchell and John Schoeffel, eds., *Understanding Power: The Indispensable Chomsky* (New York: New Press, 2001), p. 244 (emphasis in original).

63. Ibid., p. 245.

64. Norman Finkelstein, "Is Criticism of Israel Anti-Semitic?" public forum at the Vancouver Public Library, May 15, 2004, accessible at www.workingtv.com/finkelstein.html.

65. Ibid.

66. Ibid.

67. Ibid.

68. Mitchell and Schoeffel, eds., *Understanding Power: The Indispensable Chomsky*, p. 245.

69. Ibid.

70. Alexander Cockburn, "My Life as an 'Anti-Semite,'" in Alexander Cockburn and Jeffrey St. Clair, eds., *The Politics of Anti-Semitism* (Oakland, CA.: AK Press, 2003), p. 25.

71. Alexander Cockburn, "Alan Dershowitz, Plagiarist?" *CounterPunch*, September 26, 2003.

72. Alexander Cockburn, "Remembering Israel Shahak," *Antiwar.com*, July 13, 2001.

73. He compared a passage from Peters's book, which cites earlier sources, to a selection from another book (by Ernst Frankenstein), which cites those same earlier sources, and faulted Peters for not citing Frankenstein, which she in fact did. See Joan Peters, *From Time Immemorial: The Origins of the Arab-Jewish Conflict over Palestine* (New York, Harper & Row, 1984), pp. 521, 523.

74. In the twenty years since the release of *From Time Immemorial*, Peters has not authored another book.

75. "'I Won't Lie Down and Take the Insults,'" *Irish Times*, July 1, 2003, p. 13.

76. Interview with Norman Finkelstein, "The Holocaust Industry," March 10, 2004, Part 1 of DVD, accessible at www.snowshoefilms.com.

77. Finkelstein, *The Holocaust Industry*, p. 82.

78. Victor Frlke, "Shoah Business," *Salon.com*, August 30, 2000, accessible at http://dir.salon.com/books/int/2000/08/30/finkelstein/index.html.

79. Interview with Norman Finkelstein, "The Holocaust Industry," March 10, 2004, Part 1 of DVD, accessible at www.snowshoefilms.com.

80. Ibid.

81. Catalyst Radio interview with Norman Finkelstein, March 4, 2005.

82. Like Finkelstein, Chomsky has also gone out of his way to pick on Elie Wiesel and other Jewish leaders. Chomsky falsely accused Wiesel of "denying that the Armenian geno-

cide took place." He attributed Wiesel's alleged silence to his "following the instructions of the Israeli government." ("Noam Chomsky Writes to Lawrence K. Kolodney," accessible at www.chomsky.info/letters/1989----.htm). But Chomsky simply made up this charge out of whole cloth. The fact is that Wiesel has been a leader in the effort to remember what he has called "the incontestable fact of the Armenian genocide." He has described denial of that genocide as a "double killing" because it also "murders the memory of the crime." Ruth Rosen, "The Hidden Holocaust," *San Francisco Chronicle*, December 15, 2003, p. A27. For Chomsky the truth is an inconvenience to be avoided when inconsistent with his ideological biases.

83. Omer Bartov, "A Tale of Two Holocausts," *New York Times*, August 6, 2000, p. 8.
84. Interview with Norman Finkelstein, "The Holocaust Industry," March 10, 2004, Part 1 of DVD, accessible at www.snowshoefilms.com.
85. Omer Bartov, "A Tale of Two Holocausts," *New York Times*, August 6, 2000, p. 8.
86. Finkelstein, *The Holocaust Industry*, p. 64.
87. Daniel Jonah Goldhagen, "The New Discourse of Avoidance," an expanded version of an article from the *Frankfurter Rundschau*, August 18, 1997 (found at www.goldhagen.com/nda0.html).
88. Goldhagen's critique continues: "Finkelstein has gone so far as to call my book, a work of scholarship about the Holocaust, a 'hoax.' . . . He has declared that 'there is not a scratch of scholarly evidence to support Goldhagen's claims' . . . the implication of which is that all the evidence contained in my book is fraudulent, including the extensive testimony of survivors and of perpetrators. This . . . comes from a man who has arrived overnight to a scholarly field made up of a massive scholarly literature, not to mention all the documents, who, to boot, cannot read most of the sources because they are in German." Daniel Jonah Goldhagen, "The New Discourse of Avoidance," an expanded version of an article from the *Frankfurter Rundschau*, August 18, 1997 (found at www.goldhagen.com/nda0.html).
89. Norman Finkelstein, "Letters," *Nation*, February 25, 2002. Neuborne finds the charge comical: "For most of my career, I have been at odds with many Jewish organizations because, as an ACLU lawyer, I represented Nazis—and everyone else—in the free speech cases." Burt Neuborne, "Letters," *Nation*, February 18, 2002.
90. Finkelstein, *The Holocaust Industry*, p. 168.
91 Norman Finkelstein, "An Exchange with Burt Neuborne, Lead Blackmailer for the Holocaust Industry," www.normanfinkelstein.com/article.php?pg=3&ar=22.
92. Burt Neuborne, "Letters," *Nation*, February 18, 2002.
93. Norman Finkelstein, "Should Burt Neuborne Be Disbarred?" www.normanfinkelstein.com/article.php?pg=3&ar=20.
94. Finkelstein, *The Holocaust Industry*, p. 168.
95. For example, Finkelstein quotes the Volcker report that conducted an audit of the Swiss banks as follows: "[N]o evidence of systematic destruction of account records for the purpose of concealing past behavior has been found." Norman Finkelstein, "Letters," *Nation*, December 18, 2000. In his reply, Neuborne shows that Finkelstein totally made up this quotation:

> Let's look at the document Finkelstein cites—the report of the Volcker committee, which conducted an intensive audit of the banks. The Volcker report finds that records for 2.8 million accounts opened during the Holocaust era had been completely destroyed by the Swiss banks (Volcker report, para. 20). The Volcker report calls the destruction of those records an "unfillable gap." Moreover, the Volcker report finds that almost all of the transaction records for the remaining 4.1 million accounts were also destroyed, leaving a record of an account's opening and closing, but no information about the account's size, or whether it had been plundered (Volcker report, para. 21). I call that a pretty good job of systematically destroying records, especially since, in the absence of records, the banks get to keep the money because Switzerland has no escheat law.

Burt Neuborne, "Letters," *Nation*, December 25, 2000, p. 2. In his next letter Neuborne continues:

> Your charge that I "flagrantly falsify key documents in published correspondence" is a lie—and you know it. Our exchange of letters in *The Nation* [December 18 and 25, 2000] makes it clear. . . . You conveniently ignore the German foundation in your chapter, perhaps because it doesn't support your obsession. I will leave to Judah Gribetz the pleasure of demolishing your effort to mischaracterize his remarkable work as a "shakedown" of Holocaust victims. You misstate virtually everything about the allocation plan.

Burt Neuborne, "Letters," *Nation*, February 18, 2002, p. 23.

96. Finkelstein claims that Neuborne has "radically redefined the term 'Holocaust survivor.'" Norman Finkelstein, claiming that "the Holocaust Industry," in a conspiracy to blackmail the Swiss banks, put the actual figure of 100,000 survivors to nearly a million. Norman Finkelstein, "Letters," *Nation*, December 18, 2000, p. 2. For a detailed description of Finkelstein's conspiracy theory, see Finkelstein, *The Holocaust Industry*, pp. 81–139. Neuborne rebuts this charge as follows:

> Finkelstein accuses me of "making a mockery of Jewish suffering during World War II," because I have estimated that 1 million victims of the Holocaust are still alive. In order to reach such a figure, Finkelstein argues that I must be diluting what it meant to suffer during the Holocaust. But, as usual, Finkelstein's obsession with criticizing anyone who acts on behalf of Holocaust survivors blinds him to the facts. My figure of 1 million victims was intended to include all surviving victims, not merely Jewish survivors. The German foundation Remembrance, Responsibility and the Future estimates that more than 1 million former slave and forced laborers are still alive and qualify for compensation. The fact is that the Holocaust did not affect only Jews. The Swiss settlement includes Sinti-Roma, Jehovah's Witnesses, the disabled and gays. The German foundation will distribute most of the slave/forced labor funds to non-Jews. About 130,000 Jewish survivors and about 900,000 non-Jewish victims are still alive. Norman Finkelstein accuses me of being a "main party" to seeking compensation for them. Thank you, Norman. I could not be prouder.

Burt Neuborne, "Letters," *Nation*, December 25, 2000, p. 2.

97. One of Finkelstein's favorite lies is that those who seek justice for Holocaust survivors were only enriching themselves and that nothing of the settlement would go to the actual survivors. This is, of course, not true, as Neuborne explains: "[E]very penny of the $1.25 billion Swiss bank case will go to Holocaust victims." As for lawyer fees, he states that "[d]espite their enormous effort, more than half the lawyers in the Swiss bank case waived all fees" and "[t]hose lawyers who are seeking fees . . . have filed modest requests." This is why he concludes that "[t]hat is . . . the lowest fee structure in history for comparable levels of success." *Nation*, October 23, 2000, p. 2.

98. Burt Neuborne, "Letters," *Nation*, February 18, 2002, p. 2.

99. Ibid.

100. Ibid., p. 23.

101. Telephone conversation with Burt Neuborne, May 10, 2005.

102. Cockburn wrote that *The Case for Israel* is "now slithering into the upper tier of Amazon's sales charts." Alexander Cockburn, "Alan Dershowitz, Plagiarist?" *CounterPunch*, September 26, 2003, accessible at www.counterpunch.org/cockburn09262003.html. In a speech, Finkelstein complained, "The *Times* reviewed the book about a couple of months later, the *New York Times*. The book, the *Boston Globe* reviewed it. The *Washington Post* reviewed it. Your *Globe and Mail* reviewed it. The *Globe and Mail* even mentioned the controversies. And then . . . it gave the book a great review. It got great reviews everywhere." Norman Finkelstein, "Israel-Palestine Conflict: Roots of Conflict, Prospects for Peace," Calgary, April 3, 2004.

103. Feroze Sidhwa, "The Case for Israel, a Critical Review," *Electronic Intifada*, June 15, 2005, accessible at http://electronicintifada.net/v2/article3927.shtml.

104. Finkelstein has also falsely mischaracterized my reaction to his false charges that I didn't write the book. Here is *his* characterization of our encounter on *Democracy Now!*: "Several times, . . . I kept saying things like: 'The book you claim that you have written.' And I was expecting him sort of implode. If you tell somebody a book you claim to have written, there is no bigger insult. But he was actually quite calm about it. It is if he would say 'That is interesting. How do you know?'" Norman Finkelstein, "Israel-Palestine: Roots of Conflict, Prospects for Peace," Calgary, April 3, 2004.

Now, here is the truth. As soon as he called *The Case for Israel* the "book you *purport* to have written," I interrupted him and said, "I proudly wrote it." He then said I should admit, "I didn't write the book, I had no time to read it. I'm sorry." Again I interrupted: "I wrote every word of it." (The transcript of the debate can be found at www.democracynow.org/static/dershowitzFin.shtml.) Anyone who listened to the show—and it can be heard online even now—will hear that my answers were quite forceful and nothing like the "how did you know?" admission Finkelstein falsely claims I made.

105. Norman Finkelstein, "Image and Reality of the Israeli-Palestine Conflict," *Book TV*, C-SPAN2, April 11, 2004.

106. Finkelstein concocted an elaborate chart comparing the quotes from Peters's book with my own and posted it on his Web site. The *very first* box in this chart shows a quotation from the Palestine Royal Commission Report, which appears in somewhat similar form in *From Time Immemorial* and *The Case for Israel*. To use this supposed "gotcha!" as the basis of a plagiarism claim could not be any more disingenuous. The Peel Report had sat on the bookshelf behind me for years, underlined innumerable times beneath quotes that appear in my book and *not* in Peters's. I have a *whole chapter* devoted to the Peel Report. That Finkelstein and Cockburn would use the fact that I cite the same snippet of text from this report as Peters does to charge plagiarism makes it clear that their goal is to get at me and not at the truth. Peters and I both, of course, cited portions of the book that supported our arguments.

Another example is the oft-discussed quote from Mark Twain's travelogue *The Innocents Abroad*. Finkelstein and company make much of the fact that in my book I cite some (but not all) of the same passage as Peters. But I was using quotes from this Mark Twain book in my debates during the 1970s, years before Peters wrote her book. I even used this material in a debate with Chomsky in the early 1970s. Quotations from it have appeared several times in *Myths and Facts*, a book published by AIPAC almost yearly with important facts and quotations for those on the pro-Israel side of the debate. Furthermore, Finkelstein alleges that I have "the identical quote from Twain with the ellipses in the same places." That is simply false, as anyone who compares the books will see. It is not an identical quote. I omitted a few sentences from Twain that Peters included.

107. Norman Finkelstein, "Is Criticism of Israel Anti-Semitic?" public forum at the Vancouver Public Library, May 15, 2004.

108. Finkelstein, "Israel-Palestine Conflict: Roots of Conflict, Prospects for Peace," Calgary, April 3, 2004.

109. Ibid.

110. I actually cited her at least eight times.

111. Lauren A. E. Schuker, "Dershowitz Defends Book," *Harvard Crimson*, October 2, 2003, accessible at www.thecrimson.com/article.aspx?ref=349102.

112. He wrote:

Should an author (1) who wants to use a quotation from another author (2) that he found while reading the work of a third author (3) cite to the original source (2) or to the work (3) that cited it?

It is common practice in both legal and non-legal citation to cite to the original source. "Whenever possible, a quotation within a quotation should be attributed to its original source." "Authors should check every quotation against the original or, if the original is unavailable, against a careful transcription of the passage."

Peter Martin, the former dean at Cornell Law School and co-founder of the

Legal Information Institute, has developed a very well respected online guide to legal citation. According to Professor Martin, the purpose of a citation is to:

- identify the document and document part to which the author is referring
- provide the reader with sufficient information to find the document or document part in the sources the *reader* has available (which may or may not be the same sources as those used by the writer), and
- furnish important additional information about the referenced material and its connection to the writer's argument that a reader trying to decide whether or not to pursue the reference would want to know.

If a legal writer reads a passage from the Constitution or from a Restatement of the Law and wants to use that passage himself in a piece he is writing, he will not cite to the quoting work but to the original. Generally speaking, the legal reader is interested in the quality of the argument and the weight of the authority, not the trail of research undertaken by the author.

Are there exceptions? As explained by the Chicago Manual, when the original source is not available to the author, a respected transcription may be used. Furthermore, where the original source might be difficult for most readers to locate, a citation to a more accessible source—preferably additional to the original—might be a service to the reader. Situations can also arise in literary criticism where how one author uses the words of another is closely analyzed. In that case, clarity might require quoting the quotes rather than the original source. But the general rule is to cite the first source not the repeater.

I believe this was [Dershowitz's] instinct and I think [Dershowitz] is certainly correct.

113. I asked for an investigation as soon as Finkelstein made his accusation. Indeed, I brought the accusation—of which they were unaware—to the attention of the administration.

114. Accessible at www.chomsky.info/books/dissent02.htm.

115. See, for example, Rashad Daoudi, "Dershowitz Admits Plagiarism," October 3, 2003, Rense.com, accessible at http://rense.com/general42/admits.htm.

116. Norman Finkelstein, e-mail to Dean Kagan.

117. Norman Finkelstein, "Image and Reality of the Israeli-Palestine Conflict," *Book TV*, C-SPAN2, April 11, 2004. A major object of my book is to respond to the facts, figures, and arguments used by those who apply a double standard against Israel. To this end, not only do I cite the accusatory words of Amnesty and B'Tselem, but also those of other Israel detractors such as Noam Chomsky, Edward Said, and a host of others, including Finkelstein himself—literally.

118. Norman Finkelstein, "Image and Reality of the Israeli-Palestine Conflict," C-SPAN2, *Book TV*, April 11, 2004.

119. In an effort to support his false charges against me regarding the "shaking" issue, Finkelstein had his assistant threaten Dr. Michael Baden, a distinguished pathologist who has worked with Physicians for Human Rights and who performed an autopsy on Mustafa Akawai. Baden had given his opinion that the cause of death in that case was a heart attack resulting from a previously unknown and severe medical condition. When Finkelstein learned that Baden had provided me this information, he had one of his research assistants contact Baden by phone and misrepresent himself as *working for me* in an effort to try to get Baden to contradict himself. (This assistant, one Rohit Goel, has at various times represented himself or been represented by Finkelstein as working for the *Nation*, the New Press, and even for me when he now readily admits that his "boss" is "Norman Finkelstein.") Then when the *Harvard Crimson*, a student newspaper, refused to give in to Finkelstein's demands to publish what he told them to publish, he harassed the staff, calling them "liars" and threatening to include their names in his book. On November 30, 2004, the *New York Times* ran a detailed story concerning plagiarism at Harvard. The writer, Sara Rimer, interviewed me at length for the article. She also conducted her own independent examination and evaluation. On the basis of this journalistic investigation, the *New York Times* decided not to mention the false allegations of plagiarism that had been leveled against me and dismissed as

unfounded by Harvard. As the *Times* reporter explained to me, "there's just nothing to it. I don't even understand how you could plausibly be accused of plagiarism. Moreover, you were vindicated by the Harvard process." Shortly after the article appeared, Finkelstein called Rimer and began shouting threats at her over the phone. This is part of a long-standing pattern of intimidation, threats, and inappropriate academic behavior on Finkelstein's part dating back to his days as a college teacher in New York, when he was fired for engaging in similar conduct against students who disagreed with him.

120. What the High Court said was that "medical literature has not, to date, reported a case in which a person died as the direct result of having been shaken." It did reference a case, *different* from the one I discussed in my book, in which "the suspect expired *after* being shaken," but explained that "according to the state, that case was a rare exception, [where] death was caused by an extremely rare complication which resulted in pulmonary edema" (emphasis added). The difference between "died *from* the shaking" and "expired *after* being shaken" is considerable, especially since the sentence that follows in the decision attributes the death to an extremely rare complication, and the sentence before summarizes the literature as having no conclusive examples of anyone dying from shaking. In addition, Finkelstein misquotes me as saying, "he didn't die from the shaking." I actually said, "*one person died following shaking*," and he knows I was discussing a different case.

121. Norman Finkelstein, "Is Criticism of Israel Anti-Semitic?" public forum at the Vancouver Public Library, May 15, 2004, accessible at www.workingtv.com/finkelstein.html.

122. I was writing about an entirely different matter: the movement of people as part of a postconflict "political solution," such as what occurred after World War II when "approximately fifteen million ethnic Germans" were moved from Czechoslovakia and other Eastern European nations to Germany as part of an international effort to produce increased stability. This is not ethnic cleansing, but it "may constitute a human rights violation" as may the movement of Palestinians following the Arab attack on Israel in 1947–1948. That violation, considered "in the whole spectrum of human rights issues," I concluded, is "a fifth-rate issue analogous in many respects to some massive urban renewal or other projects that require large-scale movement of people."

123. Moreover, I have cared deeply about Israel since I was a child in 1948, and attended the same Zionist camp in which Noam Chomsky worked as a counselor. I also attended a Jewish high school with strong Zionist leanings and made speeches about Israel during college and wrote about it during law school. Finkelstein knows this because he has read *Chutzpah*, in which I describe my activities on behalf of Israel before the Six-Day War. I wrote, "Before [the Six-Day War], I saw—and still see—no conflict between my Zionism and my moral principles." Alan Dershowitz, *Chutzpah* (Boston: Little Brown, 1991), p. 213.

124. Norman Finkelstein, "Israel-Palestine Conflict: Roots of Conflict, Prospects for Peace," Calgary, April 3, 2004.

125. For example, in 1998, the *Boston Globe* columnist Patricia Smith was forced to resign after it was discovered that "[f]rom time to time" she "attributed quotes to people who didn't exist." "Boston Globe Columnist Resigns, Accused of Fabrications," *CNN.com*, June 19, 1998, accessible at www.cnn.com/US/9806/19/globe.columnist.resigns.

126. Finkelstein sent me the following e-mail:
   Dear Alan,
   I was just reading your latest publication, "The Committee . . ." Please be so kind as to enter these corrections in the list titled "The 10 most despicable things Finkelstein . . ."
   In item #7, please insert "cleaner" between "vacuum" and "salesman";
   In item #1, I think the "G" in "Grand" and "W" in "Wizard" should be capitalized.
   For the record, judging by the pamphlet's intellectual depth and accuracy, I've no doubt that—at any rate, in this case—you are the real author.
   Sincerely, Norm

127. Mitchell and Schoeffel, eds., *Understanding Power: The Indispensable Chomsky* (New York: New Press, 2002), p. 245.

128. Churchill has been accused of fabricating an entire historical incident, falsely attributing an alleged genocide to the U.S. Army, though the sources he cites do not support his "findings." The sociology professor Thomas Brown concluded that "Churchill fabricated the most crucial details of his genocide story. Churchill radically misrepresented the sources he cites in support of his genocide charges, sources which say essentially the opposite of what Churchill attributes to them." Brown continued: "Churchill has fabricated a genocide that never happened. It is difficult to conceive of a social scientist committing a more egregious violation." Thomas Brown, "Assessing Ward Churchill's Version of the 1837 Smallpox Epidemic," accessible at http://hal.lamar.edu/~browntf/Churchill1.htm.

Another critique, by John LaVelle, law professor at the University of New Mexico, said, "By researching those copious endnotes, however, the discerning reader will discover that, notwithstanding all the provocative sound and fury rumbling through his essays, Churchill's analysis overall is sorely lacking in historical/factual veracity and scholarly integrity." Dave Curtin and Howard Pankratz, "CU Prof's Writings Doubted. Two Scholars Say Churchill's Work Strayed from Facts on Two Issues," *Denver Post*, February 10, 2005.

In addition to those charges pertaining to his scholarship, Churchill was responsible for "making a mirror image of an artist's work and selling it as his own," a potential copyright violation. Raj Cochan, CBS4Denver, "'Original' Churchill Art Piece Creates Controversy," http://news4colorado.com/topstories/local_story_055200531.html.

Although Churchill's scholarship received a similar assessment to Finkelstein's, Noam Chomsky praised them both. It is obvious that for Chomsky ideology matters more than accuracy.

Chomsky has also praised the radical anti-Zionist writer Israel Shahak, who claimed, among other falsehoods, that Jews worship the devil, as "an outstanding scholar, with remarkable insight and depth of knowledge. His work is informed and penetrating, a contribution of great value." Quoted in Rachel Neuwirth, "The Chomsky File," January 6, 2005, accessible at www.americanthinker.com/articles.php?article_id=4157.

129. Steven Zeitchik, "Behind beyond Chutzpah: Professor's Allegations Sets Dershowitz in Motion," *Publishers Weekly Daily*, May 17, 2005.

130. According to the Web site *Solomonia* (Solomonia.com, June 8, 2005, accessible at www.solomonia.com/blog/archives/006010.shtml), the offending article is an online essay entitled "Jerusalem, a Concise History," by Rashid Khalidi. Khalidi copied from a nearly identical essay by K. J. Asali without attribution or quotation marks. For example, here is what Khalidi purported to author:

> The oldest recorded name of the city, "Urusalem" is Amoritic. "Shalem" or "Salem" is the name of a Canaanite-Amorite god; "uru", means "founded by." The names of the two oldest rulers of the city, Saz Anu and Yaqir Ammo, were identified by the American archaeologist W. F. Albright as Amoritic. The Amorites had the same language as the Canaanites and were of the same Semitic stock. Many historians believe that they were an offshoot of the Canaanites, who came originally from the Arabian Peninsula. The Bible concurs that the Amorites are the original people of the land of Canaan.
>
> > Thus saith the Lord God unto Jerusalem.
> > Thy birth and thy origin are of the land
> > of Canaan; thy father was an Amorite,
> > and thy mother a Hittite.
> > (Ezekiel, 16:1)
>
> In the second millenium BC, Jerusalem was inhabited by the Jebusites, a Canaanite tribe, and the culture of the city was Canaanite. The Jebusites built a fortress, 'Zion', in Jerusalem. Zion is a Canaanite word meaning "hill" or "height."

"Jerusalem, A Concise History," accessible in its current form at www.acj.org/resources/khalidi/c_history.htm.

Here is the original by Asali from which Khalidi obviously copied without attribution:

> Indeed, the oldest name of the city "Urusalem" is Amoritic. "Salem" or "Shalem" was the name of a Canaanite-Amorite god, while "uru" simply meant "founded by." The names of the two oldest rulers of the city, Saz Anu and Yaqir Ammo, were identified by the American archaeologist W. F. Albright as Amoritic. The Amorites, according to the Bible, are the original people of the land of Canaan. They had the same language as the Canaanites and were of the same Semitic stock. Many historians believe that the Amorites are an offshoot of the Canaanites who came originally from the Arabian Peninsula. In this regard it is apt to quote the Bible (Ezekiel:1 6):
>
>> Thus say the Lord God to Jerusalem. Your Origin and your
>> birth are of the land of the Canaanites, your father was an
>> Amorite, and your mother a Hittite.
>
> In the second millennium, Jerusalem was inhabited by the Jebusites. In the Bible the Jebusites are considered to be Canaanites. It was the Jebusites who first built the fortress Zion in the town. Zion is a Canaanite word which means "hill" or "height."

K. J. Asali, "Jerusalem in History: Notes on the Origins of the City and Its Tradition of Tolerance," *Arab Studies Quarterly*, vol. 16, no. 4, Fall 1994, accessible at www.al-bushra.org/jerusalem1/jerhist.htm. Endnotes omitted.

When Khalidi was caught, he immediately took his name off the article and substituted the following attribution: "Compiled by ACJ [American Committee on Jerusalem, of which Khalidi was president] from a variety of sources." But for the nearly four years before he was caught, Khalidi claimed authorship of the plagiarized essay. (The article with the Khalidi byline can be accessed at http://web.archive.org/web/20010227211134/http://acj.org/resources/khalidi/c_history.htm, courtesy of the Internet Archive Wayback Machine: www.archive.org/web/web.php.) No one can seriously deny that the Khalidi essay was copied from the Asali essay. Entire sentences, phrases, and paragraphs were essentially lifted without attribution. (Contrast this with Finkelstein's phony charge against me that quotations from well-known authors such as Mark Twain—which appear within quotation marks in my book and are properly cited to Twain—should have been cited to the secondary source where he erroneously claims I first came across the Twain and other quotes.) Khalidi apparently defends the plagiarism as being "mistakenly attributed to me by the defunct website of a defunct organization" (Elizabeth O'Neill, "The Complaint against Rashid Khalidi," *History News Network*, June 17, 2005, accessible at http://hnn.us/articles/12508.html), but he does not explain how such a mistake could have endured for so many years until it was caught and exposed by a journalist.

CHAPTER 17

Will Anti-Semitism Decrease as Israel Moves toward Peace with the Palestinians?

1. Alexandra Blair, "Lecturers Condemned for Vote to Boycott Israeli Universities," *Times* (London), April 23, 2005.
2. Duncan Currie, "'Kremlin on the Charles' No More?; Harvard's Student Body Is More Conservative-Friendly Than You Might Think," *Daily Standard*, July 29, 2004.
3. Daniel J. Hemel, "Israel Divestment Debate Reignited," *Harvard Crimson*, April 27, 2005.
4. "Palestinian Minister Advises 'Factions' Not to Shell Settlements, Blames Israel," *BBC Monitoring International Reports*, April 11, 2005.
5. Molly Moore, "Militants Extend Pledge Not to Attack Israel," *Washington Post*, March 18, 2005.

6. See footnote 4 in chapter 9.
7. David Levy, "Anti-Semitism Hits Highest Level in Nine Years," *Jewish Advocate*, April 8–14, 2005. It is important to note, though, that while anti-Semitic incidents have increased, the ADL finds in the same report that anti-Semitic attitudes in the United States have decreased.
8. See chapter 14.
9. *Jewish Week*, April 29, 2005, p. 30.
10. "British Academic Intolerance," *Jerusalem Post*, April 12, 2005.
11. According to the *Jewish Week*, "The Presbyterians began their divestment move just as Israel and the Palestinians were moving toward a renewed peace effort and as Prime Minister Ariel Sharon accelerated his plan for withdrawal from Gaza." James D. Besser, "Israel Caught in Sanctions Crossfire," *Jewish Week*, March 4, 2005.
12. "In general, according to a Jerusalem Media Communications Center poll taken just after Arafat's death, more Palestinians are optimistic about the future than since the beginning of the intifada in 2000, and the number of Palestinians who say they oppose attacks against Israel jumped from 26% in June 2004 to 51% in December 2004, the highest level since the intifada began." David Makovsky, "Abbas' Voice Resonates with Palestinians; Polls Show an Openness to a New Direction," *Los Angeles Times*, January 11, 2005, p. B13.
13. "British Academic Intolerance," *Jerusalem Post*, April 13, 2005.
14. "Blunt Boycott: Universities and Israel," *Guardian* (London), April 20, 2005.
15. Yaakov Lappin and Talya Halkin, "Israel Fumes at UK Academics' Boycott," *Jerusalem Post*, April 22, 2005.
16. Daniel J. Hemel, "Israel Divestment Debate Reignited," *Harvard Crimson*, April 27, 2005.
17. Ken Ellingwood, "Truce in Gaza Is Near, Palestinian Leader Says; Mahmoud Abbas says he is close to persuading militants to end attacks. Israel suggests it will curtail military moves if guerrillas halt violence," *Los Angeles Times*, January 24, 2005.
18. Ma'rouf Zahran, Palestinian Authority–appointed mayor. Isabel Kershner, "Up Against the Wall," *Jerusalem Report*, March 21, 2005.
19. Less than a week and a half after the Sharm el-Sheikh cease-fire, the president of Iran expressed support for "radical anti-Israeli groups." "Iran's Khatami Pledges Backing for Syria and Anti-Israel Groups," Agence France-Presse, February 17, 2005.
20. See the discussion of Finkelstein in chapter 16.
21. Although eventually overcoming legislative and administration hurdles, the disengagement plan faced considerable opposition within Prime Minister Sharon's own Likud Party.
    Despite broad popular support, Sharon's Gaza plan was defeated in a Likud Party referendum in May and was voted down by the party's Central Committee in August. In an unprecedented slap, 15 of the 40 Likud members of parliament voted to repudiate a speech that Sharon gave this month on the opening day of the legislative session. On Tuesday, 17 members voted against the disengagement plan, forcing Sharon to reach out to traditional opponents in the parliament, or Knesset, to ensure the plan's approval.
    John Ward Anderson and Molly Moore, "After Gaza Win, Sharon Fights Political Doubt; Israeli Leader Struggles to Keep Government Unified and Evacuation Plan on Track," *Washington Post*, October 31, 2004.
    Although politically settled, settlers remain angry, even threatening, toward the government as the disengagement approaches. Bentsi Lieberman, leader of the Yesha Settlers Council, a group representing settlers in Gaza and the West Bank, announced that "The proposal to expel Jews from their homes is an immoral decision and a breach of human rights." "Settlers 'to Resist' Gaza Pullout," BBC News, December 20, 2004, accessible at http://news.bbc.co.uk/2/hi/middle_east/4111505.stm.
    Also from the BBC:
    The Israeli Haaretz newspaper has suggested that Israeli forces may close off the Gaza Strip before Passover to head off attempts by thousands of disengagement opponents to reach the settlements in order to foil efforts to evacuate them.

The contents of the call to protest were broadcast by Israel public radio.

It says: "From Passover on, we are all mobilised for the defence of Gush Katif [a large settlement bloc in Gaza]."

Addressing soldiers directly, the document asks: "Received a reserve duty call-up order for after the Passover holiday? Received a conscription order for enlisted duty soon? Then you got an order for destruction and evacuation."

"Call for Israeli Army Gaza Revolt," BBC News, March 31, 2005, accessible at http://newswww.bbc.net.uk/1/hi/world/middle_east/4396513.stm.

22. Norman G. Finkelstein, "The Occupation's Spillover Effect," *Tikkun*, March/April 2005, p. 14.

23. Alan Dershowitz, *Chutzpah* (Boston: Little Brown, 1991), p. 163.

24. Letty Cottin Pogrebin, "In Defense of the Law of Return: It Is Israel's Compensatory Response to the Truth of Jewish Experience; Reprint," *Nation*, December 22, 2003.

25. Max Boot, "Neocons; Think Again," *Foreign Policy*, January 1, 2004.

26. Philip Green, "'Anti-Semitism,' Israel and the Left: Who's Really behind the Crude Equation between Israel and 'the Jews'?" *Nation*, May 5, 2003.

27. Gloria Borger, "Blaming the Cabal," *U.S. News & World Report*, March 24, 2003.

28. Anti-Defamation League, "Pat Buchanan: In His Own Words—on American Jews and the Pro-Israel Lobby," September 1999, accessible at www.adl.org/special_reports/buchanan_own_words/print.asp.

29. William F. Buckley Jr., *In Search of Anti-Semitism* (New York: Continuum, 1994), p. 44.

30. Brendan O'Leary, "In Defence of the Indefensible," *Times Higher Education Supplement*, October 4, 2002.

31. Kelsey Snell, "Loop Professor Takes Heat for Conduct," *DePaulia*, October 1, 2004, accessible at www.thedepaulia.com/story.asp?artid=77&sectid=1.

32. Steven Plaut, "DeNial at DePaul: The Thomas Klocek Affair," *Jewish Press*, April 13, 2005, accessible at www.thejewishpress.com/news_article.asp?article=4902.

33. Susanne Dumbleton, "Special to the DePaulia: SNL Seeks to Resolve Situation," *DePaulia*, October 8, 2004.

34. "Polish anti-Semitism remains substantial, although . . . [o]nly a few thousand Jews still live in Poland," Associated Press. "Walesa Condemned for Silence after Hearing Anti-Semitic Views in Sermon," *Baltimore Sun*, June 18, 1995.

CONCLUSION
The Contributions Peace Can Make

1. Sacha Baggili, "Middle East Conflict Knocks Biotech Sector," *World Markets Analysis*, March 22, 2002.

2. On the complex issue of water, see Franklin M. Fisher, et al., *Liquid Assets: An Economic Approach for Water Management and Conflict Resolution in the Middle East and Beyond* (Washington, D.C.: RFF Press, 2005).

INDEX

Abbas, Mahmoud
cease-fire agreement, 191
civil war threat, 93–94, 96
election of, 24
Jerusalem, 52
peace advancements, 192
provocative actions, 13
reality on the ground, 12
"right of return," 6
Tel Aviv nightclub bomb-
ing (2005), 66
terrorism, 62
Abbassi, Hassan, 113
Abudrdeina, Nabil, 96
Abu-Zayyad, Zaid, 75
academia
anti-Semitism in, 196–198
boycott of Israeli universities, 118, 129–133, 189,
191, 192
hate speech, 123–133, 136,
198
peace opponents, 4–6
academic freedom, Israel,
132
academic obstructionist case
study, 167–188
Chomsky, Noam, 170–172
Cockburn, Alexander, 175
Finkelstein, Norman,
172–175
overview, 167–169
personal attacks by,
169–170, 180–188
tactics of, 175–180
Adrangi, Sahm, 128–129
Afghanistan, 72
Ahmad, Rif'at Sayyed, 151
Al-Ahram, Massad, 126
Al-Akhbar (newspaper), 150,
151
Al-Aqsa Martyrs brigade
suicide bombers, 202
weapons, 109
Al Aqsa Mosque
Jerusalem, 52, 53–54
provocative actions, 12–13
Albany Times Union (newspaper), 53–54
Al-Dustour (newspaper), 152
Al-Gamei'a, Sheikh, 153
Algeria, Jews expelled from,
49

al-Husseini, Faisal, 89
al-Jalahma, Umayma Ahmad,
149
Al-Jazeera television, 82
al-Majali, Rakan, 152–153
al-Muslih, Ahmad, 152
Alon Plan, boundaries,
19–20
al-Oqbi, Tufful, 80
Al-Osboa (newspaper), 153
al-Qaeda, Hamas compared,
77
Al-Quds University
(Jerusalem), 131
Al-Rantisi, 'Abed al-'Aziz,
151
Al-Riyadh (newspaper), 149,
150
Altalena (ship), 94–95
ambulances, terrorism, 82,
83
American Civil Liberties
Union (ACLU), 179
American Jewish Committee,
162
Amiel, Barbara, 115, 133
Amnesty International, 130,
185
Annan, Kofi, 143, 145
Anti-Defamation League
(ADL), 128–129, 160,
178, 190–191
anti-Semitism. *See also* hate
speech; pro-Israel extremists; racism
academia, 123–133,
196–198
Arab world, 148–153
Chomsky, Noam, 171
defined, 142–143
Europe, 133–134,
138–139, 142
Finkelstein, Norman,
173–174
increase in, 190–191
Israeli policies and,
189–198
Israel-Nazi comparison,
135–136
legitimate criticism com-
pared, 139–141
nonrecognition of Israel,
115–117
one-state solution, 30–32,
33
United States, 152–153

apartheid policy, Israel
compared to, 136–138
Arab-Israeli citizens
advantages of, 201
Israel, 32
land swapping, 20–21
rights of, 137
Arab-Israeli conflict, sources
of, 9
Arafat, Yasser
Clinton-Barak proposal
rejected by, 16, 60–61,
119, 124–125
corruption of, 202
death of, 3, 9, 17, 29, 86
Jerusalem, 52–53, 55, 56
noncontiguous Palestine,
35, 36
"right of return," 18–19
Said, Edward, 124
Saudi Arabia, 69
terrorism, 61, 67, 91
two-state solution, 9, 19,
29, 44
Armey, Dick, 160
Ashrawi, Hanan, 99
Associated Press, 12–13
Association of University
Teachers (AUT, U.K.),
130–131, 191, 192
Atlanta Journal-Constitution
(newspaper), 161

Baker, Mona, 130
Bandar (prince of Saudi
Arabia), 29, 125
Bantustans
South Africa comparison,
136–137
term of, noncontiguous
Palestine, 39, 62–63
Barak, Aharon, 100
Barak, Ehud, 127, 128
boundaries, 15, 35
Camp David, 61, 90
Geneva proposals (2003),
61
Jerusalem, 54–55
noncontiguous Palestine,
39
two-state solution, 18–19
Baraka, Amiri, 128–129,
153, 195–196
Bartov, Omer, 137–138, 178
Bauer, Yehuda, 178
Bayefsky, Anne, 26, 137, 144